*The Anatomy of Loving*

Rembrandt, *Adam and Eve*, 1638.

*Martin S. Bergmann*

# THE ANATOMY
# OF LOVING

*The Story of Man's Quest to Know What Love Is*

*Columbia University Press*
NEW YORK 1987

Grateful acknowledgment is made to the following for permission
to reprint selected material:

*Literature of Ancient Egypt,* ed. by W.K. Simpson. Copyright © 1973 Yale University Press.

Oxford University Press, for *The Oxford Book of Greek Verse,* edited by T.F. Higham and C.M. Bowra. 1938.

University of California Press, for "Ancient Egyptian Literature, a Book of Reading" from *The New Kingdom,* vol. 2, by M. Lichtheim, 1976.

Dover Publications, for *The World as Will and Representation,* by A. Schopenhauer, 1966.

*The Complete Greek Drama,* edited by W.J. Oates and E.G. O'Neill. Copyright © 1938 Random House, Inc.

*Ancient Near Eastern Texts Relating to the Old Testament,* 3d ed., edited by J.B. Pritchard. Copyright © 1969 by Princeton University Press. Reprinted with permission of Princeton University Press.

Doubleday and Company, for *History Begins in Sumer,* by S.N. Karame, 1969; and for *Sappho,* by W. Barnstone, 1965.

*Inanna: Queen of Heaven and Earth,* by D. Wolkstein and S.N. Kramer. Copyright © 1983 by Diane Wolkstein and Samuel Noah Kramer. Reprinted by permission of Harper and Row, Publishers, Inc.

Indiana University Press, for Ovid's *Metamorphoses,* 1955, and *Amores,* 1958. Both translated by R. Humphries.

Penguin Books, for the *The Portable Dante,* 1947, edited by P. Milano.

Library of Congress Cataloging-in-Publication Data

Bergmann, Martin S., 1913–
The anatomy of loving.

Bibliography: p.
Includes index.
1. Love—History. I. Title.
BD436.B47 1987      155.3      86-31743
ISBN 0-231-06486-1

Columbia University Press
New York   Guildford, Surrey
Copyright © 1987 Columbia University Press
All rights reserved

Printed in the United States of America

Book design by Ken Venezio

*To Ridi for Our 40th Anniversary*

*I remember thee, the grace of thy youth,*
*The love of thine espousals, when thou*
*Wentest after me in the wilderness,*
*In a land that was not sown.*

                              —Jeremiah 2:2

# Contents

# Preface

O, learn to read what silent love hath writ:
To hear with eyes belongs to love's fine wit.
—Shakespeare, Sonnet 23

O love is the crooked thing,
There is nobody wise enough
To find out all that is in it
For he would be thinking of love
Till the stars had run away
And the shadows eaten the moon.
—from Yeats' "Brown Penny"

This book tells the story of man's quest to know what love is. To do justice to this project I had to roam over many domains guarded by specialists. Should this book be read by Egyptologists, classical scholars, Biblical or Shakespearean scholars, historians or philosophers, I hope they will agree that when I raided their respective domains I did so only when the perspective from which I was writing enabled me to say something original. To the general reader interested in love who wants to know what he is getting himself into before he plunges into the book, I suggest he read my last chapter first and see if he wishes to traverse the territory I stake out.

There is no shortage of new books coming off the press on the subject of love. The unprecedented "sexual revolution" is behind us, at least in the Western world, and there are signs that even the rigidities of Communism will be incapable of holding back the impact of this kind of revolution. We have become franker and more knowledgeable about all aspects of sex, and feel entitled to sexual happiness. But after sexual freedom came the sense of emptiness that accompanies even satisfactory sexual relationships when the mysterious ingredient called love is missing. There is a further reason for a growing new curiosity about love: ours has been called the age of narcissism, and narcissism, as psychoanalysts have discovered, stands in a complex relationship to loving. Most authors are unaware of this connection, but my book deals extensively with the history and psychology of narcissism.

One particular insight forced itself upon me in the course of this study: on the surface, love strikes us as a unitary emotion—all those who love share in this emotion, but if love is examined in depth one discovers different types of love. Some lovers fall into one or another clear-cut group, which I have delineated in the last chapter; others show in their love an amalgam of different kinds of love. The inner development of a person before he or she falls in love determines the way he or she will love and the course love will take.

Many books on love that I have read have quoted Cherubino's famous aria in Mozart's *Figaro* ("Voi che sapete che cosa e amor": "Tell us you who know if this be love"). Hagstrum (1980) noted that the question, *what is love,* is raised by the adolescent, whose gender identity is still in flux, a mixture of Narcissus and Adonis. The more ambiguous the sense of gender identity, the more puzzling will love appear. It seems to me that it was no accident that the Greeks, who repressed their homosexuality less than others, were also the first to experience love as a puzzle. We owe to the Greek and Roman philosophers and poets not only the first insights into the nature of love but some of the most profound observations made on the subject before Freud. I found that Freud's ideas on love can be understood better if we put them within the framework of Western thought going back to ancient Greece and the Bible. In my view, psychoanalysis owes much more to its humanist past than Freud and other psychoanalysts have acknowledged. At the same time, psychoanalysis has thrown new light on this humanist past.

The literary critic Harold Bloom has said of Freud that "His agon with the whole of anteriority is the largest and most intense of our century." (The term anteriority was coined by Bloom as the opposite of posteriority, that is, the struggle of every creative thinker against the oppression exercised by tradition.) He goes on to state that Freud usurped the role of the mind in our age, so that more than forty years after his death we have no common vocabulary for discussion of works of the spirit except what he gave us. My book confirms Bloom's prediction, for when I wanted to tell the story of man's quest to understand love I could see the past only through Freud's prism. As to Freud's own wrestling with the past, I find Plato to be Freud's main agon, that is, the person Freud is most influenced by and whose influence he is struggling against. The only other "agon" of a similar nature was Nietzsche.

Because I believe that there is an unconscious continuity that links myths, legends, and theories of philosophers of the classical past to dreams and neuroses of modern men and women, I have throughout the book juxtaposed classical texts with associations of analysands.

I feel confident that this book will be read by those who value psychoanalysis, whether for personal or professional reasons, including mental health professionals who need to understand as comprehensively as possible the psychoanalytic contribution to love. They will read this book to be more effective in their clinical work. It is my hope that I have also written a book of wider appeal—that has something important and new to say to those who cherish our humanist past, who find it relevant, and who wish to know how psychoanalysis fits into this long tradition.

Finally, I wish to say something to those who will read the book because they are bewildered about the outcome of their efforts to find happiness in love. One of the earliest metaphors on love compares it to a sickness that only the beloved can cure. Books have no such power. But should it happen that an understanding of our culture's long struggle to understand love, or the views of a particular author cited, or even a case presented enables a reader to see his or her difficulties in another, more helpful and hopeful light, even though the book has no curative intent, it would be a gain not only to the reader but to myself.

I am indebted to many analysands, students, and colleagues for their helpful ideas. Unfortunately, not all of them can be mentioned. Professor Peter Gay read the first version of this book. In his reading he combined the diligence of an editor with the erudition of one familiar with the literature on love. I am equally indebted to Dr. Otto Kernberg, who has contributed so much to the expansion of the analytic knowledge of this field and who read the first version and made valuable suggestions. I have profited greatly from the remarks of Dr. Arlene Richards and Mrs. Anne Rose, who also read the manuscript. My wife and my son Michael were helpful collaborators. Professor Bernard Bothmer and Mr. Lee Pomerantz gave me access to Sumerian and Egyptian sources not easily available to the layman. Dr. Giorgio DiGregorio discussed at length with me the complex chapter on Freud. Some portions of this book were written in Oxford, and the staff of the Bodleian Library were most helpful in locating many source books. I also was heartened that my two assistants, Mrs. Andrea

Madden and Miss Martha Meade, were not only skillful in the use of the word processor, but showed a lively interest in the book's content. Any writer knows the pain that the blank face of a secretary can inflict. I was spared this agony. I would like to thank Mrs. Barbara Frank for proof-reading.

I began writing this book about twenty years ago. My first paper on love appeared in 1971. Preliminary versions of some of the chapters appeared in *The Psychoanalytic Quarterly,* the *Journal of the American Psychoanalytic Association,* the *International Journal of Psycho-Analytic Psycho-Therapy,* and the *American Imago.* I thank the editors of these journals for permission to reprint sections of these papers.

I also want to thank the Postgraduate Center for Psychotherapy for giving me the privilege of "a year's distinguished psychoanalyst" to present this book in a series of lectures. The book profited from the question and answer periods.

# I

## *The Humanist Past*
### *The Growth of the*
### *Vocabulary of Love*

# 1

# *Love Poetry in Ancient Egypt*

Poetry is the plow that turns up time
so that the deep layers of time, the
black soil, appear on top.
—Ossip Mandelstam in Gibbons 1979: 18

M ost writers on love quote with approval La Rochefoucauld's statement to the effect that most people would not love if they did not
hear love talked about. La Rochefoucauld was one of the inventors of the
maxim as a literary form, but in this case he raised a crucial question
which can be paraphrased: Is love essentially a social phenomenon cultivated in certain climates of opinion and not found in others? Or does it
represent a basic human need and is it ubiquitous wherever human beings
are found? The search for clarification of this question led me to ask when
love was discovered. The search led to the new kingdom of Egypt (1300 to
1000 B.C.), where we find the first poetry of love.

### Egyptian Love Poetry

A prerequisite for a self-conscious love poetry is possession of the word
love in the language. The Egyptians had a hieroglyph for love, both as a
noun and as a verb. It consisted of three parts: a hoe, a mouth, and the
figure of a man with a hand in his mouth.*

Egyptian love poetry (Lichtheim 1976; Simpson 1973) was written on

---

*I wish to express my thanks to Dr. Howard H. Schlossman for drawing my attention to this
fascinating hieroglyph.

papyri and vases between 1300 and 1100 B.C.. It comes from the new kingdom in Egypt. They are old by our standards but late by Egyptian standards since Egyptian recorded history begins in 3000 B.C. Papyri and clay are not as enduring as writing in stone. It is therefore possible that love poetry existed earlier, but it did not survive. Fifty-five love poems have been assembled by Egyptologists, all dating from the new kingdom. When we come upon the Egyptian love poems after familiarity with other love poetry, they astonish us by the range of topics and the subtlety of the emotions they express. What is most striking in these poems is the absence of painful associations such as shame, guilt, or ambivalence that will characterize much of the later love poetry. A reader acquainted with the biblical Song of Songs will find that many of the metaphors are familiar.

A woman speaks:  My brother torments my heart with his voice,
He makes sickness take hold of me;
He is neighbor to my mother's house,
And I cannot go to him!

Mother is right in charging him thus:
"Give up seeing him!"
It pains my heart to think of him,
I am possessed by love of him.

A man speaks:  Seven days since I saw my sister,
And sickness invaded me;
I am heavy in all my limbs,
My body has forsaken me.
When the physicians come to me,
My heart rejects their remedies;
The magicians are quite helpless,
My sickness is not discerned.
To tell me "She is here" would revive me!

The sight of her makes me well!
When she opens her eyes my body is young,
Her speaking makes me strong;
Embracing her expels my malady—
Seven days since she went from me!
                                        (Lichtheim 1976:182–185)

The metaphor of love as a form of sickness is also found in the Song of Songs. "Stay with me flagons, comfort me with apples: for I am sick of love" (2:5).

The only jarring note to our ears is the universal address of sister when the man is speaking and brother when the voice is a woman's. These were normal terms of endearment in ancient Egyptian usage (Lichtheim 1976:181). Unlike the Egyptians, whose pharaohs were privileged to transgress the incest taboo and marry their sisters, we are sensitive to the association between sibling and beloved. Antiquity in general was not so strict in separating sibling love from sexual love. In the Song of Songs, which is of Hellenistic origin (Rozelaar 1954; Hadas 1959), we find: "Thou hast ravaged my heart, my sister, my spouse"; and "How fair is thy love, my sister, my spouse" (4:9 and 10). Since love is experienced as an overwhelming emotion beyond the control of the healthy ego, the metaphor of sickness is apt.

And now some fragments expressing the bliss of love:

> I found my lover on his bed,
> and my heart was sweet to excess.
> I shall never be far away (from) you
> while my hand is in your hand,
> and I shall stroll with you
> in every favorite place.
>
> How pleasant is this hour,
> may it extend for me to eternity;
> since I have lain with you
> you have lifted high my heart.
> In mourning or in rejoicing
> be not far from me.
>
> (Simpson 1973:308)

The ambivalence that lovers feel toward being caught in love found expression in Egypt in the metaphor of the trap. The metaphor was readily available in a culture that derived part of its sustenance from trapping wild foul. A woman speaks:

> The voice of the wild goose shrills,
> It is caught by its bait;
> My love of you pervades me,
> I cannot loosen it.
> I shall retrieve my nets,
> But what do I tell my mother,
> To whom I go daily,
> Laden with bird catch?
> I have spread no snares today,
> I am caught in my love of you!
>
> (Lichtheim 1976:190)

There is humor in the metaphor of the layer of traps becoming herself entrapped. The woman employs the metaphor of the trapped wild fowl and the man humorously uses a metaphor of domesticated cattle to describe his "plight":

> How well she knows to cast the noose,
> And yet not pay the cattle tax!
> She casts the noose on me with her hair,
> She captures me with her eye;
> She curbs me with her necklace,
> She brands me with her seal ring.
>                      (Lichtheim, p. 187)

Some poems are addressed to the lover's own heart. They suggest that love was already experienced as an intrapsychic event, symbolized by a metaphorical use of the heart.

> My heart flutters hastily,
> When I think of my love of you;
> It lets me not act sensibly,
>                      (Lichtheim, p. 183)

> "Don't wait, go there," says it to me,
> As often as I think of him;
> My heart, don't act so stupidly,
> Why do you play the fool?
>                      (Lichtheim, p. 184)

The Egyptians experienced the heart as an intrapsychic structure standing apart from the rest of the personality. In this poem, the heart is accused of being the organ of love. The equation of heart with love has remained with us; we say we lose our hearts when we fall in love.

There are hints of masochism and perhaps also fetishism in some of the Egyptian poems.

> I wish I were her Negro maid
> who follows at her feet;
> then the skin of all her limbs
> would be (revealed) to me.
> I wish I were her washerman,
> if only for a single month,
> then I would be (entranced),*

---

*Parentheses indicate breaks in the tablets.

washing out the Moringa oils
in her diaphanous garments . . .

I wish I were the seal ring,
the guardian of her (fingers),
then ( . . . )
(Simpson 1973:311)

Nature is alive and participates in love making. Trees compete with each
other by offering hiding places for lovers but they can also become jealous
when they discover that the lovers take them for granted. First the sycamore is speaking.

The little sycamore,
which she planted with her hand,
sends forth its words to speak . . .

Come spend the day happily,
tomorrow and the day after tomorrow, for three days,
seated in my shade,

Her friend is on her right.
She gets him drunk
while doing what he says;
and the wine cellar is disordered in drunkenness,
as she stays with her lover.
She has ample room beneath me,
the lady love as she paces;
I am discreet
and will not say that I have seen their discourse.
(Simpson, pp. 314–315)

The new kingdom was a splendid age in Egyptian history. The invading
Hyksos had been expelled and Egypt became a world power with frontiers
extending to the Euphrates. In this era the religious revolution of Akhna-
ton took place, which in Freud's view prefigured the figure of Moses and
the Israeli exodus out of Egypt. The Egyptians of the new kingdom already
had behind them the splendid pyramid age. When that age collapsed, it
was followed by an age of disillusionment and pessimism. During the new
kingdom, Egyptians were occupied with the ideas of judgment beyond the
grave. The burial graves of Memphis depict him standing in judgment
before Osiris, his earthly behavior being weighed. On one side of the scale,
Maat, the goddess of truth, is crouching. On the other, the heart of the
deceased is balanced. Should he fail to pass the test, a crocodile stands
ready to consume his heart. Spells, written on the walls of the grave, make

sure that this will not happen. A special spell enjoins the heart from testifying against the deceased.

The *Book of the Dead* contains a fascinating chapter on the so-called negative confessions, when the deceased declares what he has not done. There we find such statements as "I have not taken milk from the mouths of children. I have not falsified the scales, I have not caught fishes in the marshes of the gods." Some negative confessions deal with strictly ethical issues such as "I have not defamed a slave to his superior." Others deal with sexual relationships such as "I have not had sexual relations with a boy" (Pritchard 1969:34). These negative confessions tell us a great deal about the temptations against which the ancient Egyptians had to struggle.

Love poetry makes its appearance in a complex society, where feelings of guilt were already highly developed and techniques to combat them well established. Homosexuality and particularly the seduction of boys must have been prevalent or they would not appear in the "negative confessions."

What is striking in these poems is the wealth of metaphors. There is something in the nature of love that is conducive to metaphor formation. The emotion is intense but words fail the lovers, and their language passes into metaphor. Surprisingly, most of the Egyptian poems on love are secular in nature. The Egyptian lovers do not experience their love as the working of any god, although they ask the golden goddess to be united with their lovers and to have their love reciprocated. Nor do the Egyptian lovers know the pain of ambivalence, loving and hating at the same time. There are only mild indications of intrapsychic conflict; basically the lovers are in harmony with their feelings of love. No love seems illicit. There is no struggle between love and obedience to parents. The lovers are not tormented by feelings of guilt or inadequacy. They do not feel that they may not deserve the love they desire. A heavy burden of guilt hovers over the new kingdom in Egypt but it finds no reflection in the Egyptian love poetry.

In ancient Egypt lover-poets invented the metaphorical language we still use. The existence of love poetry 3,500 years ago in a culture that played only a peripheral role in the Western world, I take as evidence in support of the hypothesis that love is not a habit fostered in certain cultures. To make a jump to the nineteenth century, Madame Bovary's desperate search for lovers was undoubtedly influenced by her reading of romances. But the lessons I draw from Flaubert's masterpiece is not that reading evokes the hunger for love, but that reading novels evoked in Madame Bovary fantasies of love that she was unable to translate into her real world and this inability to transfer the fantasies into reality led to her undoing.

Whether preliterate primitive societies know love songs is a matter of controversy. Bowra (1962), who studied primitive song, is of the opinion that societies that live on hunting and gathering have no love songs. These appear only after a settled agricultural life has replaced hunting and nomadic existence. Bowra (p. 175) reports that the aborigines of Arnheim land associate lovemaking with the monsoons. They identify flashes of lightning with the mating of snakes. In their view, the tongues of lightning are snakes flickering and twisting, one with the other. To my knowledge, no poet has ever used lightning as a sexual symbol. And yet, in association with the violence of the monsoon, this metaphor rings true. If the aborigines of Arnheim had no love songs, they did at least know how to use similes and metaphors, which are the basic prerequisites for poetry.

Bowra was a classical scholar by training. In contrast to his view, the anthropologist Paul Radin (1957) collected a number of love poems current among aborigines.

> As the rapid flow of the current at Onoian,
> And as the swollen torrent from the valley,
> So flows my yearning heart after thee,
> O Aitofa, have compassion on thy lover, lest he die!
>
> As a great cloud obscuring the sky is his grief,
> The grief of the husband mourning for his estranged wife,
> And like the sky darkened by its rising is my distress for her.
> (Tonga, Polynesia)

> I would drown myself if you died,
> Drown myself in the river Si Tumallam,
> If you were thrust into the depths,
> Into the deep abyss
> That we cannot ascend.
> I shall endeavor
> To make a twisted cord—
> The road to death.
> (Batak, Sumatra)

And a lullaby illustrating the love between parent and child.

> Why dost thou weep, my child?
> The sky is bright; the sun is shining;
> Why dost thou weep?
> Go to thy father; he loves thee,
> Go tell him why thou weepest.
> What! Thou weepest still?

Thy father loves thee, I caress thee:
Yet still thou art sad.
Tell me, then, my child, why dost thou weep!
(Balengi, Central Africa)

Finally, they seem to know that love is not always bliss:

Love does not torment forever.
It came on me like the fire
Which rages sometimes at Hukanui.
If this beloved one is near to me,
Do not suppose, O Kiri, that my sleep is sweet.
I lie awake the livelong night,
For love to prey on me in secret.
(Maori, New Zealand)

# 2

## *Sensuous Poetry in Ancient Sumer*

The Sumerian and Babylonian epic of Gilgamesh goes back to 2000 B.C. It may well be the oldest literary work to have come down to us. When the epic of Gilgamesh was written, Sumer already had a long history. Its myths were established and it had a well-ordered pantheon of divinities. Gilgamesh was a powerful and ruthless king.* To curb his power, the gods created out of clay Enkidu, his double. We encounter here for the first time an ancient group of ideas associated with love. We will deal with them again when we analyze Plato's *Symposium*. The general mythological assumption is that long ago man was very powerful, as he was also self-satisfied, needed nobody, and did not know love. This state, which following Freud can be called the state of gratified narcissism, becomes the prerogative of the gods as religion develops. Once this wish has been projected on them, the gods are seen as begrudging this gratified narcissism to men. They therefore split him in two, and thus create longing, a characteristic of mortals but unknown to gods.

In the Gilgamesh epic, the fact that love between friends is the result of divine splits is only implied. After a short combat, Gilgamesh and Enkidu become friends for life and it is the death of Enkidu that brings about a profound change in Gilgamesh. From the ordinary hero of antiquity who is ever eager for combat with monsters, he becomes the seeker of immortality which he almost finds only to lose it again. Unlike the Egyptians, who saw the hereafter as a continuation of life and erected pyramids to make sure that the dead king would have all his needs met in the netherworld, the Assyrians had a desolate view of the world to come and their epics

*For a fuller account of the Gilgamesh myth written for the general reader, see G. S. Kirk 1970, chapter 4.

expressed openly the fear of death. In this book I will be concerned primarily with the problems of love in Sumerian mythology and literature.
    Enkidu is at first a subhuman demonic being.

> With the gazelles he feeds on grass,
> With the wild beasts he jostles at the watering place,
> With the teeming creatures his heart delights in water.
>                                                    (Speiser 1969:74)

    As the champion of the animals, Enkidu terrorizes the hunters. He fills the pits they have set for the animals and tears up their traps. The hunter consults his father, who devises a way of taming Enkidu.

> Go my hunter, take with thee a harlot-lass.
> When he waters the beasts at the watering-place,
> She shall pull off her clothing, laying bare her ripeness.
> As soon as he sees her, he will draw near to her.
> Reject him will his beasts that grew up on his steppe!*
>                                                    (p. 75)

The harlot-lass is a sacred prostitute. The hunter cheers her on during the crucial moment.

> "There he is, O lass! Free thy breasts,
> Bare thy bosom that he may possess thy ripeness!
> Be not bashful! Welcome his ardor!
> As soon as he sees thee, he will draw near to thee.
> Treat him, the savage, to a woman's task!
> Reject him will his wild beasts that grew up on his
>         steppe,
> As his love is drawn unto thee."

---

*That metaphors can remain alive over thousands of years can be seen when *Gilgamesh* is juxtaposed to the poem "Man" (Der Mensch) by the German Romantic poet, Holderlin. The translation is by Michael Hamburger:

> Soon he has grown up;
> The animals avoid him, for other than
>     They is man; he does not resemble
>     Thee, nor the Father, for boldly in him
>
> And alone are mingled the Father's lofty
> Spirit with thy joy, O Earth, and thy sorrow.
>     Gladly he would be like the mother
>     Of the gods, like all-embracing Nature!
>
> For more freely breathe the birds of the forest,
> And though Man's breast rises with greater splendour,
>     And he sees the dark future, he must
>     See death too, and he alone must fear it.

> For six days and seven nights Enkidu comes forth,
>     Mating with the lass.
> After he had had (his) fill of her charms,
> He set his face toward his wild beasts.
> On seeing him, Enkidu, the gazelles ran off,
> The wild beasts of the steppe drew away from his body.
> Startled was Enkidu, as his body became taut,
> His knees were motionless—for his wild beasts had gone.
> Enkidu had to slacken his pace—it was not as before;
>
>                                        (p. 75)

The choice of the term "ripeness' to describe a woman's body brings Rubens or Renoir to mind. Carnal knowledge estranges man from nature. For Gilgamesh and for Adam in Genesis, sexual knowledge is the end of innocence.

> She pulled off (her) clothing;
> With one (piece) she clothed him,
> With the other garment
> She clothed herself.
> Holding on to his hand,
> She leads him like a child
> To the shepherd-hut,
>
>                    (p. 77)

Symbolically, Enkidu is weaned away from the "milk of wild creatures." Although Enkidu lost his wildness, he had gained understanding. The lass comforts him.

> "Thou art wise, Enkidu, art become like a god!
> Why with the wild creatures dost thou roam over the
>     steppes?"
>
>                                        (p. 75)

The Bible too speaks of Adam knowing Eve. Enkidu has become civilized and wise through the sexual act. We should note also that in spite of the prominence given to the sexual encounter this is not yet a love poem.

In the meantime Gilgamesh has a dream anticipating Enkidu's arrival. In the dream he was vanquished by Enkidu, and his mother interprets the dream:

> (Like the essence of Anu),* so mighty his strength
> (That thou didst love him and) wert (drawn) to him
>     (as though to a woman),

*Parentheses indicated breaks in the tablets.

> (Means that he will never) forsake (th)ee.
> (This is the mean)ing of thy dream."
>
> (p. 76)

It is evident that the ancients used dreams as a supportive rather than an analytic therapy. To a psychoanalyst, the wisdom of Enkidu's mother is truly astonishing; it will take another four thousand years for Freud to discover that the homosexual falls in love with the man who has defeated him. When the boy sees no prospects of equaling or defeating his father, or the daughter of a beautiful woman cannot see herself capable of equaling or defeating the mother, Freud will discover that aforementioned rivalry turns into love. Gilgamesh's mother, like many mothers of homosexuals today, encourages the shift towards homosexuality because Enkidu is less of a threat than another woman.

The epic of *Gilgamesh* contains another episode of special significance. At one point the goddess Ishtar falls in love with Gilgamesh. This is what she promises him:

> "Come, Gilgamesh, be thou (my) lover!
> Do but grant me of thy fruit.
> Thou shalt be my husband and I will be thy wife.
> I will harness for thee a chariot of lapis and gold,
> Whose wheels are gold and whose horns are brass.
> Thou shalt have storm-demons to hitch on for mighty mules.
> In the fragrance of cedars thou shalt enter our house.
> When our house thou enterest,
> Threshold (and) dais shall kiss thy feet!
> Humbled before thee shall be kings, lords, and princes!
> The yield of hills and plain they shall bring thee as
>        tribute.
> Thy goats shall cast triplets, thy sheep twins,
> Thy he-ass in lading shall surpass thy mule.
> Thy chariot horses shall be famed for racing,
> (Thine Ox) under yoke shall not have a rival!"
>
> (pp. 83–84)

But Gilgamesh is not seduced by the goddess's offer of wealth, for he knows her history. Ishtar is the archetype of the beautiful woman who brings disaster to men. Gilgamesh recounts her history to her face.

> "For Tammus, the lover of thy youth,
> Thou hast ordained wailing year after year.
> Having loved the dappled shepherd-bird,
> Thou smotest him, breaking his wing.

In the grooves he sits, crying 'My wing!'
Then thou lovedst a lion, perfect in strength;
Seven pits and seven thou didst dig for him.
Then a stallion thou lovedst, famed in battle;
The whip, the spur, and the lash thou ordained for him
Thou decreedst for him to gallop seven leagues;

. . . .

Then thou lovedst Ishullanu, thy father's gardener,
Who baskets of dates ever did bring to thee,
And daily did brighten thy table.
Thine eyes raised at him, thou didst go to him:
'O my Ishullanu, let us taste of thy vigor!
Put forth thy "hand" and touch our "modesty!" '
Ishullanu said to thee;
'What dost thou want with me?
Has my mother not baked, have I not eaten,
That I should taste the food of stench and foulness?
Does reed-work afford cover against the cold?'
As thou didst hear this (his talk),
Thou smotest him and turnedst him into a mole."

(p. 84)

Such a courageous defiance of a goddess we will meet again in the *Iliad* when Helen defies Aphrodite. Such a defiance is unthinkable under monotheistic conditions, but it was thinkable when the relationship between gods and mortals could become a sexual one. Astarte had the same evil intentions that Circe entertained towards Odysseus and his crew. In the Greek myth, however, Odysseus overcomes Circe's magic and can enjoy her sexually. He does so with the aid of a powerful male god, Hermes.

Neither Gilgamesh nor his double Enkidu discover heterosexual love. The epos tallies well with some of Freud's findings, namely that fear of woman and her destructive and castrative power may be older and precede man's capacity to love her. The love for the double, narcissistic love in psychoanalytic language, may be older than heterosexual love.

Gilgamesh, married to the goddess of fertility, also acquires the right of the first night.

The drum of the people is free
For nuptial choice, that with lawful wives he might mate!
He is the first the husband comes after.

Freud (1918) explained the medieval "right to the first night"—in Latin "Jus prima noctis"—as a custom that symbolically gave the father the right to the daughters but it also served the function of deflecting the hostility of the woman toward her deflowerer from the husband to the king father. This custom was already established early in the history of civilization.

The noted Assyrian scholar, Samuel Noah Kramer, was examining Assyrian tablets when he made a discovery which he later reported in a book.

As I read it again and yet again, there was no mistaking its content. What I held in my hand was one of the oldest love songs written down by the hand of man.

It soon became clear that this was not a secular poem, not a song of love between just 'a man and a maid.' It involved a king and his selected bride, and was no doubt intended to be recited in the course of the most hallowed of ancient rites, the rite of the 'sacred marriage.' Once a year, according to Sumerian belief, it was the sacred duty of the ruler to marry a priestess and votary of Inanna, the goddess of love and procreation, in order to ensure fertility to the soil and fecundity to the womb. The time-honored ceremony was celebrated on New Year's day and was preceded by feast and banquets accompanied by music, song, and dance. (Kramer 1969)

Our interest in love poetry goes in the opposite direction, for we are in search of the first description of sexual love. Even as a ritualistic love song, however, the poem Kramer discovered is of interest.

> Bridegroom, dear to my heart,
> Goodly is your beauty, honeysweet,
> Lion, dear to my heart,
> Goodly is your beauty honeysweet.
>
> You have captivated me, let me stand tremblingly before
>     you,
> Bridegroom, I would be taken by you to the bedchamber,
> You have captivated me, let me stand tremblingly before
>     you,
> Lion, I would be taken by you to the bedchamber.
> Bridegroom, let me caress you,
> My precious caress is more savory than honey,
> In the bedchamber, honey filled,
> . . . My precious caress is more savory than honey.
>
> Bridegroom, you have taken your pleasure of me,
> Tell my mother, she will give you delicacies,
> My father, he will give you gifts.
>
> Your spirit, I know where to cheer your spirit,
> Bridegroom, sleep in our house until dawn,

(pp. 212–214)

Another fragment from a poem written for the same purpose reads:

> My god, of the wine-maid, sweet is her drink,
> Like her drink sweet is her vulva sweet, is her drink,
> Like her lips sweet is her vulva, sweet is her drink,
> Sweet is her mixed drink, her drink.

(p. 215)

I am led to a different interpretation of the songs. What Kramer discovered was a poem of transition between fertility hymns and poetry of love. The context is still within the religious ritual. Sexual intercourse has to take place with the priestess if the harvest is to succeed. But the language is already the language of erotic seduction. The equation of love and wine is also found in the Song of Songs: "how much better is thy love than wine! and the smell of thine ointments than all spices!" "Thy lips, O my spouse, drop as the honeycomb: honey and milk are under thy tongue" (4:10 and 11).

In early love poetry it is important that the beloved be accepted by the parents, particularly the mother. We find this also in the Song of Songs: "I held him, and would not let him go, until I had bought him into my mother's house, and into the chamber of her that conceived me" (3:4).

From a psychoanalytic point of view we can read these lines as expressing in symbolic language a wish that the beloved become a twin from whom no separation will have to take place.

Unusual in poetry is the direct reference to the female genital. Most writers have preferred a metaphorical reference. Shulamith, in the Song of Songs, says: "My mother's children were angry with me; they made me the keeper of the vineyards, but my own vineyard have I not kept" (1:6). It would seem that the few seconds it takes to decipher the metaphor of the vineyard as referring to the vagina or the metaphor of "possessing her ripeness" as referring to sexual intercourse give the reader the chance to experience what Freud called a bonus of pleasure and undo some of the moral criticism that a franker sexual reference would evoke.

Istar, whom we encountered earlier, is the Semitic name for Inanna. Inanna was the dominant divinity of the Sumerians. She stands at the dawn of history between 3000 and 2000 B.C. As Friedrich (1978) has pointed out, she is a goddess of sexual desire, a desire devoid of maternity. She is already beginning to separate herself from goddesses of fertility. It is in Inanna that we discover for the first time man's fear of the insatiable sexuality of woman. She is both a martial goddess of war and a goddess of sexual desire.

The recently published *Inanna* hymns (Wolkstein and Kramer 1983) describe the story of the courtship between the shepherd king Dumuzi (the biblical Tammus) and Inanna, the goddess of heaven and earth. The hymn opens with the sun god, Utto, promising his sister a wedding gift of flax. The coy goddess asks who will comb it for her. When Utto promises to comb it, she asks further, who will spin then braid, warp, weave, and finally bleach the wedding sheets. At every turn, the brother promises the next chore until the goddess asks the question we assume must has been on her mind all along: who will go to bed with her on the newly spun wedding sheets? At this point the Sumerian god stops short of incest and suggests that Dumuzi the shepherd will be her bridegroom. The choice of Dumuzi grew out of a competition. The farmer offers grain in great heaps, flax, clothes, and beer. The shepherds gifts are milk, wool, and cheese. Victory goes to the shepherd.

Inanna consults her mother Ningal, who assures her that the bridegroom will be both father and mother to her. She tells Dumuzi that her vulva is full of eagerness like a young moon. While her untilled land lies fallow, she asks that her vulva be plowed. At these suggestions the shepherd king's lap stood up like the rising sea and Inanna asks for his thick sweet milk. He plants the sweet seed. His fullness is her delight. Their necks are pressed close to each other.

> Sweet is the sleep hand to hand
> Sweeter still the sleep of heart to heart.

Before Inanna is ready for her nonincestuous lover, she must renounce her sexual wishes toward her brother and she needs the assurance of her mother that the lover will replace both parents. In this sense the hymn celebrates the transfer of what Freud calls the libido from incestuous love objects to a nonincestuous one.

Inanna spoke:  I bathe for the wild bull
I bathe for the shepherd Dumuzi
I perfumed my sides with ointment
I coated my mouth with sweet smelling amber
I painted my eyes with kohl

He shaped my loins with his fair hands
The shepherd Dumuzi filled my lap with cream and milk
He stroked my pubic hair . . .
He laid his hands on my holy vulva

. . . .

My beloved the delight of my eyes met me
We rejoiced together
He took his pleasure of me
He brought me into his house.

(Wolkstein and Kramer 1983:43–44, 48)

In keeping with the demands of the fertility cycle, the sweet love becomes sated. Dumuzi asks to be set free. Inanna descends to the nether world. In the accepted version of this myth, Astarte descends to the nether world in search of her murdered lover, Tammus. In the version of Wolkstein and Kramer, no motivation is given for Inanna's descent, for Dumuzi will be killed after her return to the world of the living. As Inanna descends to the nether world, she passes through seven gates, in which she is gradually stripped, first of her steppe crown, then of her necklace of lapis beads. She relinquishes all of her ornaments. Naked and bowed low, she reaches the world of the dead. At every gate, she asks, "What is this," and receives the same answer, "The ways of the underworld are perfect and they may not be questioned." While she is imprisoned in the nether world, there is desolation on earth: the bull refused to cover the cow, the ass did not approach the she-ass, in the streets the man no longer approached the maidservant. She is allowed to return by magic devices and the gods revive her. However, the demons of the underworld follow her. These demons cannot be appeased for they eat no offerings, they drink no libation, they accept no gifts, and enjoy no lovemaking. They tear the wife from the husband's arms, the child from the father's knee, and the bride from her marriage chamber. One cannot read those lines without being reminded of the medieval engravings of the dance of death where the artist also derived sadistic pleasure from showing how death approaches people in situations where nobody would expect him.

These demons demand that Inanna give them a substitute for her liberation. Various people close to her offer themselves, but Inanna cannot do without them. Finally they come upon Dumuzi. Inanna focuses upon him the eye of death. She cries out, "Take him," and the demons dismember Dumuzi with their axes.

The myth exists in two forms: In the lamentation myth, Tammus, Osiris, or Adonis are killed by wild animals or jealous competitors. In the other version of the myth, the one favored in Sumer, it is the goddess herself who kills her former lover. Annually their nuptials are celebrated, and annually Inanna's descent and Dumuzi's dismemberment are dramatized.

Probably under the influence of the image of Aphrodite, scholars call both Ishtar and Inanna goddesses of love. However, it seems to me that if we follow the record closely, it is more accurate to call them goddesses of procreation and sexual desire. Hymns to these goddesses are beautiful and sensuous but they do not reach the level of Egyptian love poetry nor do they show the interest that Aphrodite displays in the love affairs of mortals.

The evidence from Sumer allows us to reach some tentative conclusions about the emergence of love poetry. The sensual quality of these poems is evident, but can they be called love poems? My answer is no; they are precursors to the secular poetry of love. In the poetry of love, it is the lover's own love that gives rise to verse and metaphor. The lover praises the beloved in the poetry of seduction, the lover aims to lower the resistance of the reluctant partner. The woman must praise her own capacities to gratify and delight the bridegroom.

# 3

## The Birth of Aphrodite and a New Vocabulary of Love

> As man advanced in knowledge and
> control over nature, the mystery and
> godhead of things natural faded into
> science. Only the mystery of life, and
> love that begets life, remained, . . .
> utterly unexplained, and hence Aphrodite
> keeps her godhead to the end."
> —Harrison, 1903:314

In the art of prehistoric times, human figures played only an insignificant role. It seems that hunters painted the larger animals as a way of mastering their fear of them. Only when hunting and food-gathering were replaced by agriculture did there appear small figurines of females with exaggerated buttocks, breasts, and vaginas prominently displayed. These women are also frequently pregnant. Scholars (Giedion 1964) believe that these figures do not represent goddesses but potent magic symbols. The figurines go as far back as 4000 B.C. They are found in Sumer, Egypt, China, and even in the Dordogne Valley. Out of these figurines the goddesses of fertility slowly evolved. The Syrian, Astarte, is such a goddess of fertility. Her male escort is called Baal, who in biblical accounts evoked jealousy in Yahwe, the god of the Hebrews. The word *Baal* meant master and in current Hebrew means husband. Astarte's escort also had another name, Adon, which has a similar meaning. Associated with Adon are two words of considerable importance, the biblical *Adonae*, translated as lord, and the Greek *Adonis*.

Baal or Adon went hunting but wild creatures with human features and crowned with horns killed him. With the help of the all-seeing sun, Astarte found him and buried him. Several animals were sacrificed so that the god would find nourishment while in the world of the dead. His death was celebrated with sorrow and lamentations, especially when rains were delayed. Astarte kills Mot, Baal's brother, whose name means death. Baal returns annually when the earth is green, evoking jubilation (Persson 1942:313ff.).

The myth of the eternal return of the slain and resurrected god which allows mourning, lamentation, and rejoicing is one of the oldest myths. Traces of this myth can still be found in the celebration of Easter. On the subject of love this myth celebrates two extremes, the sorrow of losing and the joy of refinding.

In Egypt, the celestial cow, the all-nurturing mother, emerges slowly and increasingly takes on a human form. In Giedion's description (1964:78), she is a fertility ideal, a self-begetting goddess, a cow from the marshes of the Nile, a guardian of the Nile delta, and the goddess of the marriage bed. She bequeathes to mankind the joys of life and sexual desire. Under the name of Hathor, we find her for the first time in art history with the figure of a beautiful female. Her head, however, is still the head of the cow or else she is crowned with horns. Ritual hymns to Hathor may have been the precursors to the love poems in Egypt which I discussed earlier.

Among the ancients, the Greeks were unique in having the gods Aphrodite and Eros, whose only concern was love. The emergence of gods specifically concerned with love suggests that this emotion acquired a prominent place in the life of the Greeks, but also that it had become a puzzle.

## Aphrodite

In the course of her history, Aphrodite emancipated herself slowly from the older Semitic Ishtar, queen of heaven and consort to the king. Like Ishtar she once had a beard and probably was androgenous. Like her Semitic predecessor she was associated with a lover who dies and is resurrected. Homer fixed the number of Olympian gods and created boundaries between them. They, so to speak, respect each other's autonomy (Burkert 1985:176). Those gods that play a role in Homer become Olympians. Those who arrive later never quite shed their foreign garb. Aphrodite is an Olympian: Eros, the other god of love, is not. Homer either does not know or, as Friedrich (1978) has suggested, refuses to accept the relationship between Aphrodite and the cycle of death and resurrection.

Aphrodite's name is not of Greek origin; this fact together with her name, Cyprian (from the island of Cyprus), suggests that she came to Greece from the east (Otto 1979; Burkert 1985). Heroditus, the Greek historian, traveler, and geographer, states that the Phoenicians brought Aphrodite from Askelon, the town of the Philistines, to the Greek island of Cythera. She must have become naturalized into the Greek Pantheon long before Homer.

In Homer, Aphrodite is the wife of the lame god Hephaestus, but has as her lover Ares, the god of war. In later imagery, peace reigns on earth whenever the god of war sleeps in her arms. In the eighth chapter of the *Odyssey,* Homer lets a bard entertain the royal guests by telling the story of Aphrodite's adultery. The bard sings of how Hephaestus, Aphrodite's husband, was warned by the all-seeing sun of his wife's infidelity. The divine smith then created a wondrous net that caught "the wanton lovers as entwined they lay." All the gods of Olympus were invited to see the lovers caught in the net. Modesty prevents the goddesses from coming, but the gods laugh. Apollo asks Hermes whether he would share the shame of Ares if he could have also partaken of his joy. Hermes has no doubt that he would choose the disgrace with the joy. The whole episode illustrates how lightly the Olympians as a group treated the marital bond. Neither Aphrodite nor Ares experience guilt. It is evident that the greatest punishment that Hephaestus could think of was shaming his rival.

In the marriage to the lame god, one can hear the echo of the castrating quality of Inanna, but unlike Inanna, Aphrodite is not a martial goddess, having relinquished this aspect to Athena. In the *Iliad* Zeus admonishes Aphrodite and tells her that the works of war are not for her. She should attend to the work of marriage and leave the battlefield to Mars and Athena. I interpret these lines to mean that Homer is psychologically still engaged in separating the goddess of love from the goddess of war. The martial aspect, repressed in Aphrodite, reappears in the form of her love to Ares, the god of war. (That one can love what one has to repress in oneself is an important psychoanalytic insight into love after Freud.) When Aphrodite herself enters the Trojan war to rescue her son Aeneas, she is wounded by Diomedes. She is contemptuously told by him to leave the scene of war, for her domain is to deceive cowardly women. Diomedes may well be the first in a long line of men who look upon love as a feminine undertaking parallel to the masculine interest in war. Diomedes expresses a kernel of mythological truth, for women are more frequently Aphrodite's victims and devotees than men. Paris in the *Iliad* is an exception, since love dominates his very essence. The type reappears in Shakespeare's Romeo and

Goethe's Werther, but none of these men would be described as masculine characters.

Helen is forced by Aphrodite to abandon home, husband, and daughter for the passion the goddess has induced in her for Paris, her abductor. The involuntary nature of her passion does not free her from a sense of guilt. When not under the sway of the goddess, Helen experiences shame and guilt. To King Priam, her father-in-law, she laments: she wishes she had died before she came to Troy and became the cause of the war. She feels guilty for being false to her country, her daughter, and her nuptial bed. Later, Menelaus, Helen's husband, wins her back in a personal combat with Paris, and the Trojan War can apparently come to a happy end. But Aphrodite, indifferent to public warfare, removes Paris from the battlefield and brings him back to Helen's bedroom.

Helen takes the opportunity to challenge Aphrodite. With keen intuition, Helen suspects that Aphrodite herself may be in love with Paris. Mockingly, she invites her to part from the ways of the gods, leave Mt. Olympus and be vexed for Paris's sake, until he decides to make her his wife or, perchance, his slave. Helen keenly feels pangs of conscience as well as the blame of the women of Troy. But Aphrodite is all powerful; she threatens Helen. She might become provoked and the love that Helen enjoys now can turn into hate and she will perish. Helen's rebellion against Aphrodite is over. Meekly she enters the bedchamber.

When Paris approaches, Helen reproaches him bitterly for having boasted he could challenge Menelaus to a personal combat only to flee ignominiously. Changing her mind, she begs him not to provoke Menelaus again. She had originally spoken with her eyes turned away from Paris. The great French tragedian, Racine, noted in the margin of his copy of the *Iliad* that she had averted her eyes because she wished to scold him and was afraid that her love would return if she looked at him (Flaceliere 1970). Under Aphrodite's command, sweet desire for Paris overcomes Helen. Although Helen is responsible for the destruction of Troy, Homer does not blame her. She is not what she became to later generations, the embodiment of the dangerous temptress. Love comes from Aphrodite; it is brought about by the goddess of love. But the guilt is nevertheless experienced as her own.

Psychoanalysts might be tempted to dismiss Aphrodite as merely a projection of Helen's unacceptable sexual and destructive wishes. But to do so would be to miss the creative potential for the understanding of love that was achieved when myth created Aphrodite. The creation of Aphrodite enabled Homer to describe a subtle differentiation within the emotion of loving. Helen succumbed to Paris but she also has contempt for him. He is far from being her ego ideal. Homer does not yet know of a dangerous woman like Medea, whose love when spurned turns into deadly hatred.

Dodds (1951) has shown that Homer's heroes live in a double world: one beyond their ego control and subjectively experienced as taking place under the power of various gods; the other autonomous and subject to their own volition. Helen's love for Paris is an example of love beyond the ego's control.

In the *Odyssey,* Homer describes another type of love, that between Odysseus and Penelope. Penelope is the loyal wife who rebuffs all suitors and waits for ten years for her husband, who tarries in many ports. In psychoanalytic terms, Penelope is the embodiment of the ideal mother of what Mahler (1968; 1975) called the rapprochement subphase: the mother who waits for the infant to come back and is always ready when he returns for what Mahler (1975) called refueling. Many men and some women unconsciously expect to refind in their lifetime the ideal mother of the rapprochement subphase. Odysseus represents a mythical tale of a child enjoying life's adventures on the way home.

After Homer, the next source on Aphrodite is the fifth Homeric hymn composed around 700 B.C. There, Aphrodite moves across the woods accompanied by wolves, lions, and bears. The beasts lose their ferocity under her influence and are conquered by love. Aphrodite can invoke in Zeus himself the passion for Hera as well as for mortal women. To desire a mortal is déclassé for an Olympian, and Zeus revenges himself by making Aphrodite herself fall in love with Anchises. This union results in the birth of Aeneas. What is particularly relevant to the understanding of Aphrodite's nature is that she first suggests a marriage to Anchises but soon lets herself be persuaded to have sexual intercourse upon her first meeting with Anchises.

According to Hesiod, who was second only to Homer as the authoritative source on Greek religion, Aphrodite bore Ares three children: Daimos (Terror), Phobus (Fear), and Harmonia (Harmony). Translated into conceptual language, Hesiod associates terror, fear, and harmony with love. From Hesiod also came Aphrodite's strange parentage, a parentage that psychologically speaking must have remained buried beneath the surface whenever the Greeks evoked the image of Aphrodite. Uranus, the god of the sky and the oldest of the Greek gods, had intercourse with Ge, the goddess of the earth. While so engaged he was castrated by his son Cronos. The severed organ floated in the surging sea, creating white foam, and out of this swelling, Aphrodite emerged. Once she was born she was graciously accepted. She was driven by Zephyr, the west wind, to Cyprus, where the Hours dressed her in divine clothing. Her birth was celebrated by great rejoicing. When the Homeric hymns were written this birth is no longer mentioned. She becomes the daughter of Zeus and Dionne.

Why did the Greeks assign such a strange birth to their goddess of love? In deciphering this strange parentage, psychoanalysis can be helpful, for psychoanalysts are familiar with a type of sexual attraction which is not based on the person as a whole but rather on one anatomical feature, such as breast, penis, shape of hips or buttocks. This type of attraction is based on what psychoanalysts call "part-object" characteristics. One discovers that it is based on a disappointment in the early caretaker. It is as if the person had stopped believing that another person can be loved and only a certain easily refound anatomical feature can be the source of sexual attraction. Aphrodite, in the version of the myth given by Hesiod, is such a child of a part-object. In mythological language, the birth explains why she has no respect for the marital bond or for family life. One gets the impression that the psychic forces that molded this myth were striving to sever the connection between love and the ordinary relationships between husband and wife, mother and child. Indeed, throughout Greek literature, Aphrodite's might is emphasized but seldom is her compassion.

Aphrodite acting through Helen is the cause of the Trojan War. The relationship between the goddess and her earthly representative is written with a subtlety never reached before.

## Sappho

In Greek literary history, Snell (1953) noted that the three genres of poetry, epic, lyric, and drama, flourished in chronological order, each expressing a change in sensibility. Homer knows only requited love. The pangs of unrequited love do not concern him. Unrequited love becomes a major theme in lyric poetry. This poetry shifts the emphasis from the past heroic time to the inner emotion of the poet and his readers. In drama, intrapsychic conflict is central for the first time.

Homer flourished around 800 B.C.; a hundred years later the lyric poets appeared whose poetry was accompanied by the lyre. In lyric poetry, for the first time in Western history love alone was considered a worthy subject for poetry. Unique to this poetry is the personal voice. The names of nine lyric poets have come down to us (Bowra 1962). In the poetry of Sappho, who lived on the Greek island of Lesbos, we hear for the first time in history the voice of an individual woman.

Some say cavalry and others claim
infantry or a fleet of long oars
is the supreme sight on the black earth.
                            I say it is

the one you love. And easily proved.
Did not Helen, who was queen of mortal
beauty, choose as first among mankind
                            the very scourge

of Trojan honor? Haunted by Love
she forgot kinsmen, her own dear child,
and wandered off to a remote country.
                            Weak and fitful
                            (Barnstone translation)

Sappho sets her feminine idea of the supremacy of love against the masculine idea of war. Sappho's relationship with Aphrodite is personal and intimate.

Immortal Aphrodite, of the patterned throne, daughter of Zeus, weaver of wiles, I beseech you, subdue not my heart, lady, with pangs or sorrows, but come hither, if ever before at other times you heard my voice from afar and hearkened to it, and left your father's house and came, yoking your golden chariot. Beautiful swift sparrows brought you, fluttering their multitudinous wings, over the black earth from the sky through the middle air, and swiftly they came. And you, Blessed One, with a smile on your immortal face, asked what again is the matter with me, and why again I call, and what most of all in my frenzied heart I wish to happen: "Whom now am I to persuade to come (?) into your friendship? Who wrongs you, Sappho? Even if she flees, soon shall she pursue; if she receives not gifts, yet shall she give, and if she loves not, soon shall she love, even though she would not." Come to me now also, and deliver me from harsh cares, and all that my heart longs to accomplish, accomplish it, and be yourself my fellow-fighter.

(Quoted by Bowra 1962:199)

The fact that her love is homosexual does not evoke conflict in the poetess, but Sappho, unlike Homer, knows that love evokes ambivalent emotions. She both welcomes and hates the passion that overcomes her. "Love shook my heart, like a wind falling on oaks on the mountains." "Love the looser of limbs shakes me a creature bittersweet, inescapable" (Bowra, p. 184). "Mother darling I cannot work the loom for sweet Kypris (Aphrodite) has almost crushed me, broken me with love for the slender boy" (Barnstone, p. 7).

Sappho can also sing about the pangs of jealousy:

That man seems to me to be the equal of the gods, who sits opposite you and, near to you, listens to you as you speak sweetly and laugh at your lovely laughter.

Although reputed to be a lesbian, Sappho left a poem of great beauty describing the bliss of orgasm of the bride on her wedding night.

*Song of the Wedding Bed*

Bride, warm with rose-
colored love, brightest
ornament of the Paphian,
come to the bedroom now,
enter the bed and play
tenderly with your man.
May the Evening Star
lead you eagerly
to that instant when you
will gaze in wonder
before the silver throne
of Hera, queen of marriage.

Sappho also sings about the sadness of menopause:

*Last Praises*

If my nipples were to drip milk
and my womb still carry a child,
I would enter this marriage bed
                    intrepidly,

but age dries my flesh with a thousand
wrinkles, and love is in no hurry
to seize my body with the gifts
                    of pleasant pain.

Yet, let us sing praises to her
who wears the scent of violets
                    on her young breasts.

To the lyric poets we owe speaking of love in a personal voice.

In Greek tragedy, particularly in the works of Euripides, we find the beginning of a philosophical attitude toward love. Aphrodite now stands midway between a mythological goddess and an abstract principle.

Euripides was born in 480 B.C.; he was Plato's contemporary. His dramatis personae have the tendency to enter into a debate on the nature of Aphrodite and love in general. In his tragedy, *The Trojan Women*, we meet some of the same characters we have encountered in the *Iliad*. The

Trojan War is over, Helen has been returned to her husband Menelaus. As an adulteress and as the cause of the Trojan War, Helen should receive the death penalty. Hecuba, the queen of fallen Troy, Helen's former mother-in-law, demands this penalty. Menelaus hesitates. Hecuba reads his mind: "A lover once will always love again." Helen defends her conduct: Menelaus should not have left her alone with the stranger Paris. She did not act on her own free will but was merely the vehicle for Aphrodite's designs. In the play by Euripides, Hecuba raises questions that tell us in unmistakable terms that the world of the myth is behind us; she asks, "Why should Hera who seeks no lovers enter a beauty contest with Aphrodite? And why should Athena the virgin goddess who flees from love compete with Aphrodite?" Hecuba's challenge and logic belong to a postmythological era. Hecuba implies in no uncertain terms that Helen was guilty, and Euripides lets us know that the mantle of myth was nothing more than what we would call today Helen's rationalizations.

The *Hippolytus* by Euripides deals superficially with the destructive power of Aphrodite. The story was original to Euripides. Hippolytus is the bastard son of Theseus and the Queen of the Amazons, Hippolyta. He is a *Sophrosyne,* a Greek term that connotes chastity, temperance, self-control, and moderation. He is a devotee of Artemis, the virgin goddess of the chase. His refusal to love is an affront to Aphrodite. To make matters worse, in a moment of hubris he refers to Aphrodite as the vilest among the Olympians. He refuses to pay homage to "any god whose worship craves the night." Since he is consecrated to Artemis, Aphrodite has no direct power over him. She can, however, make the heart of his step-mother, Phaedra, be seized with wild desire for him. The queen resists heroically the incestuous temptation. However, she has a nurse who persuades her to confess her love for Hippolytus. The following exchange takes place between them:

Phaedra: What is it they mean when they talk of people being in love?
Nurse:    At once the sweetest and the bitterest thing my child.
Phaedra: I shall only find the latter half.

(Coleridge translation)

The nurse prevails and this is her argument:

Thy fate is no uncommon one nor past one's calculations; thou art stricken by the passion Cypris (Aphrodite) sends. Thou art in love; what wonder? so are many more. Wilt thou, because thou lov'st, destroy thyself? 'Tis little gain I trow, for those who love or yet may love their fellows, if death must be their end; for though the Love-Queen's onset in her might is more than man can bear, yet doth she gently visit yielding hearts, and only when she finds a proud unnatural spirit, doth she take and mock it past belief. Her path is in the sky, and mid the ocean's surge she rides; from her all nature springs; she sows the seeds of love, inspires the warm desire to which we sons of earth all owe our being.

(Coleridge translation)

A whole philosophy of love is expressed by the nurse.

In the fourth century B.C., the acceptance of sexual desire that character-ized Aphrodite is no longer acceptable. The image of Aphrodite herself undergoes a split between the celestial Aphrodite (Ourania) and a lower Aphrodite (Pandemous), a goddess of sexual life and patron of prostitutes. With the rise of Christianity this division will persist and gain strength. It is against this split that Freud (1910a, 1912) wrote his articles on love.

By the fifth century, the power of Aphrodite to generate new insights into the nature of love is waning. New insights come from philosophers, notably Plato. Aphrodite's final dethronement comes at the hands of the Roman poet, Ovid, who was alive when the Christian era began.

Like Aphrodite, Eros was dethroned by Ovid (*Metamorphoses, 10*). Ovid was to my knowledge the first poet to describe incest sympatheti-cally. The story of Myrrha and her father Simeras shows many parallels to that of Hippolytus and Phaedra. Myrrha rejects all suitors because she is sexually in love with her father. When her father asks her what kind of a husband she wants, she answers, "a man like you." The father praises her answer. Like Phaedra, she struggles against the incestuous temptation. Ovid makes the Christian distinction between sinning in mind and sinning in body. "You have so far not sinned in body, Myrrha, try not to sin in mind" (Humphries translation, p.145). Burdened by guilt, Myrrha at-tempts suicide. Like Phaedra, she is rescued by the nurse who helps her to commit incest with her father. Ovid describes Myrrha's thoughts: animals are not subject to the incest taboo; stallions and rams sire upon their own daughters. Why are humans not free to do so? Incest is a law against nature. A daughter's love for her father is a most natural love. It is evident that Ovid does not share the horror of incest that Sophocles had.

Pregnant with her father's son, Myrrha is metamorphosed into a tree. Out of this tree, the beautiful Adonis is born. At this point, Ovid tells us how Eros (Cupid) made a mistake:

> Cupid, it seems was playing,
> Quiver on shoulder, when he kissed his mother,
> And one barb grazed her breast; she pushed him away,
> But the wound was deeper than she knew; deceived,
> Charmed by Adonis' beauty, she cared no more

For Cyther's shores nor Paphos' sea-ringed island,
Nor Cnidos, where fish team, nor high Amathus,
Rich in its precious ores. She stays away
Even from Heaven, Adonis is better than Heaven.
She is beside him always; she has always,
Before this time, preferred the shadowy places,
Preferred her ease, preferred to improve her beauty
By careful tending, but now, across the ridges,
Through woods, through rocky places thick with brambles,
She goes, more like Diana than like Venus.

                                        (Humphries translation)

There is no hint yet in Ovid that Adonis will be recalcitrant and unresponsive to the love that Venus proffers. The last humiliation of the goddess will take place at the hands of Titian and Shakespeare. I will deal with the last phase of Aphrodite's humiliation in another chapter. In Ovid, for the first time in classical history, the goddess of love is herself smitten by love. Adonis is killed in the hunt by a wild boar and Venus, unable to overcome her grief, becomes a goddess of lament, converting Adonis into the anemone flower. With one stroke, Ovid undid the separation between the goddesses of fertility, worshipped throughout the Middle East, and Aphrodite, the goddess of love, a specific Greek creation. With Ovid, she returns where she came from and becomes like Astarte and Isis, the goddess of lamentation and resurrection.

Friedrich (1978) is of the opinion that Homer and Hesiod failed to mention the connection between Aphrodite and Adonis not because the myth was unknown to them but because it was repugnant to their religious feelings (p. 70).

As a personification of both love and fertility as well as the major antidote to strife and war, we encounter Aphrodite under her Roman name, Venus, in the first chapter of Lucretius' book *De Rerum Natura*. It is to her that the book is dedicated. Lucretius (94–55 B.C.) was both a philosopher and a poet, and his work is a long didactic poem.

Ah, goddess, when the spring
Makes clear its daytime, and a warmer wind
Stirs from the west, a procreative air,
High in the sky the happy-hearted birds,
Responsive to your coming, call and cry,
The cattle, tame no longer, swim across
The rush of river-torrents, or skip and bound
In joyous meadows; where your brightness leads,

They follow, gladly taken in the drive,
The urge, of love to come.

Since you alone control the way things are.
Since without you no thing has ever come
Into the radiant boundaries of light,
Since without you nothing is ever glad,
And nothing ever lovable,
I need you with me, goddess, in the poem
I try to write here, on The Way Things Are.

Since you alone can help with tranquil peace
The human race, and Mars, the governor
Of war's fierce duty, more than once has come,
Gentled by love's eternal wound, to you,
                    (Humphries translation)

A puzzling question remains. Why did the Greeks need more than one
god of love? Was it that the emotion of love was so overwhelming and so
fraught with conflict that the Greeks could not create one God of Love?
Or was it that Greek mythology came about through the amalgam of
different traditions in which there were two different gods of love and the
differences could not be entirely obliterated? One interpretation is psychological, the other is historical and anthropological; the two are not incompatible with each other. The fact that Eros was so often portrayed as a
baby could have suggested to someone before Freud that love has something in common with infancy. But no one took this hint from mythology
as a starting point for the understanding of love. The fact that the Greeks
had two gods of love gave rise to philosophical as well as psychological
speculation. Homer knew well the nature of abiding love. He described it
in the relationship between Hector and Andromache, but wedded and
abiding love was to him neither the province of Aphrodite nor Eros.

Dover (1978), a classical scholar, has pointed out that there is some
justification in regarding genital activity as the province of Aphrodite and
"the obsessive focusing of desire on one person as the province of Eros"
(p. 63). He suggests that Aphrodite was the goddess of sexual passion and
Eros was the god of love. In Hellenistic times, an attempt was made to
associate Eros with homosexuality and Aphrodite with heterosexuality.
Dover further points out that to Homer, Eros meant desire (p. 50). It could
be desire for a drink or desire for a woman. In preplatonic Greece, there
was no word for love that precluded sexuality. In *Hippolytus,* on which I
have already commented, Aphrodite and Eros work in unison. The painful
arrows are those of Aphrodite but Eros is the one who shoots them.

Psychoanalyst Michael Balint (1936) suggested that Eros represents sexual foreplay and since foreplay, as distinguished from genital sexuality, represents a link to infancy, it is fitting that it should have been portrayed by a baby or a young child. By contrast, Aphrodite was the goddess of adult genital love.

## Eros

Eros, the second god of love, is historically and conceptually very different from Aphrodite. He has no known Semitic prehistory, he is not an Olympian and has no personal mythology associated with his deeds. Hesiod made Eros the oldest of the gods, whose power extends over gods and mortals. In this capacity we reencounter Eros in Plato's *Symposium*. He is therefore more readily translated into the conceptual language of Platonic philosophy.

In Homer's *Odyssey*, Eros is described as violent physical desire that shakes the limbs of Penelope's suitors. He is conceived as capable of entering into the human body. In Homer he is himself the violent sexual desire that drives Paris to Helen, Zeus to Hera. In lyric poetry he is experienced as a violent wind that shakes his victims. Onians (1954) has noted that Homer described sexual love as the process of liquefying and melting. He speaks of "liquid desire"; by contrast, he associates hate with freezing and stiffening (p. 202). These metaphors have an unconscious appeal for we still say that we melt when we are in love and become hardened when we hate.

In early vase paintings, Eros is portrayed as striking his victims with an axe or a whip. Eros acquired the familiar arrows at the time of Euripides, in the fifth century B.C. With the acquisition of the bow and arrow, he became the god of falling in love. He does little else than shoot his arrows at random into the hearts of men and women. Unlike the Olympians he is not known to have a sustained personal relationship with any mortal. The fact that he has no interest in his victims once he has pierced them with his arrow, I interpret to mean that the Greeks separated falling in love from loving. In metaphorical language, the arrows symbolize both the random and irrational nature of love. Historically, the arrow proved to be a most powerful metaphor. The idea that love is a random event dominates Western thinking. It was dislodged only through Freud's findings. Continuing the metaphor, we can see Freud as disarming Eros. Freud has taught us that the random nature of love appeals to us precisely because we wish to deny its incestuous origins. In Greek tragedy, Eros is still a powerful god.

The chorus in *Antigone* by Sophocles speaks of the havoc that Eros causes and how he can make even the just capable of committing crimes. In the *Hippolytus* the chorus prays to be protected against the tyrannical violence of Eros.

In later developments, Eros lost ground to Aphrodite, becoming her son. He acquired a brother called Antieros, the god of requited love. Under the impact of Freud's dual instinct theory, we are inclined to understand anti-eros as hate, but to the Greeks, the opposite of love was the wish to be loved. Eros also acquired two inseparable companions, Pathos, the personification of longing, and Himeros, the personification of desire. In mythological language the Greeks tell us that love is not love unless it is accompanied by both desire and longing.

Ovid opened his *Amores* (Loves) with a comic evocation of Cupid (the Latin name for Eros).

> Arms and violent wars, with meter suited to matter,
> Arms and violent wars, all in hexameters,*
> I was preparing to sound, when I heard a snicker from Cupid;
> What had the rascal done, but taken one foot away?*
> "Why you bad boy!" I said, "who gave you this jurisdiction?
> We are the Muses' own, not your contemptible throng . . .
> So I complained, and he drew out a shaft from his quiver,
> Taking his time to choose just the right arrow to use,
> Bent the bow, moon-shaped, at his knee," and "Poet,"
> he told me, "Take what I send; this barb surely will
> sting you to song!"
>
> (Humphries translation)

Reading these lines, we know that the awe before a supernatural god of love that characterized the mythological age is over. Eros never recovered from the arrows of this great poet.

In a fascinating study, Panofsky (1939) has traced the motif of a blind cupid. We are so accustomed to the portrayal of the god of love as blindfolded that it comes as a surprise that he was never so portrayed in Greek and Roman art. He appears blind for the first time in the thirteenth century. Panofsky comments that Cupid started his career in rather terrifying company. Being blindfolded, he is the companion of the synagogue, infidelity, and death (p.111). The interpretation was most unflattering. "Cupid is blind because he deprives men of their garments, their possessions,

---

*The reference is to the change of rhythm. Wars were described in hexameters; on love Ovid wrote in pentameters.

their good sense and their wisdom" (p. 107). Once a mighty god, Cupid's mythological power wanes and he is changed from single to plural. Cupid becomes the putties that we find as a decorative motif in the friezes by Donatello in Florence. Cupid's life was nevertheless prolonged by becoming a poetic metaphor. Newbolt (1909) has pointed out that Cupid furnished the English poets with an almost too plentiful stock of metaphors, tropes, and images to suit their changing moods and fancies. Poets like Chaucer felt free to employ Cupid as a mighty god of love the way Hesiod saw him or to treat him humorously as a jailer in Ovid's style.

I assume that Aphrodite was an inspiration to the Greek and Roman poets throughout history because she had ceased to be a goddess of fertility and became associated only with passionate love. The *Iliad* was an epic written for an aristocratic, warrior class. Its subject was war, but two women play an eminent role in it: Helen, who is the cause of the war itself, and Briseis, who is the cause of the great quarrel between Achilles and Agamemnon. Other gods play major roles in Homer, but the sexual power of Aphrodite shines through the *Iliad*.

It is of interest to note that the dethronement of the two gods of love by Ovid coincides with the beginning of the Christian era. But long before Ovid, when Athens enjoyed the last days of her glory, Plato added a new vocabulary to the understanding of love.

# 4

# How Plato Changed the
# Western Way of Looking
# at Love

Most people have an inhibition against examining love rationally. Many analysands believe that their love relationship will not survive psychoanalytic scrutiny. This feeling must have been there already in antiquity. The story of Cupid and Psyche, frequently depicted in works of art, is of late origin: it was written by Apuleius, who lived in the second century A.D. Psyche was the youngest of three daughters. Eros loved her and asked Sapphire, the north wind, to carry her to a secluded spot where he visits her nightly with the proviso that she never see his face. Her evil sisters persuade her to transgress the command. She looks upon Eros sleeping. In her excitement a drop of hot wax falls upon Eros; he awakens and vanishes. After many trials Psyche refinds him and they are united once more. While it is not a genuine myth, it can be read as a cautionary tale warning us that love will vanish if, like Psyche, driven by curiosity, we dare gaze upon Cupid's face.

Among the few who sought to overcome this prohibition and face the puzzle of love, Plato and Freud stand out as the two whose epistemological interest transformed our way of looking at love. Although 2500 years separate them, they have much in common. Dodds (1951) described Plato as growing up in a social circle which took pride in settling all questions before the bar of reason. This rational point of view was challenged during Plato's lifetime by events which, as Dodds puts it, "should well induce any rationalist to reconsider his faith" (pp. 214–215). *Mutatis mutandis,* this description fits Freud.

Plato lived at a time still saturated with the mythological point of view, but under the impact of the rational philosophers myths were gradually transformed into allegories. At the same time, the Sophists systematically called into question the basic values underlying the Greek way of life.

In two dialogues, *Phaedrus* and the *Symposium,* Plato for the first time in recorded history set out to explore the nature of love. The *Symposium,* one of the great literary-philosophical works, has received adulation from posterity. Its influence on the way Western man understood love was immense. Generations of students have pondered it, compared its lofty speeches with the inarticulate stirrings of love they were experiencing themselves. The ultimate message of the *Symposium* was clear: the sexual urges, the yearnings to love and be loved, which play so major a role in daily lives, can and should be diverted to higher aims. It was as if Plato was saying to the young men and women, take hold of this troublesome sexual drive at a time in your life when it is making particularly strong demands on you and force it upward to higher aims, that offer safer and greater rewards. Plato was the first to advocate the harnessing of the sexual drive in the service of subliminatory activities. Should Plato be credited with the discovery of sublimation of the sexual drive because he advocated it? The question is difficult to answer. The concept if not the term sublimation links Plato with Freud. I will show later that the failure to acknowledge this connection was not in the best interests of psychoanalysis as a discipline. Any discussion of love, and particularly a psychoanalytic one, is bound to remain incomplete if it fails to deal with sublimation.

Plato realized that Eros will not be deflected to higher aims without an inner struggle or what psychoanalysts call resistance. To combat this resistance, Plato became an architect of a psychology of intrapsychic conflict. It was not, to be sure, a neutral psychology; Plato was not a neutral observer of human nature, but, like many philosophers, he was a pleader for a very definite set of moral values. But he did more than advocate what he wished man to reach. He was aware of the forces opposing his efforts to educate and elevate, and out of this awareness he developed a vocabulary for dealing with intrapsychic conflicts. This rich vocabulary remained largely unexplored for 2500 years until Freud found a way of harnessing it for purposes other than those Plato intended.

In the previous chapter, I have shown how much psychoanalysis owes to Greek tragedy; its debt to platonic philosophy is as great. While the tragedians were describing intrapsychic conflict, sometimes in mythological and sometimes in psychological terms, Plato built a philosophy-psychology that conceptualized a structure in which intrapsychic events can take place.

For reasons which I will discuss later, this connection between Plato and Freud remained largely unacknowledged by psychoanalysis.

In the opening passage of Plato's *Phaedrus,* Socrates and his companion find themselves on the bank of the river Ilissus, where Boreas, the north wind, is said to have carried off Orithyia. Socrates is asked whether he believes this myth. He replies cautiously, "The wise are doubtful, and I should not be singular if, like them, I too doubted. I might have a rational explanation that Orithyia was playing with Pharmacia when a north gust carried her over the neighboring rocks, and this being the manner of her death, she was said to be carried away by Boreas, the north wind. . . . "

But to go reducing chimeras, gorgons, and winged steeds to rule of probability is (to Socrates) crude philosophy. He has no leisure for such inquiries for he must first know himself. "To be curious about that which is not my concern while I am still in ignorance of myself would be ridiculous." Socrates then goes on to ask, rather surprisingly, "Am I monster more complicated and swollen with passion then the serpent Typo or a creature of gentler sort?" (Jowett translation). What is of interest is the connection between the loss of faith in myths and the command "Know thyself." This connection goes far beyond the superficial one cited by Socrates that he has no leisure for such pursuits, for as long as myths held sway over men's minds, man was not a puzzle to himself. And there was no inner need to know oneself.

Socrates believes in a daemon, an inner voice that warns him against evil and urges him toward good. In the *Apology,* Socrates explains that he heard an inner voice as a child. It always forbade but never commanded. He is not afraid of death, for either death is a dreamless sleep which is plainly good; or the soul migrates to another world where he will converse with such men as Hesiod and Homer. To this encounter he is looking forward with pleasure. The waning of a mythological age is associated with a major advance in psychic internalization. The urge to know oneself testifies to a new postmythological loneliness and a new sense of responsibility. The accusation of impiety against the Olympian gods, insofar as they embodied the age of myth, which was leveled against Socrates, did contain more than a kernel of truth. Socrates was not the first to demand self-knowledge. Sophocles, born twenty-six years earlier, made Oedipus proclaim: "Born thus, I ask to be no other man, than that I am, and will know who I am." For Oedipus, however, self-knowledge is still largely external knowledge, whereas the self-knowledge of Socrates is closer to what psychoanalysts call insight. This moment in the evolution of human thought is also a moment when love first appears as a puzzling emotion.

Pre-Socratic Greek man feared love as a destructive power of the god of love. Post-Socratic man in Greece was puzzled by love.

Unlike most subsequent treaties on love, the *Symposium* is primarily concerned with homosexual love, which it regards as higher than heterosexual love. But Plato does not recommend physical homosexuality and in his last book, *The Laws,* he even calls homosexuality unnatural and a crime against the state. It is likely that this deflection of love into homosexual channels contributed to the feeling that love is a puzzle. My psychoanalytic experience has taught me that men and women with a strong sense of gender identity are not as overwhelmed and puzzled by love as those whose gender identity has remained ambiguous.

## *Plato's* Symposium

Plato's *Symposium* contains two theories of love. Both have exerted a significant influence on the subsequent developments in the Western world. The first is assigned to Aristophanes, the master of comedy, the second to Socrates. Plato's *Symposium* (translated as "banquet" by Shelley) is called together to honor and eulogize Eros. After the intervention by Socrates it turns into a debate about the nature of Eros. The very fact that Eros, a god, is subject to debate testifies that we are moving out of the world of myth.

Phaedrus, the first orator, praises the power of Eros in mythological language. Love he says was present at the very creation of the world. All gods were created out of love. Eros is a mighty god who inspires lovers to noble deeds of unprecedented courage so that they can win the love and the admiration of him whom they love. The second speaker, Pausanias, sees happiness as combining sexual pleasure and the cultivation of the mind. Heterosexual love can give only sexual pleasure; it is therefore the domain of earthly or common (Pandemus) Aphrodite, while homosexual love combines the two and partakes of the heavenly Aphrodite. The differentiation between heavenly and earthly Aphrodite was destined to have a long history in Western thought.

The third speaker, Euryximachus, the physician, is a follower of Empedocles. To him Eros is a natural force attracting bodies to each other; following Pythagorean medical theory, he equates health with balance between contradictory elements: good is to him the harmony of opposites, bad the coming together of similars. Euryximachus believes that the attraction for the like (narcissistic love in psychoanalytic vocabulary) creates sickness, while harmony in love takes place among complementary personality types. In the name of medicine, Euryximachus introduces a philosophical view of Eros. Eros is not confined to human relationships; he is active in all of nature, animate and inanimate. Euryximachus' personality is well drawn by Plato. He is the embodiment of the professional man sure of his views, pedantic in his delivery, lacking in philosophical depth.

The next speaker is Aristophanes. The fable that Plato gave to Aristophanes contains insights into the nature of love that are so important that I will, with apology to the Platonists who consider Socrates' contribution as the pinnacle of the *Symposium,* leave the examination of this speech to the next chapter.

After Aristophanes, Agathon speaks; he has just won the Athenian prize for tragedy. In his view, love is the youngest of the gods, for had love been born earlier the prehistory of the Olympian gods would never have taken the course that it did. This is a fine insight into Greek mythology, for in the generation before Zeus created order and assigned to each god his or her domain, Cronos castrated his father and ate his children. Agathon correctly interprets this to mean that love had no dominion over him. Agathon is the father of all psychologists, including Freud, who believe that hate is older than love. All those who serve the god of love serve of their own free will, implying that love can never be forced. He also evokes the beautiful image of Aphrodite subduing the god of war and when he sleeps in her arms, peace prevails on earth. (The topic became popular with Renaissance painters.) When touched by the god of love, everyone becomes a poet, even though he had no music before. When Apollo discovered medicine, archery, and music, he did so under the guidance of the god of love. Melody, metallurgy, and weaving are all done under the aegis of the god of love. In poetic language, Agathon describes here what Freud will later designate under the term sublimation.

Plato's style is unique and accounts for the aesthetic appeal of this work. The style reflects the transition from myth to philosophy. Plato assumes that his readers, like the distinguished company that makes up the symposium, are awed by the god of love, ready to pay homage to him but not to examine him. Socrates will have the painful task of weaning them away from the mythological sense of certainty by disclosing some unflattering truths about love. With empathy for the resistance that the philosophical view will evoke, Plato lets one protagonist after another praise love only to have Socrates undercut the argument. Consciously, Socrates was representing Plato's views. For unlike a playwright like Shakespeare, Plato does not hover neutrally over his characters. Nevertheless, I suspect that to a greater degree than he would have acknowledged, Plato was also captivated by the view of love presented by the other speakers, particularly Aristophanes.

Socrates, the last speaker, surprises everybody by his assertion that love is the key to everything he has done; it is the only subject he ever pretended to have any knowledge of. Philosophy is love because the philosopher is a lover of knowledge. For Socrates this was not yet a phrase; he loved philosophy with a passion. Socrates refuses to enter the competition between the orators. He will not praise love, but if his listeners are willing to hear his message, he will tell them the truth about love. In a disarming display of modesty, Socrates does not present his views as his own but rather as lessons he learned from the Sophist, Diotima. Like the other guests, he too was captive of the mythological point of view until he was enlightened by Diotima to the philosophical one. As Socrates develops his view, love becomes an abstract, nonmythological power, equated with the creative reproductive urge that governs all nature.

Diotima uses a fable to instruct Socrates. When Aphrodite was born, a feast was held by the gods and during this feast, Resource was intoxicated and fell asleep. In this helpless state, Poverty seduced him and Eros was conceived. As a son of Poverty, Eros has neither shoes nor house to dwell in, he sleeps on bare ground under the open sky and takes his rest on doorsteps. Like his mother, he is always wanting. (We should note that the English word "want" means both desire and deficiency.) Like his father, Eros is enterprising, scheming, an enchanter and sorcerer. Even when one does not agree with Socrates, one must concede that the humorous contempt with which the strange parentage of Eros is presented captures the paradoxical feeling of many lovers: immense riches, an elation that alternates with feelings of dismal poverty when separated from or abandoned by the loved one. Plato thus put in the mouth of Diotima one of the very great insights in the history of love. Love is not a god because it is based on a need and no god can be needful. The recognition that love is a human need which when not met leaves us unfulfilled is of great importance. For centuries theologians struggled with the problem of how a god who does not need man still loves him. It is a deep philosophical paradox that no religion based on God's love has successfully resolved.

The full significance of Plato's idea will become clear in the last chapter. There I will show that love is indeed based on longing for completeness. Those who rebel against this need and cannot acknowledge it remain narcissistic. Those who feel this need so strongly that they cannot exist without the mate love neither wisely nor well.

Diotima teaches Socrates that love is not a god but a great daemon.

Daemons are intermediaries between men and gods. They communicate human affairs to the gods and convey divine messages to mortals. In Diotima's postmythological world, no god has intercourse with human beings. All mingling takes place through the intermediating daemons. It is they who appear to men in visionary states and in dreams. A man who knows this truth becomes himself a demonic man and as such superior to ordinary craftsmen who lead unimaginative lives.

Love is to Diotima not a god because it is based on the feeling that one needs someone else to feel complete. This was a new insight into the nature of love. By implication, the Greek gods who live in a state of gratified narcissism do not know such a need and are therefore incapable of loving. The Greeks were the first to develop the beatific smile in their archaic gods. This smile, which found another expression in Hindu sculpture, was the smile of gratified narcissism that has freed itself from the dependence on any other objects.

The term daemon is found in Homer, but the concept was Plato's own creation. It had an enormous influence on Western thinking. The gods that appeared, spoke, hovered, and intervened in the lives of Homer's heroes are now so far away that one can communicate with them only through intermediaries. Christianity took up the concept of the intercessors, a role usually assigned to Mary and the Hosts of Saints. The term daemon was transformed to mean supernatural evil.

All who are mortal, Diotima continues to instruct Socrates, yearn for immortality. It is the quest for immortality that moves men and women to procreate. It is also the power behind all heroic and sacrificial acts. Socrates, the relentless inquirer, does not ask why the wish to be remembered or, to put it negatively, why the anxiety of being forgotten, should be the dominant passion of mankind. Had Socrates asked himself this question, he would have come closer to Freud's world.

Diotima's teaching culminates in Plato's concept of the ladder of love. The young man is drawn to the beauty of the body. With proper guidance he can be led to see that the particular beauty of a particular body is only an example of the beautiful body in general. If he becomes aware of this, the attachment to a particular body will diminish. On the next level the disciple will discover that the beauty of the soul is more valuable than the beauty of the body. From there he will be led to discover the beauty of science and philosophy. Step by step he will then be led to contemplate absolute beauty devoid of any ugliness. Love's beginning is in the love for beautiful boys. Love's end is the contemplation of absolute beauty. What Plato presents is a theory of sublimation of homosexual love.

# 5

## *Love as a Yearning for Reunion: Plato's Second Theory of Love*

One of the ironies of literary history is the immense appeal that the fable Plato gave to Aristophanes had on subsequent generations; it is generally agreed that it is the best known and most popular piece of all Plato's writings. What was intended to be a low-level insight to be swept away by Diotima's superior understanding has retained a fascination for future generations. Why did Plato give half of the space in the *Symposium* to the representations of all the important traditional views on love prevalent in Athens before Socrates? Scholars are divided on this point: some like Taylor (1926) are convinced that Aristophanes' fable is nothing but high comedy spoken by a jester; others like Jaeger (1945) and Gould (1963) assume that Plato, a true philosopher, attempted to extract the greatest possible truth from every prevalent point of view in order to demonstrate all the more forcefully the brilliance of Socrates.

I believe that all speakers in the *Symposium* represent an aspect of Plato himself. The creative writer in Plato allowed each character to exist in its own right, but as a philosopher, he had to present a coherent world view. In this struggle, Socrates emerged as the victor, and yet the fable that Plato gave to Aristophanes touched a deep yearning in many people, and had so profound an influence that I cannot agree that it was all said in jest. Plato, I would guess, may have been ambivalent about his insight, but he was not joking. Consciously and ideologically, Plato sided with the Socratic view. However, the creative part of him, closer to the unconscious, created a fable that never lost its appeal to lovers. I will not here repeat the whole fable, only that part which is pertinent to the understanding of love. I call it a fable rather than myth, because the term myth should be used to connote stories which compel belief in the culture in which they originated. Aristophanes does not give his tale the authority of a myth. Like Diotima's fable it is an explanation, not an article of faith.

Of all the gods, Aristophanes tells the revelers of the *Symposium,* the god of love is the best friend of man. Originally, the sexes were not two but three. There were men, women, and the union of the two. Originally man had two faces, four arms, four legs, two sexual organs, and could move freely forward or backward. There were three types of these primeval human beings. Some were composed of two males, others of two females, a third was composed of men and women. These primeval humans were so powerful that they threatened the gods, and Zeus cut them in two, creating homosexual men, lesbian women, and heterosexual couples. The reason why mankind was not annihilated is ascribed to the dependence of the gods on the sacrifices brought by man.

After the division, the two parts each desiring his other half came together and, throwing their arms about one another, entwined in mutual embraces. They long to grow together into one.

Each of us when separated, having one side only, like a flat fish, is but the indenture of a man, and he is always looking for his other half . . . And when one of them meets with his other half, the actual half of himself, whether he be a lover of youth or a lover of another sort, the pair are lost in an amazement of love and friendship and intimacy, and will not be out of the other's sight, as I may say, even for a moment: these are the people who pass their whole lives together; yet they could not explain what they desire of one another. For the intense yearning which each of them has towards the other does not appear to be the desire of lover's intercourse, but of something else which the soul of either evidently desires and cannot tell, and of which she has only a dark and doubtful presentiment. Suppose Hephaestus, with his instruments, to come to the pair who are lying side by side and to say to them, "What do you people want of one another?" they would be unable to explain. And suppose further, that when he saw their perplexity he said, "Do you desire to be wholly one; always day and night to be in one another's company for if this is what you desire, I am ready to melt you into one and let you grow together . . ." There is not a man of them who when he heard the proposal would deny or would acknowledge that this meeting and melting into one another, this becoming one instead of two, was the very expression of his ancient need. And the reason is that human nature was originally one and we were a whole, and the desire and pursuit of the whole is called love.

The oration ends on a note of religious piety:

If we are friends of the god (of love) and at peace with him we shall find our own true love, which rarely happens in the world at present . . . if our loves were perfectly accomplished and each one returning to his primeval nature, to his original true love, then our race would be happy.

(Jowett translation)

The fable represents one of the most remarkable insights into the nature of love in the whole history of the subject. There is nothing in the preceding Greek thinking on love that I have described in chapter 3 to prepare us for this idea. The imagery is highly sexual but another, deeper need that can be met by one person only is stated here for the first time. Plato may have been the first to verbalize the idea that somewhere there is a perfect mate. The perfect mate, so familiar to us in the yearnings of contemporary men and women, has its historical origin in Greek idealism.

The fable gives a mythical rather than a psychological explanation of love. In its own mythological language, it does answer the question of why the finding of one person gives a sense of bliss and permanence while another offers only transitory satisfaction. The fable also captures another symptom of love, the sense of yearning and missing that both precedes and accompanies falling in love.

The association between love and melting was not original to Plato. Sophocles praises love as omnipotent, "for it melts its way into the lungs of those who have life in them" (Onians 1954:27). We should also note that the expression "dark and doubtful presentiment," when translated into psychoanalytic vocabulary, expresses a feeling that emerges when a present event, or feeling state, has established contact with a past event or a feeling state without the past event becoming conscious. I assume that Freud had this passage at least preconsciously in mind when he wrote "following a dim presentiment, I decided to replace hypnosis by free association" (Freud 1914a:19).

The fable by Aristophanes reappears with a reversed meaning when Dante enters the second circle of the inferno reserved for carnal sinners. There Francesca and Paulo appear condemned, never to separate. Francesca was married to Paolo's older, crippled brother. The couple was apprehended in flagrante delecto by the husband's brother, who pierced them both with the same sword. In Dante's version, eternal union is a punishment; the lovers are physically merged but have retained separate voices and separate individuality. What was a vision of bliss in the *Symposium* has become a torment in Dante.

One of the best known lines in the poetry of love is:

> Love that will take for answer only love
> . . . caught me so fiercely up in his delight

that as you see he still is by my side.
Love led us to one death.

Dante understood that the reading of love poetry lowers resistance against illicit love.

> One day together, for pastime, we read
>   Of Launcelot, and how Love held him in thrall.
>   We were alone, and without any dread.
> Sometimes our eyes, at the word's secret call,
>   Met, and our cheeks a changing colour wore.
>   But it was one page only that did it all.
> When we read how that smile, so thirsted for,
>   Was kissed by such a lover, he that may
>   Never from me be separated more
> All trembling kissed my mouth. The book I say
>   Was a Galahalt to us, and he beside
>   That wrote the book. We read no more that day.
>                               (Milano 1947, Canto V)

The fable that Plato assigned to Aristophanes originated in India, where bisexuality was one of the privileges of divinity. Freud learned about the Indian origin of the fable from Gomperz (1896), who was one of Freud's ten favorite authors (Eissler 1951). He did not, however, notice the basic difference between the Indian and the Greek version (Freud 1920:58n). The fable in Plato's hand underwent a typically Greek transformation.

In the *Upanishads,* Purusa, the primeval man, looked around him and saw nothing but himself. At first, he said, "I am," and thus the word "I" was born. He did not rejoice and therefore one who is alone does not rejoice. He willed himself to fall into two separate pieces, and from this husband and wife were born. They united, and from this mankind was born. She reflected, "How can he unite with me after engendering me from himself? For shame; I would conceal myself." She became a cow and he became a bull and united with her and from them all cattle were born: she became a mare and he a stallion, etc. (O'Flaherty 1975:34).

In the Indian version, primeval man like the biblical Adam is lonely. He asks that two be made out of one. The homosexual variant is absent. But what is most striking is that the remerger and the yearning for reunion as an expression of love is absent. The Indian version introduces the incest motif into the story of the reunion after the split, or at least the incest fear is experienced by the woman. It is through her incest fear that the animal kingdom was created. We should note that unlike the biblical story, the creation of man precedes the creation of animals. In the Greek version the homosexual theme overshadows the fear of incest.

If the myth of Purusa offers an explanation for the population of the world by humans and the creation of the animal kingdom, a parallel myth dealing with the god Siva is of greater psychological complexity. Brahma the creator, being male, had great difficulty in creating a woman; he became enraged by this failure and out of his rage, Siva was born. Unlike Brahma, who was all male, Siva was half male and half female. Brahma, eager to go on with the work of creation, commanded Siva to eject the feminine part of himself. Thus Parvati was created. Soon after her creation she emanated a mirror image of herself and returned back into Siva. It is the image of the original Parvati that lived on as the external goddess. Therefore, her complex history as the daughter of the king of the mountain is really only the history of Parvati's image. No sooner did Siva fall in love with the now externalized Parvati that he began to practice austerities in order to liberate himself from her influence; Parvati, not to be outdone by him, also practiced austerities. The whole story seems to be a mythological reenactment of the conflict between narcissism and love which ends on a very interesting compromise. Parvati begets children but not with Siva (Kramrish 1983:personal communication). The myth may be interpreted symbolically as portraying the difficulty of parting with one's bisexuality. In psychoanalytic practice, Freud found many examples of continuous yearnings for bisexuality in both men and women. Indeed this was one of the most intriguing subjects in the exchange of letters between Freud and his friend Fliess (Freud 1950).

In the *Puranas,* written later than the *Upanishads* and composed after the *Symposium,* Siva Ardhavisavara, who is male on the right and female on the left, divides himself into Siva and Sava. Once so divided the two parts of him make ardent love for a thousand years (Kramrish 1981).

Nunberg (1926) reports a clinical case with a striking similarity to Plato's fable.

One patient had the feeling that he was turned, back to front and upside down, as if he were made up of two people. He thought that one of these people looked forward and the other backward. He was afraid to walk in the street, for he thought that his toes peeped out of his heels, and so he was afraid of tripping over his own feet. When he spoke he always had to take hold of the top of his head to convince himself where his head and face were, and so forth. He pictured that if he were cured the man in him who looked forward would disappear. This symptom was overdetermined; its deepest significance was an identification with the mother, who was embodied in him in the person looking backward. (pp. 78–79)

A fragment of a dream of a woman undergoing psychoanalysis will illustrate that Plato's fable is still alive in the unconscious of contemporary men and women. She dreamt that her lover said to her: "Let us try the Milky Way." The patient in the dream objected: "I have never been there before." The lover replied: "Neither have I." They were then shown a place where the people of the future lived and the patient was surprised to discover that they were all hermaphrodites. What Plato relegated to the past this patient assigns to the future. In the primary processes future and past are interchangeable. Analysis of the dream revealed that the Milky Way was a dream symbol for fellatio, a wish the dreamer had but also feared, for it associated the man too closely with the nursing mother.

A case of a seven-year-old boy was reported by Bird (1958). The case shows how Plato's fable as well as the androgenous Shiva can be recreated by an anxious boy who has difficulty in distinguishing his sexual wishes and accepting his masculine gender identity.

As the mother's pregnancy advanced, and particularly when it was discovered she would have twins, Joey could not help showing jealousy and anger. At the same time he expressed pleasure about having twins and was sure they would be a boy and a girl. This certainty that the twins would be boy and girl was part of his bisexual theory of birth and was not merely a hope. He simply had no other thought and was surprised I should even ask what sex they would be. The meaning behind the twin-birth idea was not revealed until later, but briefly it was that every birth produces a combination kind of hermaphrodite, which then divides into two parts, one part getting the penis, the other none. (p. 290)

. . . Finally he looked searchingly at the genital area of the doll and, with a relieved grin, said he had solved the problem: the baby was half boy and half girl and would grow up that way. It would have long hair on one side of its head, short hair on the other; it would have a dress on one side, long pants on the other, etc. When I drew attention to the fact that he had not described the genitals of this half-and-half baby, he became confused all over again and tried hard to find an answer. Perhaps, he ventured, it would have a penis side by side with a crack; or it would have half a penis (split down the center) and half a crack. But nothing satisfied him until at last he hit upon the perfect solution: the baby would have a regular crack, and inside of that crack would be a regular penis. He was completely satisfied with this solution. He danced with joy. He called the baby he-he, she-she, then struck upon he-she. With the utmost glee he said he-she could have a baby all by himself-herself—no one else would be needed. (p. 297)

Aristophanes' fable found an unexpected "confirmation" when Charles Darwin reasoned in the *Descent of Man* (1871) that some extremely remote progenitor of the whole vertebrate kingdom appears to have been a hermaphrodite. The sexologist, Krafft-Ebing, who greatly influenced Freud, thought that constitutional bisexuality was at the basis of the riddle of homosexuality. Carl Claus, one of Freud's teachers, discovered that some crustacea live part of their lives as males and the second as females. Freud, before he became a psychoanalyst, worked in the laboratory of Brücke. There he dissected the spinal nerves of a petromyzont, also a bisexual animal (Bernfeld 1949).

If we translate Plato's mythological language into a psychological one, we will substitute infancy for the original state of man. We will then see that Plato had an equivalent theory to that of psychoanalysis, where the infant takes bisexuality for granted. Only slowly and painfully does the infant accept his or her own gender identity. If the feeling that one is only a half persists into adult life, gender identity has not become consolidated, the person will feel insufficient, inadequate, and incapable of being alone.

The platonic fable was often quoted by romantic philosophers in the nineteenth century to demonstrate the fundamental bisexuality of human beings (Ellenberger 1970:204). Lewin (1952), a psychoanalyst, interpreted the fable as a denial of the original attachment to mother and the substitution for the mother of a union between two siblings who were separated from the mother but not from each other, and who both shared the same uterus and the same maternal breast (p. 209). In Lewin's interpretation, the *Symposium* (a drinking party) is more than a literary device for the discussion of love, for orality (drinking) and love are, psychologically speaking, related subjects.

Plato feared the power of emotions raging beyond control. In the *Republic* he devised a well-calculated scheme, according to Freud, to prevent the capacity to love, for Plato suggested that the child be raised by interchangeable wet-nurses. Such a child, Plato argued, will regard all older citizens as parents and will not know the power of erotic love nor the torments of jealousy. It seems uncanny that even in this respect Plato anticipated Freud.

# 6

## On the Affinity Between Greek Tragedy and Psychoanalysis

I n Greek tragedy, for the first time we find a full portrayal of intrapsychic conflict. A typical tragic hero is Orestes, the subject of tragedies by Aeschylus and Euripides. It was Apollo's oracle and not Orestes' own wishes that prompted Orestes to avenge the murder of his father Agamemnon and kill his mother Clytemnestra. After the matricide, it was not his own guilt that haunted him, but rather he was persecuted by the avenging Erinyes. In spite of his externalization of an inner conflict, the world of Homer is far behind us. The intervention of gods only disguises the psychological sphere within one person. The tragic hero is in conflict, lonely, and usually unsupported by the community. The subject matter of tragedy is much closer to the subject matter of psychoanalysis than that of any other literary genre that preceded tragedy. Due to psychoanalysis, the world of Greek tragedy is closer to us than Virgil's *Aeneid* or Dante's *Divine Comedy*. The tragedies abound in patricide, matricide, incest, and murder of children. They portray what Freud would call the wishes of the id. In Aristotle's view, tragedy evokes catharsis, consisting of fear and pity. Freud expanded the Aristotelian view to mean that the tragic hero expresses feelings an ordinary civilized person would never dare express. As an example, I quote Clytemnestra's description of how she killed her husband Agamemnon.

> Then smote him, once, again—and at each wound
> He cried aloud, then as in death relaxed
> Each limb and sank to earth; and as he lay,
> Once more I smote him, with the last third blow,
> Sacred to Hades, saviour of the dead.

And thus he fell, and as he passed away,
Spirit with body chafed; each dying breath
Flung from his breast swift bubbling jets of gore,
And the dark sprinklings of the rain of blood
Fell upon me; and I was fain to feel
That dew—not sweeter is the rain of heaven
To cornland, when the green sheath reams with grain.
(Aeschylus' *Agamemnon,* lines 1385 ff.; Moreshead translation)

The metaphor in which Clytemnestra equates the blood of the murdered husband with rain freshly falling on sweet corn is poetic but horrifying. The passage is followed by a bold assertion of her right to a new love.

This man lies sacrificed by hand of mine,
I do not look to tread the hall of Fear,
While in this hearth and home of mine there burns
The light of love—Aegisthus—as of old
Loyal, a stalwart shield of confidence—
As true to me as this slain man was false,
Wronging his wife with paramours at Troy,
(Ibid., lines 1430 ff.)

We shudder to hear Clytemnestra's open acknowledgement of the pleasure with which she murdered Agamemnon. We the listeners to the tragedy would have felt too guilty to express such feelings at the moment of murder. Two thousand five hundred years later, Freud will discover that, through a special atmosphere that psychoanalysis has created, when free associations are encouraged and repressions lifted, even ordinary men and women can speak with the ferocity that we encounter in Greek tragedy.

I will now attempt a psychoanalytic interpretation of *Hippolytus* by Euripedes. I have already alluded to this tragedy in the chapter on Aphrodite. I invite the reader to suspend disbelief and look upon Hippolytus as a patient undergoing psychoanalysis. The fact that Hippolytus is a narcissist and resists love will become the central theme of this analysis. In due time the patient Hippolytus will tell the analyst something or a great deal about his mother, Hippolyta, the Queen of the Amazons. The reader as well as the audience before whom the tragedy was played knew unconsciously, if not consciously, that Hippolyta must have hated her son. The audience is dimly aware of the connection between the phallic nature of his mother, the queen of the Amazones, and her hatred of everything male, and the inability of Hippolytus to love women. In the course of the analysis Hippolytus will have to face the difficult task which he undoubtedly denies that he was hated by the very mother upon whose love he was dependent. One would expect a great resistance to his accepting this fact. All the anger and hatred once experienced against his mother will now appear in the transference as a hatred toward the analyst. When the transference is at its height, Hippolytus will have paranoid fantasies and suspect the analyst of wishing to kill him.

A greater resistance is still to come. For Hippolytus resorts to what psychoanalysts call a sublimation. He became a devotee of Artemis, the virgin goddess of the chase, whose domain is everything wild that has not been subdued by the plough of man. His devotion to Artemis has undoubtedly helped him to cope with his depression. The aggression he expresses in hunting may well be a protection against suicidal wishes prevailing in his unconscious. These suicidal wishes may have to be faced when he realizes how hated he was by his mother. The psychoanalyst will then be forced to examine the relationship to his favorite goddess, Artemis. By doing so, the psychoanalyst runs the risk of undermining Hippolytus' sublimation. He may become the subject of a clinical conference and there will be those who will believe that since his childhood was so traumatic he will not be strong enough to undertake psychoanalysis. Supportive therapy with a great deal of empathy for what he suffered may be the only therapy that he can accept.

Assuming that the idea that he is analyzable prevails, the therapist will bring up the relationship between Artemis and his mother. Hippolytus will have to face the astonishing similarity between Artemis and his mother, Hippolyta. Did not Artemis, like his mother, use the bow, did she not, like his mother, resist being subdued by men? Does she not, like his mother, hate the very thought of a sexual encounter? True, unlike the goddess who remained a virgin, his mother was subdued by a man but would not she rather have retained her virginity? The psychoanalyst will slowly, step-by-step, get Hippolytus to admit that the worship of Artemis is a disguised form of love and loyalty to the very mother who was incapable of returning his love as a baby and child.

"Who is Phaedra?" the psychoanalyst will ask Hippolytus, prodding him to associate further. "She is the stepmother," would be the reply of the analysand. But if the analyst presses on, Hippolytus would have to face that she too represents another part of his own unconscious wishes. For in his early childhood, Hippolytus had the fantasy that Hippolyta, his mother, was in love with him. He assumed that she sexually desired him because he could not face his own oedipal wishes for him. Like the biblical Joseph, Hippolytus resisted temptation to have sexual intercourse with a thinly disguised mother-substitute. Theseus, the father, like the biblical Potiphar, does not believe that Hippolytus is innocent. For Theseus remembers unconsciously, if not consciously, that he too as a child had similar oedipal wishes. At this point a further task awaits the psychoanalyst. He would have to work through the so-called negative oedipus: the love that Hippolytus has for his father Theseus. For like many children who had an unloving mother, he must have turned early in the search for love to his father. In such a case, the negative oedipal constellation would be particularly strong. It may have led to a latent or overt homosexuality.

I asked the reader earlier to suspend disbelief and to treat Hippolytus as if he were a psychoanalytic patient. I have done so only in order to demonstrate how a tragic hero can be understood in terms applicable to a contemporary psychoanalytic patient. I want to stress that Greek tragedy presents people whose intrapsychic problems we comprehend. They represent archetypes we encounter in the course of psychoanalysis. Hippolytus is an archetype of a narcissistic personality.

*Oedipus Rex,* the play by Sophocles that gave the oedipus complex its name, is not a tragedy that deals with love. Many critics of Freud have observed that Oedipus is not in love with his mother, Jocasta; he merely marries her in order to ascend to the throne. Freud, at the time he discovered the oedipus complex, was steeped in dream interpretation, and would not have been persuaded by this argument since he differentiated between manifest and latent contents in dreams as well as in myths. Oedipus need not show his love to his wife-mother, for the audience will subconsciously assume it on the basis of the universality of the oedipus complex. Had Sophocles depicted Jocasta and Oedipus as an amorous pair, the tragedy may have evoked excessive resistance. Only by eliminating all manifestations of love scenes between Jocasta and Oedipus could the dramatist hope to evoke sympathy for Oedipus in spite of the incest committed.

The description of the self-blinding and the speech by Oedipus that follows it are among the most terrible found in Greek tragedy:

> For a sword he begged and cried:
> "Where is that wife that mothered in one womb
> Her husband and his children! Show her me!
> No wife of mine!" Then—oh sight most terrible—
> He snatched the golden broaches from the queen,
> With which her robe was fastened, lifted them,
> And struck. Deep to the very founts of sights
> He smote, and vowed no more those eyes should see.

The wrongs he suffered, and the wrong he did
"Henceforth" he cried "be dark—since you have seen
Whom you should ne'er have seen."

(lines 1255–69)

Following his blindness, Oedipus explains the act.

Nay, give me no counsel. Bid me not
Believe my deed, thus done, is not well done.
I know tis well. When I had passed the grave,
How could those eyes have met my father's gaze,
Or my unhappy mother's—since on both
I have done wrongs beyond all other wrong?
Or live and see my children?—Children born
As they were born! What pleasure in that sight?
None for these eyes of mine, forever none.

Cast me, where you shall look on me no more.
Come! Deign to touch me, though I am a man
Accursed. Yield! Fear nothing! Mine are woes
That no man else but I alone must bear.

(lines 1372–82)

Aristotle interpreted the fall of Oedipus as due to a mistake. Such a mistake did not originate in the depravity of character but in the ignorance of circumstance. Therefore, the act should be pardoned. In the tragedy itself the ultimate responsibility for the murder and incest is due to the Delphic oracle that can never be evaded. Here, too, the Greeks used an external force to designate what Freud would call unconscious wishes.

Freud said about Oedipus: "His destiny moves us only because it might have been ours—because the oracle laid the same curse on us before our birth as upon him. It was the fate of all of us, perhaps to direct our first sexual impulse towards our mother and our first hatred and our first murderous wish against our father. Our dreams convince us that this is so" (Freud 1900:262).

This was new and it was revolutionary. Until Freud, the tragic hero was the exceptional man. Now he became everyman. An important difference remained, however. The Greek hero portrays events which for most of mankind are merely wishes, and wishes that have undergone repression. There are two aspects to Oedipus. In the myth, he has slain his father and married his mother. In the mythopoetic rendering of Sophocles, Oedipus became the tireless seeker after truth. In a well-known letter to Goethe, Schopenhauer wrote: "It is the courage of making a clean breast of it in the face of every question that makes the philosopher. He must be like Oedipus who, seeking enlightenment concerning his terrible fate, pursues his indefatigable inquiry, even when he devines that appalling horror waits him in the answer. But most of us carry in our hearts the Jocasta who begs Oedipus for God's sake not to inquire further" (quoted in Ferenczi 1912:254).

When Sophocles transformed the myth of Oedipus into the tragedy, the incest was counterbalanced by the portrayal of Oedipus as the relentless seeker of truth. It was with this quality that Freud identified himself when he discovered the oedipus complex. The discovery itself should be looked upon as an act of sublimation. Out of this sublimation, psychoanalysis was born.

It must, however, be admitted that Oedipus never captured the imagination of the Western world. The real oedipal hero, the Titan who defied the reigning gods, the one who inspired the largest number of plays and poems, was Prometheus. Why did he rather than Oedipus capture the imagination? I do not believe that the greater popularity of Prometheus should be used as an argument against Freud's discovery. I suspect that only very few could identify with Oedipus the solver of riddles and the searcher for the truth. Most readers recoil from identifying with the story of the oedipal crime and its punishment. Prometheus—the Titan who was punished for giving mankind mastery over fire—admirably met the needs for identification with the powerful and suffering rebel. Prometheus' defiance of Zeus was the archetype for all fighters against tyranny, and on a personal level the part of the oedipus complex which often remains conscious when the other part, the sexual desire for the mother, undergoes repression. Only during the latest "transvaluation of values" associated with the sixties did Marcuse (1955:161) transforms Prometheus' image from that of a heroic rebel to a culture hero, devoted to toil, productivity, and progress, a mythical figure that personifies not rebellion but the repressive powers of man. Marcuse presented not Prometheus but Orpheus, Narcissus, and Dionysus as objects for identification to the New Left.

In 1913, when Freud wrote *Totem and Taboo,* he turned to Greek tragedy with a new understanding; he now saw the tragic hero as the father and the chorus as a representative of the murderous sons. It was they who in primeval times were guilty; in Greek tragedy their role was transmuted into that of the observers and commentators on events in which they no longer participated. We might add that the chorus in Greek tragedy represents what psychoanalysts call the observing ego. We identify ourselves at times with the tragic hero and then seek refuge from this identification by identifying ourselves with the Greek chorus. Freud was able at this point to bring about a synthesis between Greek tragedy and Pauline Christianity. Both are parallels of the same process. In tragedy the father becomes the guilty hero and the sons become the observers. In Christian theology, the son was killed for crimes he never committed. In Freud's view, whether we follow the Greek model of tragedy or the model of Christianity, unconsciously we still are the reenacters of the drama in which the band of rebel sons kill the father, a drama which has come down to us from primeval time.

# 7

# The Roman Contribution:
# The Discovery of Narcissus

In his recently published history of sexuality, Foucault pointed out a basic shift in interest that took place in the attitude toward love and sex when Rome replaced Athens as the cultural center. The Greeks, as Foucault sees it, were essentially preoccupied with the compatibility of passive homosexuality with virility. In Imperial Rome, when the community of men was no longer the center of public life, the interest shifts to the compatibility between spouses, to heterosexual love as an ideal within marriage. Plutarch, Pliny, Seneca, and Lucian all show the extent to which marital love has become the center of a new interest. Marriage is the natural state in which love grows because it alone promotes reproduction.

Of the many Roman poets who have written on love, I select a few lines from the refrain in the anonymous poem "Perviglium Veneris," celebrating Venus and the arrival of Spring in Rome.

> Cras amet qui nunquam amavit,
> Quinque amavit cras amet.
>
> Tomorrow let him love who never loved,
> He who loved let him love tomorrow.

Catullus (87–57 B.C.), who was Lucretius' contemporary, must be credited with the discovery of ambivalence among the most painful of human emotions.

An abbreviated version of this chapter was read before the Michigan Association for Psychoanalysis as the Seventh Annual Richard and Edith Sterba Lecture on March 31, 1984, with Dr. Richard Sterba as discussant. It appeared as a separate essay in the *American Imago*, Winter 1984, 41 (4):389–411.

> Lesbia loathes me night and day with her curses,
> "Catullus" always on her lips,
>     yet I know that she loves me.
> How? I equally spend myself day and night
> in assiduous execration
>     knowing too well my hopeless love.
>                         (Whigham translation)

And finally, the famous *Odi Et Amo:*

> I hate and I love. And if you ask me how,
> I do not know: I only feel it, and I'm torn in two.
>                         (Whigman translation)

When, in 1910, Bleuler coined the term ambivalence, it appeared as a novel psychiatric term destined to play a significant role in psychoanalysis. Looking back at the poetry of Catullus we can say that ambivalence has been explored in depth in the poetry of Catullus 2000 years earlier.

## Dido and Aeneas

To the stock of Western love stories, Imperial Rome added one that was destined to exert a considerable influence on subsequent thinking on love. Virgil's last work, the *Aeneid,* or the story of Aeneas, was left incomplete when the poet died in 19 B.C. Book Four tells the story of the tragic love between Dido and Aeneas, which became a favorite subject in painting. Dido's regal suicide by Rubens in the Louvre is probably the best known painting on this theme.

Approaching this story from a psychoanalytic point of view, we note that the lovers were in mourning when they met. Aeneas had just lost his father, the father he had carried out of burning Troy upon his back. It is a powerful symbol for the reversal of roles between father and son. Loyalty to the father and the commitment to his destiny is at the core of the character of Aeneas. This typical Roman hero conquers love in the name of duty. While the Greeks idealized the all-conquering power of love, the Romans glorified the anti-erotic sense of duty.

Dido too is in mourning for her husband, Sychaeus, killed by the hand of her brother, and in his name she rejects the new love. Psychoanalysts, as we shall see, lay special stress on the connection between love and mourning. In Dido's case, love overcomes the mourning.

The queen, for her part, all that evening ached
With longing that her heart's blood fed, a wound
Or inward fire eating her away.
The manhood of the man, his pride of birth,
Came home to her time and again; his looks,
His words remained with her to haunt her mind,
And desire for him gave her no rest.
(Fitzgerald translation; Book 4, lines 1–7)

The traditional woman who counsels the hesitant lover is in this case Dido's sister Anna who persuades her to love again.

This counsel fanned the flame, already kindled,
Giving her hesitant sister hope, and set her
Free of scruple.
(Book 4, lines 45–47)

T.S. Eliot (1951) showed that Aeneas is a new kind of hero who prefigures the Christian ideal. His protestation of love has a hollow ring. He's much better at describing resistance to love. The capacity to love, Eliot discerned, is the important ingredient Virgil lacks. Indeed, Aeneas has virtue and a sense that he has to fulfill the destiny the gods have commanded which, in this case, is making Rome and not Carthage the ruler of the world. Like Odysseus, Aeneas is a seafarer but it is not for him to dally in foreign ports, erotic adventures "leave no canker in his conscience." After one night of nuptial delight, he is summoned to leave Dido.

Duty-bound,
Aeneas, though he struggled with desire
To calm and comfort her in all her pain,
To speak to her and turn her mind from grief,
And though he sighed his heart out, shaken still
With love of her, yet took the course heaven gave him
And went back to the fleet.
Book IV, lines 93–100

And just as when the north winds from the Alps
This way and that contend among themselves
To tear away an oaktree hale with age,
The wind and tree cry, and the buffeted trunk
Showers high foliage to earth, but holds
On bedrock, for the roots go down as far
Into the underworld as cresting boughs

> Go up in heaven's air: just so this captain,
> Buffeted by a gale of pleas
> This way and that way, dinned all the day long,
> Felt their moving power in his great heart,
> And yet his will stood fast; tears fell in vain.
>
> (Book 4, lines 441–453)

Many generations admired his virile strength and his obedience to destiny. If we admire it less, it is because after Eichman, any blind following of commands has acquired a sickening connotation.

Dido has been described as the noble embodiment of passionate love. Psychoanalytic estimation would put her in a less formidible category—the speed with which her love turns into hate, a hate that endures even when the lovers meet in Hades; the fact that she rushes full speed to suicide may add drama to the narrative but it casts a shadow on her real capacity to love. All too often, the rapid turn of love to hate and self-hate was taken as a sign of great love. In a psychoanalytic perspective, this character suggests a desperate interlude of passionate love between melancholia and suicide.

Eliot was right to stress that Virgil himself lacked the capacity to portray love but we can go even further and say that he could not illuminate character from within. The kind of analysis I did with Hippolytus could not be undertaken with either Aeneas or Dido. His appeal is to morality, not to the workings of the human mind.

In the story of love, Ovid ranks second only to Plato in the way he enlarged our vision of love. Ovid was in many ways Plato's opposite. Living 400 years after Plato in the dissolute society of imperial Rome, he had a mocking rather than an idealizing attitude toward love. In his books, *The Loves (Amores)* and *The Art of Love (Ars Amatoria)*, Ovid sets out to teach lovers how to attain a harmonious enjoyment in which both partners will find equal delight without letting the partner affect too radically the inner balance of the lover. Some of the advice he has given remains part of the wisdom of love. Avoid criticism, he argues, always emphasize to the partner his or her best features. Do not hesitate to magnify them, even beyond what you yourself believe. In this chapter, I will deal with three quasimythological figures created by Ovid: Narcissus, Pygmalion, and Hermaphroditus. I call them quasimythological because they do not compel belief, and therefore are not genuine creations of myth. Nevertheless, their impact on subsequent generations was great.

## The Myth of Narcissus

According to Ovid,* Narcissus was a youth of wondrous beauty. His mother, the nymph Leirope, was ravished by the river god Kephissos, who encircled her with his winding streams. Leirope consulted the prophet Tiresias whether Narcissus would reach old age. The seer answered, "only if he never knows himself." Edwards (1977) pointed out the significance of the seer's answer, *si se non noverit,* was Ovid's ironical reversal of the classic Greek ideal: "Know thyself" inscribed on the temple in Delphi.

The beautiful youth has many suitors, men, women, water nymphs, and mountain nymphs. He rebuffs them all. One of the dejected suitors prays to Nemesis, the goddess of vengeance, imploring her to afflict Narcissus with the pain he had caused those who loved him. Nemesis grants the wish. Among those inflamed by love for Narcissus is the unhappy nymph, Echo, whose story is of special relevance to the myth. While Jupiter was dallying with nymphs, Juno, driven by jealousy, was looking for him. Echo detained her with stories long enough for Jupiter to escape. As a punishment, Juno condemned her to be unable to converse, never to be able to utter the first word, but also never to remain silent when someone else was talking. This is how Ovid describes the meeting:

> Out of the woods she came with arms all ready.
> To fling around his neck, but he retreated: "Keep your
> hands off" he cried "and don't touch me, I would die
> before I would give you a chance at me." "I'd give you
> a chance at me", is all that poor Echo could reply.
> (*Metamorphoses,* Book 3, Humphries translation)

The reader will note that the nymph has some residual power to decide where she would begin to echo. She uses this power to the utmost to communicate her feelings. She repeats only what she wishes to communicate.

Returning from the hunt, exhausted from the summer heat, Narcissus reaches a fountain whose waters are unruffled, never having been disturbed by man or beast. He looks into the smooth and silvery water and while he quenches his thirst a new thirst seizes him, for now he is smitten by love for the image that stares at him from the water. At first he does not recognize the image as his own. Then comes the moment of truth: "I

---

*Ovid was not one of Freud's favorite authors. Freud quotes him only once in discussing the wishful aspects of dreams (1916–1917: 215). "Though the strength is lacking, the will deserves to be praised." The irreverent mocking great poet of Roman decadence, the dethroners of the gods probably had little appeal to the serious-minded young Freud.

am he"———is the crucial phrase. Now he knows that it is his own reflection he is in love with, but he still cannot tear himself away. Even at the banks of the Styx (the river that in Greek mythology segregates the dead and is their abode), he gazes into the water at his own image. Before he dies, Echo once more appears to him but is unable to tear him away from the watery image. When those who loved him wish to give Narcissus a proper burial they discover a flower with a saffron-colored rim and white petals that had appeared on the spot he died. The flower is still named after him. Bunker (1947) noted the etymological relationship between "Narcissus" and "narcotic." The flower was believed to have a stupefying vapor that could induce a death-like sleep. He also notes that the name daffodil, a genetic variant of the narcissistic flower, derives its name from the Greek *asphodel,* the abode of the departed souls.

We should note that it was Nemesis, the goddess of revenge, and not Aphrodite, the goddess of love, that punished Narcissus. This was Ovid's way of including self-love under the domain of Aphrodite, that is, to see self-love as a form of love. And, as such, it has remained up to later developments. It was due to the heritage from Ovid that Shakespeare can take it for granted that self-love is a sinful form of love but nevertheless a form of love (Sonnet 62). Narcissus can love only his own image in the water. This image can mimic the lover but cannot reach out and embrace him. It is therefore a particularly unresponsive type of love object.

According to Wieseler (1856), statues of Narcissus were erected in Roman times near waters as well as on graves. At times, the statue of Narcissus was accompanied by a statue of Eros holding the torch upside down signifying death.

In another variation (not by Ovid), Narcissus kills himself out of guilt. He had been particularly cruel to one of his suitors when he sent him the sword with which the lover killed himself at Narcissus' door. In this version, the myth became a cautionary tale, in the sense in which Sharpe (1943) used this term, warning the adolescent Eronemus not to be haughty and spurn the love of Erastes.

In still another version, Narcissus was the son of Endymion and Semele, the goddess of the moon. Endymion was given a special boon by Jupiter— to die only when he so desires. So favored, Endymion fell in love with Juno and even had intercourse with her reflection in a cloud. For this oedipal transgression he was sent to Hades. The boon, however, could not be undone. He is therefore condemned, or especially blessed, as the case may be, by being able to sleep eternally. Hence his affinity with the moon. The love between Endymion and the goddess of the moon had great attraction for poets and was the subject of a long poem by Keats. For poets, love dreamt or imagined has always been a powerful rival to love in real life. Having Endymion as a father suggested to Wieseler (1856) that Narcissus was a personification of death. Like death, he was cold and indifferent to all who loved him. That Narcissus is the son of Endymion, the eternal sleeper, fits well into Freud's view that during sleep we all regress back into primary narcissism.

Another variation on the myth is reported by Pausanias (fl. c. 150 A.D.), the famous traveler and geographer who has left us ten volumes describing his travels in Greece. In this version, Narcissus did not know at first that he was looking at his own image for he was mourning the loss of a beloved twin sister: the siblings grew up close to each other and they regarded themselves as mirror images. They dressed alike, grew their hair in the same fashion. It was the sister's image that Narcissus first believed to have rediscovered in the water; the discovery that he was looking at himself was a relief from his mourning for the lost twin. A number of writers have found this variant of the myth inferior to Ovid's. We shall see that if understood properly, variants of myths contribute to the understanding of the myth itself.*

The eternal mourning by a brother for a lost sister or its reverse, a theme Shakespeare used frequently, introduces the theme of Hermaphroditus into that of Narcissus. Narcissus represents the archetype of love for one's own body; Hermaphroditus represents the wish to be both sexes.

---

*In psychoanaltyic work we encounter misremembering of myths and fairy tales, or alternatively, condensations of two or more stories into one. These can be understood as private variations on the myth. Such distortions are of special interest to the psychoanalyst because they suggest that the personal need of the analysand did not coincide perfectly with the psychological need of the teller of the myth. Under such conditions, the analysand creates his own version without being aware of having created a distortion (Bergmann 1953). An example of such a distortion may be of interest in the current context.

While free-associating, my analysand told me that Rome was founded by the twins Romulus and Regulus. Of the two, my patient continued, only Regulus survived because he was so punctual and regular in his daily habits, including his toilet training, that his parents allowed him to survive.

Unknowingly, my analysand substituted Regulus for Remus. In history, Regulus was a Roman Consul. He was captured by the Carthaginians and was freed temporarily to carry a message back to Rome with the proviso that he return to captivity if the proposals were not accepted. When he came to Rome, he urged his countrymen to reject these proposals even though this meant his own death. Living up to his promise, he returned to Carthage where he was tortured and killed. This heroic and sacrificial conduct must have impressed my analysand, but in his unconscious, the masochistic morality of the consul was transformed into the punctuality of toilet training, hence the misremembering. What analysands do unconsciously, poets do when they write a variation on the myth that they had received. The variation meets their own psychological needs more accurately than the original myth.

The fact that the hermaphroditic theme was introduced by Pausanias into the myth of Narcissus by making him mourn the loss of his twin sister shows that the ancients, like contemporary psychoanalysts, felt that the love for the self and the wish to be both sexes are psychologically related. At this point, I will introduce two psychoanalytic concepts. My aim is twofold: to illuminate the myth, and to introduce to readers not familiar with psychoanalytic terminology two concepts significant in the story of love. The variation of the myth of Narcissus by Pausanias makes Narcissus capable of narcissistic love. When his twin died, Narcissus regressed from narcissistic love to narcissism proper. A further distinction can be made. In Ovid's version, Narcissus dies of primary narcissism (never having loved anyone besides himself). In Pausanias's version, he dies of secondary narcissism, which results from a regression of the flow of the libido back to the self after the loss of a narcissistic love object.

The first to use the myth of Narcissus for philosophical purposes were the neoplatonists. For Plotinus (the founder of neoplatonism 205–270 A.D.), Narcissus was an example of a youth who was lured away from divine beauty by the deceptive beauty of appearance. He had not yet learned to close his eyes to the beauty of the body and open them to the beauty of the soul. In the writings of Ficino, the leading neoplatonist of the Renaissance, Narcissus is the soul of a bold but inexperienced youth, who falsely admires the weak body and seeks its reflection in flowing water. His fate is a warning for the soul not to desert its own beauty and search in vain to catch it in a shadowy body.

Freud's concept of narcissistic love can solve some of the riddles associated with the myth of Narcissus. It enables us to understand the connection between Narcissus and Echo. So far as I know, this connection has remained unexplained by mythographers. Echo could neither start a conversation nor remain silent after another stopped talking. To be unable to start a conversation is a symbolic way of saying that Echo lacks an independent self. To be compelled to comment when someone else is speaking is a symbolic way of saying that Echo clings and cannot separate. To love a woman who has no independent self burdens the narcissist less than the demands made by a woman who has an independent personality and will.  Bunker (1947) notes that Narcissus was not even capable of a narcissistic object choice, which led to his doom.

Chekhov, in a masterly short story called "The Darling," describes such a woman. She marries a number of times and her interests and philosophy alter completely with every new love without a trace of an inner struggle. Chekhov's Darling is a delightful figure but in clinical practice we encounter her as Helene Deutsch's (1942) "as if." Chekhov's Darling turns out to be a severely disturbed person.

The individual's whole relationship to life has something about it which is lacking in genuineness and yet outwardly runs along "as if" it were complete. Even the layman sooner or later inquires, after meeting such an "as if" patient: what IS wrong with him or her?

To the analyst it is soon clear that all these relationships are devoid of any trace of warmth, that all the expressions of emotion are formal, that all inner experience is completely excluded. It is like the performance of an actor who is technically well trained but who lacks the necessary spark to make his impersonations true to life. (pp. 263–266)

Mythical Echo becomes the clinical "as if" which we understand as a developmental failure to internalize, to build through identification an independent psychic structure.

## The Myth of Pygmalion

Ovid recounts another tale that deals with the subject of narcissistic love that ends happily. The story of Pygmalion, which antedates Ovid, comes from Hellenistic times and is found in Philostephanus. According to this version, Pygmalion was a Cyprian king or king-priest who fell in love with the statue of Aphrodite. Ovid transformed this tale and made Pygmalion a sculptor who was so upset at the behavior of the priestesses of Aphrodite that he resolved to remain chaste. These priestesses had denied the divinity of the goddess and had been punished by her by losing all sense of shame. Once they lost shame, they practiced incest.

Sacred prostitution was part of the worship of the goddess of fertility throughout the Middle East. Both the Hebrews and the Greeks, however, found the institution of sacred prostitution morally offensive. This is reflected in the myth of Pygmalion, which transforms the sacred prostitutes from Aphrodite's priestesses into rebels against her.

After Pygmalion decided to remain chaste, he created an ivory statue of a woman that surpassed all living women in beauty. He fell in love with the statue, caressed it, kissed it, bought it gifts of flowers and ornaments, and covered it with precious garments. He called the statue his wife. At a festival to Aphrodite, Pygmalion timidly made an offering to the goddess and prayed: "If you can give all things, oh gods, I pray my wife may be— (he almost said my ivory girl, but dared not)—one like my girl." Aphrodite granted the wish. Under his kisses and embraces the statue came to life. "He kissed her and she seemed to glow, he stroked her breasts and felt the ivory soften under his fingers" (Humphries translation). Thus, Aphrodite granted what Pygmalion preconsciously desired but did not dare request. He was granted the right to create his love and bring her to life in the sexual act.

The full impact of the Pygmalion story becomes clear if we combine the two versions. Aphrodite grants Pygmalion, who may have been her priest, the wish to have sexual intercourse with herself by bringing her statue to life. If art and religion are sublimations of the sexual drive, as Freud thought, then Aphrodite's gift is an example of desexualization. In the Middle East, sacred prostitutes symbolized Aphrodite and were her substitutes. The Greek Pygmalion refused this compromise and became chaste; by refusing the symbolic representation of Aphrodite, he obtained the goddess herself by a desexualization of his work of art.

What is tragic in the story of Narcissus has a happy ending in Pygmalion. As long as Pygmalion loved merely a statue, Ovid hints, the relationship was masturbatory. When she came to life, it was transformed into a narcissistic relationship. Narcissus and Pygmalion were both narcissists, but while Narcissus could not even love Echo, Pygmalion can love his own creation. Hermaphroditic wishes are probably also latent in the Pygmalion tale. We may assume that Galatea represented the artist's own feminine aspects. If this is true, then the artist was trying to bring his own feminine wishes to life. The hermaphroditic wish is a greater stimulus to creativity than the self-absorption of Narcissus. A Pygmalion type of love is evident in many relationships where the beloved is not idealized but one of the partners tries to transform or mold the mate to become the ego ideal. Mild Pygmalion wishes are common among contemporary lovers. Some wish to change the way the partner speaks or dresses.

Weissman (1969) demonstrated the extent to which Pygmalion fantasies are alive among contemporary men and women. He described a concert pianist who as an adolescent:

when left alone at home—occasions to which he looked forward with pleasure—he drew female nude figures which he caressed and touched as "real" love objects in his masturbation. Later in life, similar intense hallucinatory and delusional fantasies preoccupied him during his concert performances. He would then fantasy with intense realistic conviction that some female whom he selected from the audience loved and worshipped him and was ready to gratify any sexual desire he might have.

Another patient:

An actor who often played romantic leads repeatedly acted out in real life his last dramatic role with the very actress with whom he had actually played it. It is of interest that the four actresses with whom he was intensely involved professionally and personally had the same hallucinatory and delusional capacity as he had to transform the unreal created role into a real role. (pp. 114–115)

The cases discussed by Weissman found their artistic counterpart in Woody Allen's recent motion picture, *The Purple Rose of Cairo.* Metaphorically speaking, many men and women in love have tried to step out of their ordinary life and have discovered that the return to reality can be difficult and sometimes no longer possible.

The psychoanalytic understanding of perversions opens still another door to the interpretation of the tale of Pygmalion, for what happened to Pygmalion is the very opposite of what happens in fetishism and transvestitism. In these perversions, the disappointment is so great that the inanimate object matters more than the person. Unlike the living partner, the fetish does not change, has no wishes of its own, and makes no demands. Pygmalion may have been a fetishist before his wish was granted. Aphrodite can be seen as a magical therapist who guides Pygmalion from fetishism to heterosexuality. Ovid gives no further details. Did Galatea become a real woman with her own personality, or did she remain a statue endowed with locomotion and sexual responsiveness? If she did become a real woman, would Pygmalion be capable of accepting her individuality? Was he able through this miracle to develop a human relationship that he was not capable of tolerating before? Did the statue acquire life only or also human independence? Can one expect Galatea to love her creator or will she have to find her own man once her birth into womanhood has been accomplished? To all these questions, Ovid gives no answer. In his rendering of the myth of Pygmalion, Bernard Shaw showed that, psychologically speaking, divine intervention is not always necessary for narcissistic love. It is accomplished, in the play *Pygmalion,* through Professor Higgins' transformation of a gutter snipe into a duchess. Shaw should be credited with the insight that Pygmalion is a variant on the theme of Narcissus. The character of Professor Higgins is a component of the two.

When Freud wrote the study of Leonardo (1910), he assumed that Leonardo refound on Mona Lisa's lips the smile of his lost mother. Ordinarily, Freud observed, such a refinding leads to falling in love with the model. But Leonardo, whose capacity to love was blocked, fell in love not with the sitter but with the painting. He could not part with it (Bergmann, 1973). Gombrich (1960) quotes Leonardo. "If the painter wishes to see beauties to fall in love with, it's in his power to bring them forth . . . he is their Lord and God. It happened to me that I made a religious painting which was bought by one that so loved it that he wanted to remove the sacred representations, so as to be able to kiss it without suspicion" (p. 95). We know that it is evident that the behavior of this man did not strike Leonardo as strange or unnatural. This passage may be read as a veiled confession of Leonardo's own Pygmalion wishes. Leonardo went on to give the same mysterious smile not only to other women but also to males such as John the Baptist in the Louvre. The smile became bisexual.

The poem "My Last Duchess" by Robert Browning is a chilling obverse of Pygmalion. The Duke introduces a visitor to a painting of the Dutchess "looking as if she were alive," her crime was "a heart too soon made glad, too easily impressed; She liked what e'er she looked on, and her looks went everywhere . . . Oh Sir, she smiled, no doubt, whene'er I past her; but who passed without much the same smile?" To possess her completely, to put an end to her "promiscuous" smile, the Duke killed her and can now be the sole possessor of her painting. Love drove Pygmalion from the inanimate to the animate. Jealousy drove the Duke to prefer the inanimate to the animate.

The Pygmalion story so delightfully told by Ovid rests on deeper anxiety-evoking foundations. For an inanimate object coming to life evokes feelings of the uncanny. In an essay on the uncanny, Freud (1919) recapitulated Hoffmann's story in which the student Nathaniel, already engaged to a real woman, falls in love with the mechanical doll Olympia. In Freud's interpretation, the mechanical doll (created by Nathaniel's father in the split image of the all-bad father, the evil magician) represents the student's own feminine wishes toward his father. Because these passive wishes are so strong, he falls in "senseless and obsessive love" with Olympia. Freud concluded that the relinquishing of real love for a real woman in favor of a doll that represents Nathaniel's own femininity is a form of narcissistic love. Freud concluded ruefully: "The psychological truth of the situation in which the young man, fixated upon his father by his castration complex, becomes incapable of loving a woman, is amply proved by numerous analyses of patients whose story, though less fantastic, is hardly less tragic than that of the student Nathaniel" (Freud 1919:232n).

Psychoanalysts found that the creative urge in men is to a significant degree a sublimation of men's envy of women's capacity to bear children. When this envy becomes too strong, the artist may wish that his work of art come to life, then sublimation may be partly or entirely done. One of the reasons why we admire Van Gogh's paintings is that they suggest the intensity of being alive. Yet Van Gogh himself complained, "Why am I so little an artist that I always regret that my pictures are not alive?" (quoted in Gross and Rubin 1973: 353).

After his psychotic break, the painter Edvard Munch (1863–1944) arranged his paintings like sentries to protect him from the outside world. He also mistreated them, exposing them to cold weather. He could not bear to be separated from them. In Munch's psychosis, the inanimate world came to life.

In Ovid's tale no trace of the uncanny feeling associated with the inanimate becoming animate has survived. We acquire the line of demarcation between animate and inanimate slowly in the course of development. Where artists succeed in presenting the inanimate to us as if it were alive, we experience it as uncanny. In childhood the line of demarcation is still fluid. A nine-year-old girl told Kestenberg:

"What I believe about dolls," she said, "is that they can do things they will not let us know about. Perhaps Emily (the doll) can read, talk and walk, but she will only do it when people are out of the room. That is her secret. If people knew that dolls could do things they would make them work. So, perhaps they have promised each other to keep it a secret. If you stay in the room, Emily will just sit there and stare. But if you go out, she will begin to read perhaps or go and look out of the window. Then if she heard either of us coming, she would just run back and jump into her chair and pretend she had been there all the time." (Kestenberg 1968:468–469)

The subject could be pursued further to include the creation of the Golem by the twelfth-century rabbi of Prague and the story of Frankenstein's monster by Mary Shelley. Less has been written about the fate of Galatea in real life. There are many young women whose lovers are also their mentors. In felicitous circumstances it can lead to a happy relationship. However, since many of these mentor-lovers are much older, these relationships are vulnerable. When a break in the love relationship occurs, the young woman faces the additional task of separating what she has learned and acquired during the relationship from the man she loved. An analysis of such cases shows the close association between Pygmalion, the mentor-lover, and a very early representation of one or both parents. The mentor continued the task left unfinished by the parent.

## The Myth of Hermaphroditus

I have already indicated that Narcissus and Hermaphroditus are related both mythologically and psychologically.

The story of Salamcis and Hermaphroditus also comes from Ovid. The water nymph, Salamcis, did not enjoy the hunt, preferring to look at herself in the water mirror and comb her lovely hair. Hermaphroditus, the son of Hermes and Aphrodite, was a beautiful lad fifteen years old. Like Narcissus he came to a pool translucent to the very bottom. It was the same pool that Salamcis was using to mirror her own self-love. She sees Hermaphroditus, admires his beauty, desires him, and pleads for kisses. Hermaphroditus is reluctant. Salamcis lures him to the water and once there, serpentlike, she coils herself around him. She prays to the gods, "May no day ever come to separate us." Her prayer is answered. Their bodies merge, becoming one person, both man and woman. While she finds happiness in this merger, Hermaphroditus prays that all who enter the accursed pool emerge from it with half their masculine strength. This story is an obvious variant of the fable told in Plato's *Symposium*, but there both lovers desire to become one. In Ovid's version only the woman is made happy through the union. The man feels castrated by it. Before Hermaphroditus appeared, Salamcis was a narcissa. United forever with the male figure, she is transformed into the hermaphroditic pair.

The myth has a homosexual bias; both the nymph and Hermaphroditus are narcissists, but the woman, upon seeing the man and presumably recognizing her own castration, wishes to be permanently united with the man. Hermaphroditus, containing both sexes, cannot reciprocate her love.

The origin of the Hermaphrodite in Greek culture was rooted in their pronounced bisexuality and in the general fear the Greek men had of women. In many Greek provinces there was a custom that on the wedding day brides and bridegrooms exchanged their garments. In other provinces, it was the custom for the bride to enter the nuptial bed dressed as a man. In Cyprus, Aphrodite was worshipped as a bearded goddess. There are a number of stories where men are transformed into women, and vice versa. The stories of Iphis and Tiresias are the best known. In the fourth century, statues of Hermaphroditus became popular. Hermaphroditus was usually depicted as a full-breasted young woman with a penis.

Basic psychological themes, what Jung called archetypes, undergo little if any change in the course of history. Sibelius put to music a nineteenth-century poem which reflects the same theme.

### The Tresses

He told me: "Last night I dreamed.
I had your tresses around my neck.
I wore your locks like a dark chain
Around my neck and on my breast.

I caressed them and they were my own;
And we were thus forever united,
By the same tresses, lips upon lips,
As two laurels often have but one root.
And gradually, it seemed to me,
So much were our limbs entwined,
That I became you,
Or that you entered into me, like my dream."
When he had finished,
He gently laid his hands upon my shoulders,
And he looked at me with a glance so tender
That I cast down my eyes and trembled.

I suspect that most readers will respond negatively to such a frank expression of Hermaphroditic love. They may even find it offensive. The poem, however, convincingly demonstrates that hermaphroditic love is a form of love.

In a sublimated form, we find the same wish in Elizabeth Barrett Browning's *Sonnets from the Portuguese:*

Go from me. Yet I feel that I shall stand
Henceforth in thy shadow. Nevermore
Alone upon the threshold of my door
Of individual life,

. . . What I do
And what I dream include thee, as the wine
Must taste of its own grapes. And when I sue
God for myself, He hears that name of thine,
And sees within my eyes the tears of two.

Elizabeth Browning's love feelings are more acceptable to us because although she feels united with her lover, the two have not become one.

While Narcissus resides so to speak in the center of the psychoanalytic edifice, Hermaphroditus occupies a peripheral position. The difference between the two is due to an accident of psychoanalytic history. Under the influence of Fliess and before he discovered the oedipus complex, Freud came close to assigning to bisexuality the major role in the etiology of neuroses as well as of the perversions. Had this view prevailed, Hermaphroditus as a mythological image would have occupied the place of honor now held by Oedipus. Some of these formulations survive in Freud's *Three Contributions to the Theory of Sexuality* (1905b). The neurotic is described as suffering from the repression of the other half of his hermaphroditic self while the pervert exhausts himself in a hopeless attempt to live out this impossible position. In a well-known passage (1905b:141–149), Freud rejected psychic hermaphroditism as the basic explanation for neurosis and perversion. Nevertheless, bisexuality remains an important component in every neurosis. In 1908, Freud emphasized that in psychoanalytic treatment we must always be prepared for any symptom to have a bisexual meaning (1908b, p. 166). Masturbation in particular retains its hold over many people as the preferred form of sexual expression because it lends itself to the feeling of being both genders. Freud (1908b) cited a case of a woman who with one hand pressed her dress down defending herself against a sexual attacker, while with her other hand she played the role of the man and tried to tear her dress off.

In her memoirs, Helene Deutsch (1973) recalled a dream she had while in analysis with Freud in which she had both a masculine and feminine organ. "Freud told me only that it indicated my desire to be both a boy and a girl. It was only after my analysis that it became clear to me how much my whole personality was determined by the childhood wish to be simultaneously my father's prettiest daughter and cleverest son" (p. 132).

This is an interesting example of self-analysis carried out after the termination of the analysis with Freud. One can observe in this passage how Helene Deutsch subordinated her bisexual wishes to her oedipus complex. As she puts it, she wished to be both boy and girl to capture the total love of her father; is the bisexuality the powerful urge or the wish to be loved by father? Was she following an implicit suggestion of Freud?

In 1974, Kubie published a long paper, "The Drive to Become Both Sexes." The title itself is of interest, for psychoanalysts do not speak lightly of drives. Since drives are psychological forces that operate below the surface and never emerge directly in the psychoanalytic relationship, all that psychoanalysts actually deal with are drive derivatives, which appear in the form of wishes and dreams. For Kubie to assign to the wish to be both sexes the status of a drive was by itself a challenge to the traditional psychoanalytic way of formulating psychoanalytic theory.* Kubie took Virginia Woolf's (1928) *Orlando* as his basic text. Orlando has had the capacity to fall into a trance and be reborn anew as a woman. Kubie describes how after Orlando's gender transmutation "she" lives as both man and woman. "Thus in this fantastic marriage to herself-himself, she

---

*The wish to be both sexes is so powerful in perversions and it is given up with so much difficulty even in neurotics that there is at least a kernel of truth in Kubie's reformulation. It is possible that Freud minimized the role of bisexuality after his break with Fliess.

achieves the transmutation so often sought with tragic futility in sex and marriage, especially in neurosis and psychosis."

One would assume that in the course of evolution, gender identity had become permanently engraved. But every psychoanalyst discovers that even heterosexual men and women harbor the wish if not the drive to be both sexes. The wish is dominant in all perversions (p. 355). Kubie concludes with the observation that, throughout his life, the human being is destined to search for an idealized image of a bisexual father and mother which will replace the parents. The wish to remain forever the bisexual infant cared for by this imaginary bisexual partner is part of everybody's unconscious and as we shall see is a serious impediment to loving.

Like Plato before him, Ovid expressed his psychological insights through fables. The concept of narcissistic love enables us to see similarities between a number of fables by Ovid which would otherwise not be seen as having a common theme. In most variations on the myth of Narcissus, there lurks in the background a narcissistic love object which takes the mythical form of Echo or a lost twin sister. The abode of the nymph Salamcis is so similar to that of Narcissus that Ovid must have been at least preconsciously aware of the fact that the two stories have much in common. I call such love hermaphroditic.

The fact that the mother of Narcissus was the water nymph Leirope has suggested to McDougall (1980:301) that the pond into which he is gazing in vain represents the nonresponsive mother. Leirope's unresponsiveness has resulted in a deficit of love; Narcissus is to make up for this loss of love by loving himself before he can love another. The fable then represents a self-cure that has failed. An analysand of mine recalled how, during long stretches of a desolate childhood, she yearned for a twin sister. Particularly when she was alone in crowds or in a movie, she expected her twin sister to materialize and cry out, "I have been looking for you everywhere." They will both love each other and be happy. This daydream was resorted to whenever the patient felt lonely.

# 8

# Narcissism and Ego Ideal in the Hebraic and Greek Cultures

Western culture grew out of the confrontation and confluence of two basically irreconcilable cultures: the Hellenic and the Hebraic. The two cultures held very different views on the subject of love and reacted differently toward homosexuality. Although well known, the differences between the two cultures should be recalled. The Hebrews were iconoclasts, who destroyed idols and were prohibited from worshipping graven images. The Greeks created an art that shaped the art history of the Western world, an art which, in Winckeleman's words, was dedicated to "noble simplicity and serene greatness." The Hebrew culture produced prophets, the Greek poets.

In this chapter I will pass from the Greco-Roman world of ideas to the Hebraic-Christian one. I propose to examine the differences between the two cultures and their attitudes toward love. I will do so with a concept created by Freud called the ego ideal. The ego ideal was conceptualized by Freud in 1914 as an agency of the personality that is at the same time the heir to the narcissism of the very young child and the result of identification with the parent.*

It has often been commented upon (Cornford 1950) that as the Greeks had poets rather than priests as their teachers, the Greek culture retained a vitality and flexibility. Priesthood tends with time to become increasingly compulsive and exacting in the pursuit of the ritual; poets speak in individ-

---

*Although superego and ego ideal are interrelated, psychoanalysts draw a line of demarcation. The superego is a forbidding agency charged with enforcing the incest taboo. The ego ideal on the other hand, allied with narcissistic aspirations, demands personal achievement. Every culture stresses its own typical supergo demands, but every culture also creates its own ego ideal. I will show in the chapter on Freud how important the ego ideal was to Freud's understanding of love.

ual voices. With Homer as their teacher and the heroes of the *Iliad* and the *Odyssey* as their ego ideals, the Greeks had a better chance to develop the ego and the ego ideal and escape the yoke of a punitive cultural superego.

The Greeks assumed that the gods play with the lives of men as they please. Paradoxically, this attitude led to a dignified pessimism in the face of death. The lyric poet Bacchylides sings:

> "No living man can turn away
> The purpose which the gods display"

> Bold-hearted Ares takes no heed
> Of friends in war, but blindly flies
> His shaft against all enemies;
> Death is the gift he brings to all
> Whose fated hour is to fall.

> "Tis best for man not to be born
> Never to see the light of morn.
> But since by tears is nothing won,
> A man must say what may be done."
> (Bowra's translation, in Higham and Bowra 1938: 339 and 341)

In their myths, the Greeks created the family of the Olympians. Their gods, at least in Homer, if not in some of the tragedies of Aeschylus, are amoral and narcissistic, leading a carefree life in which nearly all desires are gratified. The Greek gods have sexual relations with mortals, begetting the intermediary category of heroes that stand midway between gods and men. The Greek gods have their own favorites whom they promote and protect against the favorites of other gods. The Hebrews knew one god, strictly speaking, a god devoid of personal mythology. He knows jealousy, anger, and love, but no sexual passion. His love and his jealousy are desexualized and infused with moral fervor. He has an ambivalent relationship with his chosen people Israel, and in the New Testament, he has an unambivalent relationship with the church. The God of the Jews, particularly after the revolution brought about by the prophets, rewards every man according to his merits.*

The children of Israel did regard themselves as specially chosen by God, but the term was used in a quasimetaphorical way. When Jesus literally claimed to be the Son of God, the Jews reacted to it as a blasphemous

---

*In Christian theology the term "Hebrews" refers to the chosen people of the Old Testament. The term Jews is used for those who rejected Christ. *Rex judeorum*, the king of the Jews, was inscribed on the cross. I, however, employ the terms interchangeably.

statement. The Gospels merely introduced a commonplace Greek concept into the orbit of Hebraic thinking.

Both Jews and Greeks regarded themselves as superior to their neighbors: the Jews because they felt chosen among the families of the earth and chosen by the one and universal God. The Greeks felt superior to the Barbarians around them, because they had developed a higher culture that found expression in poetry, art, sports, science, and philosophy. Both cultures therefore faced the problem as to what to do with the excessive narcissism that emerged from their sense of superiority. The Hebrews dealt with the problem by subjecting their narcissism to a strict moral code, a code that Freud compared to an obsessional neurosis.

Yahwe was at first a mere tribal God but after the Babylonians' exile in the fifth century B.C. and the ethical revolution wrought by the prophets, he became a universal God. Unlike the Greek gods, Yahwe does not play arbitrarily with the destinies of mankind, but maintains an ethical, contractual, and reliable relationship with mortals. He rewards the righteous and punishes iniquity. This was in essence the religious revolution that was brought about by the prophets: "You only have I known of all the families of the earth: therefore I will punish you for all your iniquities" (Amos 3:2). The Hebrews dealt with the narcissism of being chosen and brought it under control by imposing upon themselves a strict moral code. Anti-Semites disregard the impact of the teaching of the prophets and see Jews as feeling superior and devoid of a moral code.

The Greeks, on the other hand, attempted to subdue their narcissism through identification with the tragic hero. The cathartic experience which, according to Aristotle, is the aim of tragedy was also a way of dealing with narcissism evoked by the Greeks' hubris. The term hubris had both a religious and a civil connotation. It implied (according to Dover 1978: 34), an arrogant confidence that one can treat other people as one pleases and escape penalty for violating the moral laws acceptable to society. On a religious scale, it found expression in a belief that one is equal to or in some way better than one of the gods: an act of insolence that was punished severely. Hubris was therefore a sin that applied not only to the relationship between man and God but between one man and another. The frequency with which deeds of hubris have to be punished in Greek mythology tells us that narcissism was an ever-present danger in Greek culture.

One may hypothesize that this greater emphasis on ego ideal rather than on the superego in Greece also made it possible for the Greeks to be more tolerant toward homosexuality than the cultures that surrounded them.

The Greek idealization of one particular form of homosexuality, that between an adolescent boy called Eronemos, loved passively by a middle-aged active lover called Erastes (Dover 1978), has puzzled many observers. Plato took homosexual love as a starting point for the development of his metaphysical theory of love. Whether the more permissive attitude toward homosexuality had any relationship to the unusual creativity of the Greeks is an intriguing question. It should be noted that almost every form of violation of the incest taboo occurs somewhere in Greek mythology. Zeus, the father of the gods, himself takes the form of an eagle or sends one to earth to snatch the beautiful youth Ganymede and makes him his cup-bearer—a thinly disguised allusion to his homosexuality.*

By contrast, the Bible explicitly forbade and condemned all forms of incest, adultery, and homosexuality. Chapter 18 of Leviticus opens with the declaration "I am the Lord your God." The Hebrews are prohibited from walking in the ordinances of the people whose land they will conquer and keep only their Lord's ordinances. A strict code of sexual prohibitions follows.

None of you shall approach to any that is near of kin to him, to uncover their nakedness: I am the Lord.

Moreover thou shalt not lie carnally with thy neighbor's wife, to defile thyself with her.

Thou shalt not lie with mankind, as with womankind: it is abomination.

For whosoever shall commit any of these abominations, even the souls that commit them shall be cut off from among their people.

(Leviticus 18: 6, 20, 22, 29)

Social commandments follow the sexual ones—keeping the Sabbath, not gleaning the vineyard but keeping the remnants of the grapes for the poor, not swearing falsely. The high point of this ethical system culminates in "Thou shalt love thy neighbor as thy self" (Leviticus 19: 18).

And ye shall be holy unto me: for I the Lord am holy and have severed you from other people, that ye shall be mine.

(Leviticus 21:26)

In a well-known footnote added in 1910 to the *Three Essays,* Freud said: "The most striking distinction between the erotic life of antiquity and

---

*In a remark that shows how deeply Ovid understood the nature of narcissism, he said:

The King of the gods once loved a Trojan boy
named Ganymede; for once, there was something found
That Jove would rather have been than was
    (*Metamorphoses,* Humphries translation)

our own no doubt lies in the fact that the ancients laid stress upon the instinct itself, whereas we emphasize its object. The ancients glorified the instinct and were prepared on its account to honor even an inferior object; while we despise the instinctual activity in itself and find excuses for it only in the merits of the object" (p. 149).

As I have shown in the chapter on Aphrodite, the problems were more complex, for the Greeks knew all too well what the glorification of the object can be. In this book, I follow a similar line of demarcation: when the instinct was glorified I spoke of sensuous poetry; when the object was idealized I spoke of love poetry.

Freud connected Greek homosexuality to his ideas on bisexuality.

It is clear that in Greece, where the most masculine men were numbered among the inverts, what excited a man's love was not the *masculine* character of a boy, but his physical resemblance to a woman as well as his feminine mental qualities—his shyness, his modesty and his need for instruction and assistance. As soon as the boy became a man he ceased to be a sexual object for men and himself, perhaps, became a lover of boys. In this instance, therefore, as in many others, the sexual object is not someone of the same sex but someone who combines the characters of both sexes; there is, as it were, a compromise between an impulse that seeks for a man and one that seeks for a woman, while it remains a paramount condition that the object's body (i.e., genitals) shall be masculine. Thus the sexual object is a kind of reflection of the subject's own bisexual nature. (1905b: 144)

Freud also had some interesting things to say about the sublimation of homosexual feelings into concern for the welfare of the community. He noted that many homosexuals have developed an unusually high concern for the fate of others. He attributed this heightened concern to the fact that early in their lives the homosexuals give up rivalry feelings with other men in favor of loving them. Heterosexual persons too sublimate their latent homosexuality into concerns of social welfare (Freud 1922: 232). Psychologically, the radicalism of many young people can be explained by the urgent need to sublimate homosexual urges at that age when gender identity is not yet firmly established. Even in homosexuals, Freud believed a portion of the homosexual impulses undergo sublimation. In ancient Athens the feelings for the city (*polis*) were highly developed during the height of Greek civilization.

In Greek art, gender identity remains strong, even when the Greeks portray a hermaphrodite. The statue in the Uffizi in Florence is of a bisexual, not of an effeminate man. We have to go to the Renaissance to find works of art that combine not the genitals but the characteristics of both sexes. One thinks of the David of Donatello in Florence or of the St. John by Caravaggio in Rome. The David of Donatello was described by Janson (1963) as "Le beau garcon sans merci conscious only of his sensuous beauty . . . not an ideal but an object of desire, strangely androgenous in its combination of sinew angularity with feminine softness and fullness" (p. 85).

A comparison between Greek and Indian mythology is of interest. The Indian Pantheon, like the Grecian, contains a number of gods. But unlike the Greeks the Indian gods are in a continual struggle with each other for supremacy. The adherents of Siva know of many legends in which the superiority of their god over his rivals is demonstrated. The followers of Vishnu have no difficulty in demonstrating the superiority of their deity. What I wish to stress is that Homer and Hesiod succeeded in building a mythology in which highly narcissistic gods nevertheless recognize the special prerogatives of the other gods. Greek mythology was therefore also a lesson in how narcissistic individuals can get along with each other. Of special interest to my topic is the fact that while a Greek god like Zeus can transform himself into a bull to abduct Europa, and even into gold when he wishes to impregnate the mortal Danae, he nevertheless retains his gender identity. By contrast, the Indian gods are not confined to the human form; they can have not only many arms but also many heads. They never lost their theomorphic aspects. Nor are they restricted to the identity of one gender. The god Siva for example can be both man and woman.

While the Bible stressed that man was created in the image of God, the Greeks took it for granted that their gods have human form. In their psychology the gods are no different from men and women except that they are exempt from aging and death.

The difference between the Hebraic and the Greek point of view ultimately manifests itself in a different attitude toward man. For Sophocles "wonders are many but nothing is more wonderful than man." To be sure not all Greeks thought like Sophocles, but to my knowledge no biblical person was engaged in wondering about the nature of man. By contrast the psalmist sees men as "here today and gone tomorrow," his attitude is "who is man that thou shalt remember him . . . a thing of naught even as a dream when one awakens." The Greek attitude was conducive to a psychological interest in the nature of man. The Hebraic was concerned with his moral development.

Before Alexander the Great entered Jerusalem there are no signs that the Greeks knew the Jews by name or had any information about them. The great historian and traveller Herodotus came as far as Tyre but did not consider it worthwhile to visit Jerusalem, an interesting lesson in the capacity of even great men to anticipate what will be important in world history. After the conquest by Alexander, Jewish assimilation into Greek language and culture proceeded rapidly, particularly among the upper classes. Jews acquired Greek names, gymnasia were built in Jewish cities, and hybrid Jewish philosophers like Philo appeared in Alexandria. Assimilated historians like Josephus wrote Jewish history on Greek models. The Jews learned from the Greeks the art of hermeneutics, which remained a most important branch of specifically Jewish learning throughout Jewish history. Greek inscriptions were common in Judea and a passage in the Talmud speaks of 500 students of Greek wisdom and 500 students of Hebrew wisdom (Momigliano 1981).

A famous Talmudic passage speaks of four rabbis who entered the Hellenistic orange grove: one died, one was blinded, one was converted, and only the great rabbi Akiba entered the grove in peace and emerged in peace. The story testifies to the fear with which the Jewish rabbis responded to Hellenistic influence. Directly as a result of this influence, the rabbis forbade gnostic speculation: "Whoever speculated on these four things, it were better for him if he had not come into the world—what is above? what is beneath? what was before time? and what will be hereafter?"

The extent to which Jews became Hellenized would be of minor interest, were it not for the fact that St. Paul, generally regarded as the founder of Christianity, was such a Hellenized Jew.

Judaic law was declared obsolete by St. Paul. All dietary laws were abrogated and circumcision, to Jews the sign of the covenant with God, was replaced by baptism. The pagan world was totally condemned. The Old Testament retained validity insofar as the coming of Christ was prefigured there. St. Mathidius, one of the early fathers of the church (270–309 A.D.), credited the "old law" with man's progress from incest to monogamy (Steinberg 1983: 156).

The psychoanalyst Kohut (1972: 364), employing a somewhat different vocabulary than the one customary in psychoanalysis, suggested that Christianity curbed all manifestations of the grandiose self (the self that is activated in the act of hubris), but allowed by way of compensation a greater degree of merger with the omnipotent image of the divine Christ. The direct contact between the believer and Christ was experienced in the act of communion.

Butcher (1904) observed eighty years ago that the Jews would have been barbarians to the Greeks and the Greeks idolators to the Jews. It was not until ancient Hellas ceased to be an independent nation that it became one of the moving forces in world history. With the Greeks as with the Hebrews, the day of their political abasement was the starting point for fresh spiritual and intellectual conquest (p. 43).

Most of the time, the two cultures were in a state of war with each other, but in a rare moment of synthesis, they produced a progeny that showed what geneticists call hybrid vigor. This vigor occurs when related species are crossed and the offspring are stronger than either of the two parents. Christianity, which vanquished paganism and returned Judaism to a pariah religion in the Western world, was the offspring, and the synthesis that was simultaneously a rebellion against both cultures occurred in the mind of a Hellenized Jew, St. Paul. St. Paul's views on love hence exerted an enormous influence on the way the Western world looked upon love. It was a synthesis based on an aversion to both:

> But we preach Christ crucified, unto
> the Jews a stumbling block and unto the
> Greeks foolishness;
> (1 Corinthians 23.)

Because Latin became the universal language of the Church, the influence of Greece and Rome persisted even during the Middle Ages. Some of the most renowned church fathers struggled in vain against the magic of the Greek culture and language. St. Jerome, the translator of the Bible into Latin, confessed that for a long time the uncouth style of the prophets grated upon him, even after a night of contrition and agony. He felt compelled to reach for Plautus, a Roman playwright, as a man reaches for his pipe (Waddell 1955). He nevertheless declared that ardent love even for one's own wife is adultery. Waddell quotes a letter written by a ninth-century abbot who became frightened when he realized he quoted too much from the Roman poet Virgil. His letter is a document of ambivalence toward Greek culture.

Let us leave him, my father, let us leave him, liar that he is, sunk with Apollo and the muses in the foulest swamp of the Styx. There let him hug Persephone and listen to Orpheus fiddling for his Eurydice from the infernal gods . . . the king of heaven sets his curse on such like . . . why then do I harp on them . . . since evil dung spread upon the fields enriches it to good harvest, so the filthy writings of the pagan poets are mighty aid to divine eloquence. (p. xxii)

The good abbot may have persuaded himself that he is a devout Christian and that he had found acceptable reasons to quote the classics but there is no mistaking the style. It is saturated with Greek mythology and made beautiful by it. Dante, too, living at the high point of Medieval

Christianity, makes Virgil his guide into a most Christian journey that leads him to Inferno, Purgatorio, and Paradiso.

Panofsky (1955) showed us that Durer was the first northern artist to feel "the pathos of distance" from the Greeks. Durer's attitude toward classical art was neither that of an heir nor that of an imitator, but rather, as Panofsky beautifully puts it, that of the conquistador. There were many others during the Renaissance and later who experienced the Greek heritage as a conquest.

The difference of style between Homer and the Bible has intrigued many observers. Heinrich Heine, observed:

In Homer, that other great book, the presentment is a product of art, and though the substance itself, as is the case with the Bible, is taken from reality, it is cast into poetic form, transfused, as it were, within the crucible of the human mind. It has been refined by means of the spiritual process which we call art. In the Bible no trace of art is evident. Its style is that of a notebook, in which the Absolute Spirit, seemingly without the assistance of any individual human being, has jotted down the events of the day, almost with the same factual accuracy with which we list our laundry. One cannot pass judgment on that style. One can only observe its effect on our minds (Ewen 1948: 411).

A hundred years later, Auerbach (1946) compared the return of Odysseus to his wife Penelope after a ten-year absence with the biblical account of Abraham's sacrifice of Isaac. He too noted how Homer's records are accurate to the smallest detail. We learn that when Odysseus does not want his secret to be discovered, he holds the old nurse by the throat with his right hand while he draws her closer to him with his left. The Homeric style, says Auerbach, leaves nothing which it mentions half in darkness and unexternalized. Homer's heroes vent their innermost hearts in speech, what they do not say to others they say aloud to themselves. Much that is terrible takes place in Homer but little takes place wordlessly. The Homeric style, Auerbach concludes, knows only a uniformly illuminated foreground. By contrast, when God calls upon Abraham, he answers: "Behold here I am." (In the Hebrew it is one word, *hineni*.) We are told what Abraham was doing when God called him. We do not know from where God is coming, whether the encounter took place indoors or outdoors, all the externals are unimportant. They fade away before the majesty of the encounter. In my view Auerbach carried the concept to an extreme. There are other scenes in Genesis, for example when Jacob first meets Rachel, where God is not involved which are less austere than the one described by Auerbach. Even so, a fundamental difference in style between Homer and the Bible is undeniable. The same impulse that prohibited the Hebrews from making graven images affected their way of seeing the world; concentrating on God, the external world lost significance.

Why are monotheistic religions less tolerant of each other than the polytheistic ones? In contrast to the West, Indian religious history shows how easy it is for divergent religious traditions to merge with one another and produce a new mythology. Why was that not possible in the West? It seems that monotheism, by eliminating other gods, gives rise to religious fanaticism, one god becoming the only god. Judaism created and bequeathed it to its daughter religions, Christianity and Islam, a jealousy based on the feeling of being chosen which manifests itself in the conviction that one is the only holder of the truth.

It seems that being chosen was the compensation that the monotheistic believer received in return for the submission to an all-powerful god and its earthly intraspsychic representative: a powerful superego. Monotheism begot religious fanaticism.

The inescapable conclusion seems to be that when too great a portion of love and the sexual drive is directed toward the love for God, aggression finds an outlet by persecution of those who worship another variant on the monotheistic theme. It seems that human beings cannot be asked to deflect too much of their pursuit of earthly love, however disappointing, toward divine love without increasing their aggression toward fellow men.

# 9

# *Love in the Old Testament*

The Hebrews felt both chosen and loved by their god, Yahwe. In the present world, they believe a gulf exists between God and his chosen people. The gulf is due not as it appears in Christian theology because of Adam's sins, but because the Israelites were incapable of loving their God with all their heart, all their soul, and all their being. But this state of separation will end someday. Harmony between Yahwe and his chosen people will be restored

Yahwe strictly speaking has no mythology. Attempts to compare the biblical stories with other mythologies have been made by Frazer (1918) and more recently by Graves and Patai (1963). To support the idea that Hebrews like other nations had myths, Graves and Patai rely on sources other than the Bible—namely on rabbinical and cabbalistic lore. True, at the beginning of biblical history, Yahwe had a personal relationship with the patriarchs. He had a particularly strong relationship to Moses and showed special favors to King David. He never had a relationship to a woman, not even a desexualized one.

Through the revolution brought about by the prophets, individual relationships were sublimated into a desexualized love between God and Israel. Thus the prophet Hosea:

> When Israel was a child, then I loved him,
> and called my son out of Egypt.
> (Hosea 11:1)

In a beautiful passage, God tells Hosea:

> I will even betroth thee unto me in faithfulness:
> and thou shalt know the Lord.
> And it shall come to pass in that day, I will hear,
> saith the Lord, I will hear the heavens, and they
> shall hear the earth;

*Deborah?*

And the earth shall hear the corn, and the
wine, and the oil; and they shall hear Jezreel.
And I will sow her unto me in the earth and I will
    have mercy upon her that had not obtained mercy;
and I will say to them which were not my people, Thou
art my people; and they shall say, Thou art my God.

                                 (Hosea 2:20–30)

In poetic passages such as this one, God through his prophets holds out to his nation a promise of a cosmic love without ambivalence in which every part of the universe will be responsive to every other part in a state of cosmic oneness. The whole passage vibrates with cosmic responsiveness. In the Hebrew original this passage has even a stronger sexual connotation. For what the translators have rendered "as I will hear" can more accurately be translated as "I will respond." The King James translation somewhat mitigated the sexual connotation. There can be no question that this is a form of love—desexualized, making moral demands, but love nevertheless.

The first statement in the Bible of earthly love occurs in Genesis 2:24. "Therefore shall a man leave his father and his mother, and shall cleave unto his wife; and they shall be one flesh." The next chapter follows another tradition and contradicts this statement, for Adam and Eve had to endure the Fall before they discovered genital intercourse. Only after the expulsion from the Garden of Eden, and after the catastrophic eating from the tree of knowledge, did Adam know Eve. The biblical metaphor of knowing for sexual intercourse indicates that the Bible regarded intercourse as a deep emotional experience.

Graves and Patai (1963), quote an American source to the effect that Adam fought for three hours against the temptation to follow Eve and eat the apple but at last he said "Eve, I would rather die than outlive you." There is an astonishing similarity between the Armenian account and the scene described by Milton in *Paradise Lost*. The Midrash, a postbiblical Jewish source, tells that Adam and Eve tried to cover their nakedness by plucking leaves from many trees but the trees drove them off, calling out "Begone thief who disobeyed your creator. You shall have nothing from us." Only the tree of knowledge had compassion for them because they preferred knowledge to immortality and thus provided the needed fig leaves (Graves & Patai, p. 77).

Genesis recounts that God created Eve out of Adam's rib. This myth flies flagrantly in the face of everyday experience that man comes out of woman and not vice versa. On psychoanalytic grounds we may assume that the myth grew out of man's envy of woman to bear children,* an envy that has been demonstrated clinically (Jacobson 1950; Llleuwen 1966). The story of man's Fall and expulsion from paradise contained many contradictions. How did it happen that an omniscient God did not foresee the Fall? Why did he so maliciously put temptation in the path of the first couple? Even more alarming is the idea that a benevolent deity punished us for our thirst for knowledge. From a psychoanalytic point of view the Fall is less puzzling if we assume that it was not God that was disappointed in man but man who was disappointed in God when his infantile wishes failed to materialize. In a psychoanalytic perspective, nearly every child experiences paradise in infancy, a state referred to in psychoanalysis as the symbiotic phase which precedes the separation from the mother (Mahler et al. 1968; 1975). Furthermore, every child has to discover that he cannot forever partake in the imaginary omnipotence of his parents. As the child grows older he or she acquires a sense of gender identity which also means the acceptance of permanent differences between the sexes. Paradise means having "everything." And everything stands for bisexuality. The vicissitudes of personal life history determine how early and how powerful the disappointment in one's own omnipotence and the omnipotence of one's parents will be. If this disappointment comes too early and is too strong, psychoanalytic experience has demonstrated that the capacity to love will be impaired. Since the mother is the most important first person in everybody's life, the biblical accusation against Eve, unfair as it is, rests upon a powerful psychological basis. In Freud's view (1927a), religious man transfers the persisting need for an omnipotent parental figure from the earthly father or mother to the heavenly one. The number of scenes in the Bible that express tender feelings between man and woman are rare. I will quote one:

Jacob loved Rachel; and said, "I will serve thee seven years for Rachel thy younger daughter . . . and Jacob served seven years for Rachel; and this seemed unto him but a few days for the love he had to her. (Genesis 29: 18–20)

This passage was often quoted by the courtly lovers during the Middle Ages as the prototype of what they called "love service." If ever a Hebrew

---

*The myth is responsible for many beautiful metaphors. One I particularly cherish occurs in Proust's *Swann's Way:* "Sometimes too just as Eve was created from the rib of Adam, so a woman would come into existence while I was sleeping, conceived from some strain in the position of my thigh . . . my body conscious that its own warmth was permeating hers, would strive to become one with her, and I would awake" (C.K. Scott Moncrieff translation).

lad braved storms to meet his beloved, if he ever had to overcome monsters to get her hand, or if he ever faced social ostracism for the love of a maiden of an alien religion, the Bible did not consider it worthwhile to record it. The love demanded by Yahwe superseded all other love. The whole Hebrew genius exhausted its need for love in an effort to sublimate love into the love for the one and only God.

The reader of the Bible is more likely to become acquainted with the destructive aspects of lust than with the healing power of love. There is the story of David's sin with Bathsheba, a topic that has intrigued many painters from Rembrandt to Picasso. The king spied her bathing. She was the wife of one of his officers, Uriah, the Hittite, a particularly virtuous officer. David took her and she bore him his heir, King Solomon. To get rid of her husband, David ordered Uriah to be placed in front of the battle and to be deserted by his comrades in the face of the enemy, and he was killed. At this juncture, the prophet Nathan appears, one of the first of a long line of prophets to become the voice of conscience. David was punished. He had to endure the rebellion of his beloved son Absalom. Absalom lay with the king's wives, but the Hebrew version of the oedipal myth ends with the victory of the father and his mourning over the loss of the rebellious son (Samuel 2:15).

Popular too was the story of Susanna and the Elders told in the Apochrypha. The two elders lusted after her and when they could not get their way they accused her of adultery. This scene was also a favorite topic among painters. The painter Degas had reportedly exclaimed, "When I think that the painters of the past were able to paint the chaste Susanna . . . whereas I am condemned to painting a housewife in her bathtub." (quoted in Licht 1979: 91).

The Bible knows the dangers of narcissism. It recounts the story of why Joseph felt superior to his brothers.

Now Israel loved Joseph more than all his children, because he was the son of his old age: and he made him a coat of many colors.

And when his brethren saw that their father loved him more than all his brethren, they hated him, and could not speak peaceably unto him.

And Joseph dreamed a dream, And he told it to his brethren: and they hated him yet the more.

And he said unto them, Hear, I pray you, this dream which I have dreamed:

For, behold, we were binding sheaves in the field, and, lo, my sheaf arose, and also stood upright: and, behold, your sheaves stood round about, and made obeisance to my sheaf.

In due time, Joseph became the hero of negative love.

And it came to pass after these things, that his master's wife cast her eyes upon Joseph; and she said,   Lie with me.

But he refused, and said unto his master's wife, Behold, my master wotteth not what is with me in the house, and he hath committed all that he hath to my hand;

There is none greater in this house than I; neither hath he kept back any thing from me but thee, because thou art his wife: how then can I do this great wickedness, and sin against God? (Genesis 37)

Ranelagh (1979: 4) pointed out that Potiphar's wife is a minor incident in Joseph's story. The emphasis is on Joseph's obedience to God and the woman as evil. The presentation is flat, without sensuality or erotism. Paradoxically, it interested many painters who gave to the scene the erotic quality lacking in the Bible.

The story is swiftly told in subsequent Jewish writings. Particularly in the Midrash, the need was felt to embellish upon it. Joseph's irresistibility is enhanced. Not only Potiphar's wife but all her women friends are smitten by love for him. In the Midrash, Rabba, a post-biblical Jewish book, Potiphar himself is portrayed as a eunuch, making his wife's infidelity more understandable. He has bought Joseph for sodomy; Joseph is desired by husband and wife.*

The Koran contains a Yusuf Sura in which there occurs an interesting variation on the theme.

He [Joseph] raced her to the door, but as she clung to him she tore his shirt from behind. And at the door they met her husband.

She cried: "Shall not the man who sought to violate your wife be thrown into prison or sternly punished?"

Joseph said: "It was she who sought to seduce me."

"If his shirt is torn from the front," said one of her people, "she is speaking the truth and he is lying. If it is torn from behind, then he is speaking the truth and she is lying."

And when her husband saw Joseph's shirt rent from behind, he said to her: "This is one of your tricks. Your cunning is great indeed! Joseph, say no more about this. Woman, ask pardon for your sin. You have done wrong." (Ranelagh 1979:10)

Thomas Mann, who retold the story of Joseph, retraced in some detail the evolution of Joseph's character from naked narcissism to a narcissism in the service of society as a whole. I believe that Thomas Mann's treatment of the theme of narcissism in turn influenced Kohut (1971) in his delineation of narcissism as having a developmental line of its own.

*To be desired sexually by both father and mother is a fantasy frequently encountered in psychoanalysis when the child is exposed to sexual intercourse between the parents and feels excluded.

The Bible also knows a number of women that psychoanalysis would describe as castrating. There was Delilah who delivered Sampson to his enemies, first symbolically emasculating him by cutting his hair; there was Yael who killed the sleeping and fleeing Sisera, an enemy of the Jews who sought her hospitality; and finally, in the Apocrypha, there was Judith who beheaded Holofernes. That castrating women have a great appeal to the unconscious is indicated by the fact that these scenes, while not central to the biblical theme, were so frequently selected as subjects for painting.

There is one book in the Bible in which the delights of sexual love are evoked freely without a sense of guilt. The Song of Songs or the Song of Solomon is a collection of love and marriage songs also known as the Canticles. Any perceptive reader of the Bible will note that the atmosphere in this poem is at variance with the tenor of the Bible as a whole. Indeed, it was in danger of being expurgated. It was rescued only by being interpreted allegorically. Disguised as an allegory, it was admitted to canonical rank because it was interpreted as a love song between God and Israel, and by the Christians as a love song between Christ and the church. The Hebrew scholar Rozelaar (1954) has assembled impressive evidence demonstrating beyond doubt that the canticle belongs to a Hellenistic tradition of erotic lyrics.

In the Jewish tradition, the Song of Songs became closely associated with welcoming the Sabbath, personified as the bride. Consequently, sexual intercourse was encouraged on the Sabbath in Christian tradition. St. Origen (185–284 A.D.) considered the canticle to be an epic celebrating the drama of the incarnation in the marriage chamber of the Virgin. In his view, the canticle was a drama of four participants: the bridegroom, the bride, the chorus of the companions of the bridegroom (consisting of angels and saints), and the chorus of the bride (consisting of the faithful of the church). The church fathers were still sufficiently versed in Greek poetry to recognize the affinity between the canticle and Greek poetry. However, since it was a biblical book, they assumed that the Hebrews passed on to the Greeks the art of love poetry and not vice versa. I am selecting a passage from this book that conveys the ecstasy of love:

Many waters cannot quench love, neither can the floods drown it: if a man will give all the substance of his house for love it would utterly be contemned.

His left hand should be under my head and his right hand should embrace me.
(Song of Songs 2:6 and 8:3)

In the apse mosaic of the twelfth-century church of Santa Maria in Trastevere in Rome, the Madonna and Christ are enthroned together as consorts in heaven; Mary displays a scroll where a love verse from the Song of Songs appears, "His left arm under my head, his right arm will embrace me." The Medieval artist found it possible to describe a mother-son relationship in a disguised sexual vocabulary. St. Bernard, who also lived in the twelfth century, devoted no less than eighty-six sermons to the Song of Songs. He quoted the same passage and transformed it into allegory: "Happy the soul who reclines on the breast of Christ and rests between the arms of the Word" (quoted in L. Steinberg 1983). No amount of allegorizing can disguise the sensual quality of such lines. Who the Hellenized Jew was who either translated Hellenistic love poetry into Hebrew or composed an original Hebrew love poem under Greek influence, we do not know. Nor do we know the deeper reasons why the compilers of the Bible allowed this poem into holy writ. But because it survived, generations of Jews and Christians could respond to a love poem without feeling that they were jeopardizing their soul or allowing it to be ensnared by Satan. There is poetry in many psalms in other parts of the Bible. But the poetic impulse was harnessed in the service of the glorification of God, asking his help, and seeking his love and forgiveness. The Song of Songs is a precious exception.

# 10

## Love in the New Testament

On the subject of love within the New Testament, a differentiation must be made between the Gospels, which on the whole are closer in spirit to the Judaic ethos, and the great upheaval that took place on the road to Damascus when Saul became St. Paul. To begin with the Gospels, one of the differences between the Old and the New Testaments was the reinterpretation of Jesus' statement in Genesis. Responding to a challenge by the Pharisees, Jesus says:

> For this cause shall a man leave father and mother
> And shall cleave to his wife; and they shall be one flesh
> Therefore they are no more twain but one flesh.
> (Matthew 9:5)

The differentiation between twain and one is novel within the Hebraic orbit of thought, but it is familiar to us from Plato. Jesus goes on to draw a harsh conclusion from the premise of oneness in Genesis. He prohibits divorce:

What therefore God has joined together let no man put asunder.

In the same chapter Jesus says:

There be eunuchs which have made themselves eunuchs for the kingdom of heaven's sake. He that is able to receive it let them receive it. (Matthew 12)

The act of religious self-castration in the worship of the goddess of fertility was a familiar rite performed by priests in a state of ecstacy in the Near East. To the Hebrews it was an abomination. God had commanded men to multiply. It must therefore have struck the Jewish listeners as odd that Jesus praised self-castration. The statement was not meant of course literally but metaphorically. Nevertheless, the cult of virginity and the assumption that sexual intercourse as such pollutes was a doctrine that set the early Christians apart from the majority of Jews.

Of particular relevance to the topic of love is the encounter between Jesus and the woman taken in adultery.

> And the scribes and Pharisees brought unto him a woman taken in adultery; and when they had set her in the midst,
> They say unto him, Master, this woman was taken in adultery, in the very act.
> Now Moses in the law commanded us, that such should be stoned: but what sayest thou? . . .
> So when they continued asking him, he lifted up himself, and said unto them, He that is without sin among you, let him first cast a stone at her. . . .
> And they which heard it, being convicted by their own conscience, went out, one by one, beginning at the eldest, even unto the last: and Jesus was left alone and the woman standing in the midst.
> When Jesus had lifted up himself, and saw none but the woman, he said unto her, Woman, where are those thine accusers? hath no man condemned thee?
> She said, No man, Lord. And Jesus said unto her, Neither do I condemn thee: go, and sin no more. (John 8: 3–5, 7, 9–11)

The scribes were testing Jesus' adherence to the Mosaic law. Jesus evaded the challenge but the moral impact transcends the historical moment. The scene, one of the most powerful in the New Testament, was a favorite one among artists: "Let him who is free of sin cast the first stone." The statement contains a new concept of morality that has left a mark on the Western way of thinking. It is a compassionate statement implying that no man is free of sin and no one is entitled to sit in judgment over another. However, the statement had further implications, for those who commit adultery and those who commit it in their heart were judged equally guilty. A deepening sense of sin is descernible in a number of passages in the New Testament. The obliteration of the difference between action and wish contributed to the strengthening of a punitive superego. Psychoanalysis has demonstrated repeatedly that most guilt feelings are not based on acts committed, but on wishes that have undergone repression, under the pressure of the superego. A major part of every psychoanalysis deals with making the unconscious sense of guilt conscious and helping the analysand differentiate between wish and act, which in turn leads to greater tolerance of hitherto unacceptable wishes, which need no longer be repressed.

While many of the sayings of Jesus contain messages of love and absolution from guilt, there are some that are notorious for their harshness. One of these deserves special comment:

Wherefore if thy hand or thy foot offend thee, cut them off, and cast them from thee: it is better for thee to enter into life halt or maimed, rather than having two hands or two feet to be cast into everlasting fire.

And if thine eye offend thee, pluck it out, and cast it from thee: it is better for thee to enter into life with one eye, rather than having two eyes to be cast into hell fire. (Matthew 18: 8–9)

Fortunately most Christians have taken this admonition metaphorically rather than literally. However, among psychotics cases of self-multilation based on the idea that the offending organ should be severed have been described in psychiatric literature. The self-punitive removal of an organ which symbolizes the evil penis has usually been attributed to guilt feelings based on the oedipus complex. The psychoanalyst Kohut (1972: 375–376) has suggested a different interpretation. In schizophrenia a breakup of the body-self takes place. Each organ, as it were, then represents a subaspect of the personality. The organ which is removed has lost its narcissistic libidinal significance and is no longer regarded as part of the self. It therefore can be discarded as if it were a foreign body.

In the nineteenth century, when the power of Christian religion began to wane, the equation of the wish with the deed could be used as seduction, as in a poem by Thomas Moore (1779–1852).

> I've oft been told by learned friars,
>     That wishing and the crime are one,
> And Heaven punishes desires
>     As much as if the deed were done.
> If wishing damns us, you and I
>     Are damned to all our heart's content;
> Come, then, at least we may enjoy
>     Some pleasure for our punishment!

While Jesus was teaching, the Jewish temple was still standing. It was to purify the temple that Jesus expelled the money changers from it. That God allowed his temple to be burnt down was a trauma to the Jews as well as to the early Jewish-Christian sect. By way of mastering the trauma the Jews replaced sacrifice by prayer. In psychoanalytic terms, this was an attempt to cope with the trauma by internalization and an increase in the severity of the superego. For the sacrifice is a tangible act that easily convinces the believer that he has atoned for his sin. The prayer, more intellectual, accomplishes the same task, with greater psychic effort.

St. Paul also reacted to the trauma of the temple's destruction. He converted the body into the very temple that was destroyed.

The body is not for fornication, but for the Lord; and the Lord for the body.
                                          (1 Corinthians 6:13)

In St. Paul's writings, all forms of sexuality are condemned with a ferocity encountered neither among the Jews nor among the Greeks.

Know ye not that the unrighteous shall not inherit the kingdom of God? Be not deceived: neither fornicators nor idolators nor adulterers nor effeminate, nor abusers of themselves with mankind . . . shall inherit the kingdom of God. (1 Corinthians 6:9)

St. Paul condemns with equal severity the worship of idols, adultery, homosexuality, and masturbation.

The Greeks knew of two virgin goddesses, Artemis and Athena, but chastity as such was neither a Greek nor a Jewish symbol of perfection. For the first time in Western history, chastity became a virtue; to abstain from sexual intercourse became a sign of holiness. St. Paul himself struggles valiantly against sexual temptation:

I find then a law, that, when I would do good, evil is present with me.
For I delight in the law of God after the inward man:
But I see another law in my members, warring against the law of my mind, and bringing me into captivity to the law of sin which is in my members.
O wretched man that I am! who shall deliver me from the body of this death? (Romans 7:22)

St. Paul never knew that Plato existed but St. Augustine did. He accepted Plato's basic assumption that man yearns for goodness, that he is eager to possess the object of his desire. God alone is perfect greatness, therefore, God alone can satisfy man's desire for love. God is more abstract than a mortal partner, but less abstract than Plato's good. To mystics, God is a very concrete object of love.

Freud had his own interpretation of the victory of Christianity. It was based on ideas he had formulated in 1913 in *Totem and Taboo*. These ideas reached further clarification in his last book, *Moses and Monotheism* (1938). In that book, Freud interpreted Judaism as a religion of the father and Christianity as that of the son. The latent content of Christianity he saw as the dethronement of the father by the son, that is, as fulfillment of the oedipal wishes in a disguised form. It was St. Paul whom Freud credited with the idea of converting the parricidal and oedipal son into the saviour. Through this disguise the rebel son became the innocent victim. Cleansed of his own guilt, he can atone for the guilt of those who believe in him. In Christianity, as distinguished from Greek mythology, all traces of the patricidal impulses were ruthlessly repressed. Only the guilt remained. Freud interpreted Holy Communion, in which the believer incorporates the saviour's flesh and blood, as a repetition of the totem meal now purged of all cannibalistic and aggressive wishes.

To Freud's remarks, I would like to add the following. Within the Hebraic world of thought any sexual liaison between a god and a mortal was considered blasphemous. The Immaculate Conception is a strikingly felicitous example of a compromise between the two worlds, for here sexual intercourse between God and a mortal woman has both taken, and not taken, place at the same time. Ernest Jones (1914) has shown that in the Immaculate Conception the ear had replaced the vagina. (Arlow [1964] has reported a case where a religious woman experienced in psychoanalysis conception through the eyes.) The Immaculate Conception is an example of what Freud called primary process thinking. It fulfills a basic childhood wish for a mother who had no sexual intercourse with the father.

The story of the Nativity and particularly Christian iconography offers additional evidence. King Herod's fear of the baby Jesus—the order to massacre all babies born in Bethlehem—shows that we are dealing with an oedipal story. Further evidence comes from the menial and servile role that Christ's earthly father, Joseph, plays in the drama. The three Magi, exalted father representatives, come to pay homage. Christ has no sibling, his mother is a virgin who lives entirely for him. In heaven she will receive from him her coronation and reign like a spouse by his side. Artists like Michelangelo devined intuitively this secret when in the great Pieta in Rome he rendered mother and son as if they were the same age. With sexuality ruthlessly expurgated, with both mother and son remaining free of sin, and with crucifixion as punishment, the Christian myth allowed, in a disguised form to be sure, the fulfillment of oedipal wishes.

In its monotheistic zeal, Judaism repressed all reference to a female deity. Only among the Kabbalists was a feminine emanation of God called the Schechina allowed to persist. Even then it occupied the lowest level of God's emanations (Sephiroth in Hebrew). In Christianity, particularly during the Middle Ages, Mary reemerges as a powerful goddess in her own right. The most beautiful churches in Western Christendom, like Chartres, are dedicated to her. Freud alluded to this return of the mother-goddess in a short paper "Great is Diana of the Ephesians" (1911a).

In a recent publication, the art historian, Leo Steinberg (1983), assembled an astonishing body of evidence to illustrate that from the twelfth century until the counter-Reformation, Christian art emphasized the phallus of Christ both as an infant and during and after crucifixion. Psychoanalysts, if not the author himself, will read these findings as further proof that Freud was right to equate Christ's with Oedipus.

# 11

# *Romantic and Narcissistic Love from the Middle Ages to Milton and Shakespeare*

The Middle Ages enlarged the vocabulary of love by the creation of a new species of love—romantic love. Hitherto it was taken for granted that the lovers' journey ends in lovers meeting, that is, in their sexual union. In romantic love, unconsummated love was idealized. Typically, the lover is a knight in love with a married woman of a higher social rank. For her sake, he endures hardship. His love either remains unrequited or mounting obstacles usually created by the lovers themselves prevent the consummation of this love. A high point of romantic love is the inability of the lovers to live without each other. The union they did not achieve in life they find in a joint death. The English language has resisted the coining of the appropriate word, so that the German *Liebestod* meaning death love has acquired international meaning. The *Liebestod* is the substitute for orgasm in normal love. Romantic love sexualized death and conversely endowed love with aggression. Clinically, romantic love survives today as a species of neurotic love. Once articulated, romantic love remained in the mainstream of Western sensibility. The nature of romantic love was captured succinctly in a poem by Andrew Marvel, 1621–1678.

### The Definition of Love

My Love is of a birth so rare
As 'tis, for object, strange and high:
It was begotten by despair
Upon impossibility.

Magnanimous despair alone
Could show me so divine a thing,

Where feeble hope could ne'er have flown
But vainly flapped its tinsel wing.

And yet quickly might arrive
Where my extended soul is fixed,
But faith does iron wedges drive,
And always crowds itself betwixt.

For faith with jealous eyes does see
Two perfect loves; nor let them close:
Their union would her ruin be,
And her tyrannic power dispose.

In the Middle Ages, romantic love gave rise to courtly love that C.S. Lewis (1936) called the religion of love.

Andre the Chaplain (Andreas Cappellanus) brings us to love in the Middle Ages. He is the theoretician of courtly love. C.S. Lewis, whose book *The Allegory of Love* (1936) was highly influential in interpreting courtly love, defined this love as a highly specialized sort, consisting of humility, courtesy, adultery, and religion of love. The doctrine appears in an alleged letter of Countess Marie of Champagne, who ruled the court of love in Poitiers in the eleventh century. Particularly noteworthy are the following precepts of love. "No woman even if she is married can be crowned by the rewards of the King of Love unless she had been enlisted in the service of love outside the bounds of wedlock." Love is defined as "an inordinate desire to receive passionately a furtive and hidden embrace." "The marriage agreement limits the partners to satisfy each other's desire and therefore does away with the freedom necessary for love." Two other precepts are noteworthy: "No one can be in love with two men" and "He who is not jealous cannot love" (quoted in Kelly 1975: 37–38).

Andre the Chaplain is the theoretician of courtly love. Visible beauty is to Chaplain the only source of love. That is why he mistakenly believed that the blind cannot love. For a time "The Religion of Love" almost took on the character of a heresy. In the English language it inspired poets like Wyatt, Sidney, Spenser, and Raleigh to write love poetry of great beauty and intensity.

Dante (1265–1321), the great poet of the Middle Ages, created his own synthesis out of the various ideologies of love available to him. He is the poet of love deflected to higher aims. He therefore belongs to the tradition of romantic love, but at the same time his work is also a creative descendant of Plato's *Symposium*. He is the great poet of aim-inhibited love. Dante has played a unique role in the history of love in the Western world, for he showed that a love for a woman, like religious love, can exist in pure form inflated by the contact and personality of the beloved. Although the beloved has a name, his love comes close to being without a love object. The poet was nine years old when love entered his life, and from that time on it governed his soul. Dante feels so much in love that all he need do is to write down the words that love dictates to him, just as the Evangelists wrote down what the Holy Spirit dictated. For Dante, even the name of the beloved has to be kept secret and when the beloved casually salutes the poet, he reaches the very limits of blessedness. Here, "when she appeared in any place, it seemed to me, by the hope of her excellent salutation, that there was no man mine enemy any longer; and such warmth of charity came upon me that most certainly in that moment I would have pardoned whosoever had done me an injury" (*La Vita Nuova,* in Milano 1947: 559).

Lovers in this view know no aggression. Shakespeare made dramatic use of this view of love when Romeo refuses to fight Tybalt, but Shakespeare understood that life is not viable when all aggression is purged. He made the scene end tragically with Mercutio's death.

In the eighteenth Canto of *Purgatory,* Dante learns from Virgil what love is. Man loves, he is told, because he is created apt to love. He is stirred to action and quick to move the moment the mind encounters an object pleasing to it. This is perhaps the simplest theory of love proposed, but Virgil adds a complication. The mind creates within itself an image of the loved person, and by creating this inward image, it is captured by love. This insight is one of the most important ones in the history of this subject. For Dante knows that one doesn't fall in love with a person in the real world unless an inward image has been created intrapsychically before this person was ever met. The relationship between the inward image and the real person will be a recurrent topic in this book. Dante was still alive when Petrarch was born in 1304. Petrarch was not only a great lyrical poet but also the first humanist. For love he developed new images and metaphors. He found a vocabulary to celebrate melancholy love.

That the myth of Narcissus has abiding unconscious meaning is further demonstrated by the fact that it has intrigued generations of writers in the Christian era. The first Christian version of this myth comes from an unknown Norman French poet in the twelfth century. It has been beautifully retold by Frederick Goldin (1964). I will follow his account although my understanding of the story differs from his. The name of Freud does not appear in Goldin's books. In this medieval version, Narcisus (there is a change in spelling of the name) is an ordinary mortal. The nymph Echo is replaced by a princess named Dane. At first Dane does not know that she has fallen in love, she only suffers from insomnia. She wakes her nurse to change the sheets because she feels that her bed is too hard. Slowly she recognizes that her sickness is love, and Narcisus the only cure. She implores him to requite her love and when she is rebuffed, she prays to the God of Love that Narcisus be punished like herself. The punishment of Narcisus does not come from Nemesis but directly from Amor, the god of love. (His fate is thereby brought in line with that of Hippolytus.) He is punished because he refused to love. To the Christian poet, self-love is not a form of love but an act of disobedience of love's commands.

Narcisus comes to a fountain, falls in love with an image he believes to be that of the nymph who guards the fountain. The homosexual motif in Ovid has become heterosexual. Narcisus cannot take his eyes from the image he sees. "Her" face, figure, hands, every part of her body is bewitching. He calls on the image in the water in terms taken directly from Ovid.

Come here! Why do you hold back? Why are you haughty towards me? I am hardly less beautiful than you. My love has been sought by many. Now I feel clearly how it was with them ... Speak to me, come forward! Wretched me ... She doesn't hear what I am saying ... Her lips are moving, but I cannot hear what they are saying ... When I sigh she sighs, when I weep, she does the same ... Either she wants to mock me or else she is unable to come ...

This is followed by the moment of recognition.

I well know that the seer spoke the truth, my death is near ... I have put my love in a mad place ... Now that I know the truth I cannot have any hope ... Before at least the sight was a pleasure to me ... now I know I see nothing ... I love myself, it is madness.

At this point the differences between the pagan and the Christian Medieval view become manifest. Narcisus continues his soliloquy:

Why does my mother not know anything about this? If she came she could at least pity me and weep for me.

She might comfort me somewhat—at least there is that maiden whom I found so beautiful the other day ... who begged me to love her ... I was so hard-hearted and villanous she could never please me ... perhaps she would be able to save me, more than my mother, father or sister, if I could turn my heart to her, and so bend my heart that I will forget this frenzy ... If I had seen someone other than myself (in the water) I would not be in this predicament ... If only she would by chance come now! She could be quite sure that she would win my love and she would cast me out of this languishing. (Goldin 1964)

Dane rushes back, but she comes too late; Narcisus has fainted. He has lost his power to speak. (In this version, Narcissus becomes Echo.) By his gestures he conveys to her that he had repented his harshness. He holds out his arms, moves his lips to show her that he is now capable of loving. Dane cannot stand the thought that her own cruel prayer was the cause of his death. There is no comfort for her; she must die with him. Guilt, remorse, and *Liebestod* differentiate the medieval Narcisus from the classic. In a truly Christian fashion, Narcisus dies a repentant sinner.

Another Medieval version of the myth of Narcisus is found in the "Romance of the Rose" by Guillaume de Lorris. In this story the hero is a dreamer who in his dream walks in a garden and discovers the fountain of Narcisus. A plaque explains that Narcisus died here; the dreamer is pierced by Amor's arrow. Because the dreamer knows the story of Narcisus, he will escape death but he has to go through a long inner struggle. "This is a pernicious mirror where proud Narcisus gazed upon his face . . . In a painful moment I saw myself there, misery! How much I have sighed since I became aware of it." Goldin (1964) beautifully illustrates how a number of poets of courtly love understood the similarity between narcissism and their worship of "the lady." They see that they only love themselves when they worshipped her.

Alas how much I thought I knew about love and how little I really know! For I cannot keep myself from loving her from whom I shall have no requital. She has all my heart, and me, and herself, and all the world; and when she has thus taken all from me she leaves me with nothing but desire and longing of the heart. Never have I had power over myself nor been mine own, from that moment when she let me look into her eyes into a mirror that pleased me so much, till now, since I beheld myself in you, my deep sights have killed me, for I have lost myself as the beautiful Narcisus lost himself in the fountain. (Bernard de Ventadorn, in Goldin 1964: 95)

The eyes of the beloved were the treacherous mirror in which he saw only himself.

The story of Narcisus continues into the Renaissance. Spenser (1552–1599), in the *Faerie Queene*, Book 3, tells the story of Britomart, a feminine knight of chastity who innocently looked into an enchanted glass which was given to her father by the magician Merlin; the glass had the power to reveal anything wished for by a lover. At first, Britomart saw only her own image but when she thought of what would pertain to herself an image of an unknown knight, Artegal, rose in the mirror. At that point the "false archer" shot her, but so slyly that, before she even felt the wound, signs of love appeared: she became anxious and melancholy without realizing she was in love. Again, an old nurse recognized her symptoms, tried to comfort her but Britomart insisted that her situation was hopeless. Her reasoning shows how much Spenser knew about narcissism, for he makes Britomart feel hopeless because her knight is nothing but a mirror of her own fantasy. She never met the knight of her love but only saw his semblance in the mirror. Spenser thus shows a deep understanding of the dangers of narcissistic love.

One analysand disappointed in the woman he had chosen ruefully observed, "When I fell in love I wrote the whole scenario myself and only later looked around for a cast of characters."

## The Themes of Narcissus and Hermaphroditus in Shakespeare

A long popular tradition has it that Shakespeare is the foremost poet of love. This tradition asserts that love was to him so naturally strong that it needs the invasion of an alien power to prevent the bliss of perfect fulfillment. Unlike Dante's intellectual love, Shakespeare is seen as the poet of the earthly felicity of love; for this sunny view of Shakespeare the sonnets pose a problem. Some critics like Croce saw the sonnets as a momentary overclouding of the mirror of the plays (Murray 1921), but there were always a number of plays that did not fit with this optimistic view: *Hamlet, Measure for Measure,* and *Troilus and Cressida,* to name only the outstanding ones. With the advent of psychoanalysis and its insistence on separating manifest from latent content, this view of Shakespeare was challenged (Holland 1966). In my analysis of Shakespeare's work, I will peruse the relationship between love and narcissism in his works, a theme that has not received the attention it deserves.

*Venus and Adonis.* The reader will recall that in chapter 3 I interpreted Ovid's story of Venus and Adonis as a dethronement of the once powerful goddess of love. I have also suggested that Ovid returned Venus to the place of her birth, that is, he made her once more what she was in antiquity before the Greek genius has metamorphosed her into a goddess of love, the goddess of fertility who laments the loss of her lover. Shakespeare carried the humiliation of Venus a step further. In his poem, the goddess of love herself has not only stooped to love but she cannot even command her child Cupid to force the youth she loves to reciprocate her love. We find her telling Adonis:

Venus: I have been woo'd, as I entreat thee now,
　　　　Even by the stern and direful god of war,
　　　　Whose sinewy neck in battle ne'er did bow,

> Who conquers where he comes in every jar;
>     Yet hath he been my captive and my slave,
>     And begg'd for that which thou unask'd shalt have.
>
> (lines 100 ff.)

As part of the seduction strategy the myth of Narcissus is evoked by Venus to warn Adonis that unless he loves her he will end as Narcissus did. We have seen that the myth of Narcissus has already in antiquity been used as a cautionary tale to those who refuse to love. Venus argues:

> Venus: Is thine own heart to thine own face affected?
>     Can thy right hand seize love upon thy left?
>     Then woo thyself, be of thyself rejected,
>     Steal thine own freedom, and complain on theft.
>         Narcissus so himself forsook,
>         And died to kiss his shadow in the brook.
>
> (lines 105 ff.)

The fate of Narcissus is used by Venus as an argument in favor of procreation.

> Things growing to themselves are growth's abuse:
>     Seeds spring from seeds, and beauty breedeth beauty;
>     Thou wast begot; to get it is thy duty.
>     By law of nature thou art bound to breed,
>     That thine may live when thou thyself art dead;
>
> (lines 160 ff.)

This is Shakespeare's standard argument against the narcissist who refuses the sexual encounter. We encounter it in *Twelfth Night* when Viola argues with Olivia:

> Lady, you are the cruell'st she alive.
>     If you will lead these graces to the grave
>     And leave the world no copy.
>
> (I.5)

We will reencounter the same argument in the sonnets.

Panofsky (1969) is of the opinion that Shakespeare changed the "leave-taking Venus" into "the flight-taking Adonis" under the impact of a painting by Titian then in England. This painting, now in the Prado, shows a naked Venus clinging to a fully-dressed Adonis who holds on the leash two dogs impatient to start the chase. Why Titian, a heterosexual painter, should have departed from Ovid's model, Panofsky does not explain.

In chapter 2, I have, based on Sumerian evidence, differentiated between the poetry of seduction and the poetry of love. I suggest there that poetry of seduction is likely to be the older of the two. *Venus and Adonis* is a poem of seduction. Venus praises her own sexual charms.

> Venus: Graze on my lips, and if those hills be dry,
> Stray lower, where the pleasant fountains lie.
> 'Within this limit is relief enough,
> Sweet bottom-grass and high delightful plain,
> Round rising hillocks, brakes obscure and rough,
> To shelter thee from tempest and from rain:
>    Then be my deer, since I am such a park;
>    No dog shall rouse thee, though a thousand bark.'
>
> (lines 230 ff.)

Equally seductive are the lines:

> Venus: A thousand honey secrets shalt thou know:
> Here come and sit, where never serpent hisses;
> And being set, I'll smother thee with kisses:
>
> (lines ff.)

The beautiful metaphors that condense deer and dear and equate the vagina with a shelter full of honey secrets, a place safe from dogs and serpents, are designed to counteract the castration anxiety of the homo-sexually inclined Adonis. Venus fails, but Shakespeare has endowed her failure with magnificent language. She addresses another fear of Narcissus, the fear of boredom.

> And yet not cloy thy lips with loth'd satiety,
> But rather famish them amid their plenty,
> Making them red and pale with fresh variety;
>
> (lines 15 ff.)

The metaphor Venus uses is familiar to us from another context but there it is said in admiration of Cleopatra:

> Enobarbus: Age cannot wither her, nor custom stale
> Her infinite variety; other women cloy
> The appetites they feed, but she makes hungry
> Where most she satisfies
>
> (*Anthony and Cleopatra*, II.2)

In the poem *Venus and Adonis,* the seduction stays firmly within heterosexual boundaries. In *The Passionate Pilgrim,* she does not shrink from using homosexual ways of seduction to seduce Adonis, she becomes Mars.

> Venus, with young Adonis sitting by her
> Under a myrtle shade, began to woo him:
> She told the youngling how god Mars did try her,
> And as he fell to her, so fell she to him,
> "Even thus," quoth she, "the war-like god embrac'd me,"
> And then she clipp'd Adonis in her arms;
> "Even thus," quoth she, "the war-like god unlac'd me,"
> As if the boy should use like loving charms.
> "Even thus," quoth she, "he seized on my lips,"
> And with her lips on his did act the seizure;
> And as she fetched breath, away he skips,
> And would not take her meaning nor her pleasure.
>
> (Verse II)

In this poem too, Venus fails. The youth fears that he will be "clipped" by her. Shakespeare, I will argue later on, shared all the fears of Adonis but being the poet that he was, he could endow the suit of the tragic Venus with beautiful language.

*The Theme of Narcissism in the Comedies.* In *Much Ado About Nothing* there are two narcissistic lovers, Benedick and Beatrice. Both are tricked into loving each other by a deliberately staged social conspiracy in which each is told that they are doted upon by the other; convinced that they are adored, they overcome their reluctance to love. By exposing the narcissistic base of love, Shakespeare mocks love.

The same subject is expanded and deepened in *Twelfth Night.* In this play, a hermaphroditic pair of twins are separated from each other by a storm. The sister, Viola, disguised as a man, enters the services of the local duke, Orsino. Orsino uses Viola's services to woo Olivia, who responds to the messenger and the beauty of his message rather than to his master. Homosexual love replaces hermaphroditic love. The brother, Sebastian, is saved by a sea captain, forming a second homosexual pair. To fall in love with a man one saves is a homosexual variant on the old heterosexual theme of the man falling in love with the woman he saves. Mischief is created when the twins are mistaken for one another but all ends well when the disguise is recognized.

The twins are the hermaphroditic pair of Plato's *Symposium.* As in Plato's *Symposium,* the twins were separated traumatically, and the sea storm expresses this trauma. The heterosexual twins condense two symbols, for the twin is psychologically speaking a substitute for the mother from whom the infant must separate. But the twin also symbolizes the hermaphroditic longing for the mirror image that must be given up if an adult love object is to be found. The shipwreck is followed by a pair of homosexual lovers. What Viola says to Olivia is so much more genuine than anything that the melancholy Orsino actually feels for Olivia that we need not be surprised that Olivia falls in love with the messenger.

Viola: If I did love you in my master's flame,
   With such a suffering, such a dreadly life,
   In your denial I would find no sense;
   I would not understand it.

Olivia: Why, what would you?

Viola: Make me a willow cabin at your gate,
   And call upon my soul within the house;
   Write loyal cantons of contemned love,
   And sing them loud even in the dead of night;
              (I, 6)

Orsino himself has too high an opinion of his own love for us to take his love for Olivia seriously.

Orsino: There is no woman's sides
   Can bide the beating of so strong a passion
   As love doth give my heart; no woman's heart
   So big, to hold so much; they lack retention
   Alas! their love may be call'd appetite,
   No motion of the liver, but the palate,
   That suffer surfeit, cloyment, and revolt;
   But mine is all as hungry as the sea,
   And can digest as much. Make no compare
   Between that love a woman can bear me
   And that I owe Olivia.
             (II. 4)

Once more we note the strength of the oral imagery in the metaphors of love. Orsino may be in love with love but he is not in love with Olivia. Too much narcissism is present for us to think that he loves her. He is so impressed with his own love and so mistrustful of woman's capacity to love that we sympathize with Olivia's refusal of this proffer of narcissistic love. The real love in *Twelfth Night* is between Viola and Olivia, that is, homosexual love.

In another part of the forest, as it were, seemingly without connection to the main plot, Shakespeare gives the audience an opportunity to discharge the aggression that has accumulated while witnessing the struggle against narcissistic and incestuous love; he achieves his aim by heaping scorn on the man who loves because he mistakenly believes that he is loved. Malvolio is the original narcissist capable only of self-love. Maria describes him as:

> the best persuaded of himself; so crammed, as he
> thinks, with excellencies, that it is his
> ground of faith that all that look on him love
> him;
>
> (II. 3)

Once more Shakespeare uses the device of mocking persons who love only because they think they are loved. But how different are Orsino, who exchanges Viola for Olivia, and Olivia herself, who takes Sebastian in lieu of Viola, from Malvolio? On the surface, only Malvolio is mocked. Below the surface, subtly, love itself is Shakespeare's target for mockery. Shakespeare's message is clear: we love not what is, but what we fools imagine exists.

*The Sonnets.* John Dover Wilson (1966), one of the best known interpreters of the Sonnets, calls the Sonnets the greatest love poetry in the world. He also quotes C. S. Lewis to the effect that the Sonnets were not only unique in the English literature of the Renaissance but constitute the supreme love poetry in the world. Wilson goes on to note that Shakespeare's language "is too lover-like for that of ordinary male friendship; . . . I have found no real parallel to such language between friends in sixteenth century literature. Yet, on the other hand, this does not seem to be poetry of full bloom pederasty" (p. 15).

In Freud's opinion the Sonnets were self-confessions (Jones 1957: 455). In my view the Sonnets can be read as a magnificent example of a split between homosexual love and heterosexual sex. All homosexual loves must forgo the wish for progeny. The Sonnets show that the poet's need for children must have been strong. Since his male lover is described as a narcissist, his appeal for him to reproduce is stated in terms of reproducing his own beauty that otherwise cannot be preserved. The attempt to solve the problems through homosexual love and heterosexual sex creates its own tragedy and the Sonnets illustrate this dilemma.

The Sonnets have been tilled by many hands. Scholars have spent years deciphering and rearranging them with the hope that should we know the true sequence in which they were composed, we could decipher their secret. These scholars in my view fail to take into account the possibility that the Sonnets may reflect not a sequence of events in the outside world but cyclical moods of the poet himself.

I do not suggest that my interpretation of the Sonnets represents Shakespeare's biographical reality. What I do suggest is that we read the Sonnets differently if we understand the nature of narcissism and the bisexual conflict which accompanies it. In the context of this chapter we are less interested in Shakespeare's biography and more in the way he had reconstituted and transformed the heritage of Ovid.

The Sonnets are traditionally divided into the first 125 which are love sonnets for a younger man of higher social rank and the second group of 25 sonnets addressed to a woman known as the Dark Lady. In a psychoanalytic study of the Sonnets, Silver (1983) has come to the conclusion that Shakespeare's love for the Dark Lady represents a refinding of his own depressed mother. It is known that Shakespeare's mother lost her own mother during infancy and her father when she was eight years old. She also lost four daughters, two before the poet was born and two afterwards. It seems plausible as Silver suggests that the Dark Lady represented not only mother's depression but that this depression was condensed with feelings of jealousy and disloyalty which the pregnancies evoked. The fact that the daughters did not survive would then have suggested to Shakespeare, as similar events suggest to contemporary analysands, that siblings die because of the omnipotence of his death wishes, contributing to Shakespeare's guilt feelings.

Wilson, whom I have quoted earlier, believes that Shakespeare was happy for a time; he loved a young man of noble origin with a desexualized and highly idealized love; he also had a mistress. Then the calamity happened; "the young man has come to know the mistress whom the poet had loved dearly, and the two had betrayed him" (p. liv). As proof of the betrayal Wilson cites Sonnet 33, which opens triumphantly with

> Full many a glorious morning have I seen
> Flatter the mountain tops with sovereign eye,
> Kissing with golden face the meadow's green

These lines are a poetic transmutation of the bliss of love. The sonnet ends darkly with:
> But out alack! He was but one hour mine

It is possible, as Silver suggested, that we are dealing not only with an adult love betrayal, but also with a child's disappointment with its mother.

In a state of love, real time gives way to psychological time which always converts bliss into less than an hour. Further proof of the calamity Wilson finds in Sonnet 144:

> Two loves I have of comfort and despair,
> Which like two spirits do suggest me still,
> The better angel is a man right fair:
> The worser spirit a woman coloured ill,
> To win me soon to hell my female evil,
> Tempteth my better angel from my side,
> And would corrupt my saint to be a devil:
> Wooing his purity with her foul pride.
> And whether that my angel be turned fiend,
> Suspect I may, yet not directly tell,
> But being both from me both to each friend,
> I guess one angel in another's hell.
> > Yet this shall I ne'er know but live in doubt,
> > Till my bad angel fire my good one out.

A reading of this sonnet suggests to me what psychoanalytic experience with so-called bisexual loves so often confirms, that Shakespeare suffered from a split between love and sexuality. He was heterosexual in his sexuality and homosexual in his love. Such betrayals are often unconsciously engineered by bisexual men and women. If the lover and the mistress have indeed betrayed him, the blame is most unevenly meted out. Shakespeare makes every effort to exonerate the man and blame the woman. Bisexual men or women often evoke jealousy in both the man and the woman they are involved with. They provoke by their own behavior the two to come together and betray them. Psychoanalytic experience has shown that bisexual men and women reenact the primal scene of sexual intercourse between the parents, but now the bisexual person is no longer the excluded child but the central figure in the triangle. The bisexuality is a way of transporting the anger and jealousy evoked in the child who witnessed sexual relations between the parents. It is an answer to the humiliation and pain of the primal scene. The betrayal is in turn an unconsciously engineered return of the trauma of the primal scene (see Grunberger 1971; McDougall 1980; Chasseguet-Smirgel, 1970 and 1983).

Sonnet 143 shows that Shakespeare was not always averse to sharing his mistress with the young man. He could master his jealousy when he equated her with his mother and the lover with a sibling.

> Lo as a careful housewife runs to catch,
> One of her feather'd creatures broke away,
> Sets down her babe, and makes all swift dispatch
> In pursuit of the thing she would have stay:
> Whilst her neglected child holds her in chase,
> Cries to catch her whose busy care is bent,
> To follow that which flies before her face:
> Not prizing her poor infant's discontent;
> So runn'st thou after that which flies from thee,
> Whilst I thy babe chase thee afar behind,
> But if thou catch thy hope, turn back to me,
> And play the mother's part, kiss me, be kind.
> > So will I pray that thou mayst have thy Will,
> > If thou turn back and my loud crying still.

Wilson interprets "thy Will" as indicating that the name of his rival was also William.

Sonnet 143 can be read as a temporary truce between homo- and heterosexual conflicts, or willingness to settle for a triangular relationship.

In the figure of Cleopatra, Shakespeare portrayed a woman who both loves her Antony and betrays him. In the light of Sonnet 143 we can see Antony and Cleopatra as an attempt to explain this dual nature of the woman.

I arrive at a different interpretation of the Sonnets than the one suggested by Wilson. I assume that the basic problem for Shakespeare was his inability to surmount his own self-love. The crucial sonnet is, in my interpretation, Sonnet 62, which beautifully expresses the danger faced by Narcissus.

> Sin of self-love possesseth all mine eye,
> And all my soul, and all my every part;
> And for this sin there is no remedy,
> It is so grounded inward in my heart.
> Methinks no face so gracious is as mine,
> No shape so true, no truth of such account,
> And for myself mine own worth do define,
> As I all other in all worths surmount.
> But when my glass shows me myself indeed
> Beated and chopt with tanned antiquity,
> Mine own self-love quite contrary I read:
> Self, so self-loving were iniquity.
> > 'Tis thee, (my self) that for my self I praise,
> > Painting my age with beauty of thy days.

Shakespeare struggled valiantly against the dangers of self-love, and one of the solutions he found was what Freud (1914) would call narcissistic love, the love for what one once was.

The bisexual nature of Shakespeare's narcissistic solution is found in Sonnet 20:

> A woman's face with nature's own hand painted
> Hast thou, the master-mistress of my passion;
> A woman's gentle heart, but not acquainted with shifting change,
> As is false woman fashion;

The sonnet ends with Shakespeare's renunciation of the sexual aspect of his love for the young man.

> But since she (nature) tricked thee out for woman's pleasure,
> Mine be thy love, and thy love's use their treasure.

The differentiation between love and sex has been stated eloquently. The anger at the Dark Lady in the Sonnets reflects the fact that Shakespeare's attempt to separate homosexual love from heterosexual sex has failed.

We note that in his plays the argument that the narcissist should reproduce himself is made by women and within the heterosexual sphere it makes sense. The woman offers the narcissist the opportunity to reproduce himself in exchange for giving her the chance to bear his child. Within the homosexual context this argument makes no sense. It is indeed surprising that Shakespearean scholars never seriously raised the problem why one man in love with another would urge him to reproduce. Two interpretations are possible. The first would suggest that Shakespeare identified himself with a woman and pleaded with his lover as a woman would. The other and to me more convincing interpretation is that Shakespeare is addressing this demand not to the male beloved but to the narcissistic part of himself to establish or consolidate a loveless procreating heterosexual union. Shakespeare uses the mirror very differently from Ovid, to control his self-love. It is the mirror that forces him to face his own "tanned antiquity." It is the mirror that urges the lover to reproduce himself because he cannot remain young forever. The very same mirror which led Narcissus to his doom Shakespeare suggests can be used to curb narcissism. In *Julius Caesar,* the mirror is suggested as a way of enhancing narcissism. Brutus is depressed. He confesses to be "with himself at war." Cassius asks:

Tell me, good Brutus, can you see your face?
  *Brutus:* No, Cassius; for the eye sees not itself,
But by reflection, by some other things.
  *Cassius:* 'Tis just:
And it is very much lamented, Brutus,
That you have no such mirrors as will turn
Your hidden worthiness into your eye,

(II. 1.49ff.)

Shakespeare here anticipates a psychoanalytic finding that a healthy narcissism is a protection against depression.

In a psychoanalytic perspective one can hypothesize a connection between Sonnet 144, in which there is an almost paranoid attitude toward a woman, with Othello, in which a man's succumbing to paranoia is so powerfully described. Our understanding of Othello has deepened after Freud (1922) showed the connection between repressed homosexuality, jealousy, and paranoia. In that paper Freud differentiated three types of jealousy: (1) competitive or normal jealousy; (2) projected; and (3) delusional jealousies. Othello's jealousy is of the delusional type. But Freud quotes Desdemona to illustrate projective jealousy.

I called my love false, but what said he then
If I court more women, you'll couch with more men.

Freud observed that such a jealous person treats a flirtation as if it were an actual art of disloyalty.

Wangh (1950) has pointed out that the magic of Othello lies in its hidden context of Iago's jealousy of Desdemona because he is unconsciously homosexually in love with Othello. A considerable psychoanalytic literature has grown around the insight that Othello and Iago are bound to each other by an unconscious homosexual tie, the tie that brings about Desdemona's death.

Unfortunately, we have no reliable data on the question of whether Sonnet 144 was written before or after *Othello*. It seems more likely on the basis of the publication dates that the sonnet was written earlier than *Othello*. If so, it would represent an insight by Shakespeare into the dangers of paranoia based on a homosexual tie. If *Othello* was written first, then it would indicate that the play failed to heal the poet's suspicion of women.

A number of observers have noted that Shakespeare hinted that Othello was impotent. Othello gives a strange explanation for his wish for Desdemona to accompany him to Cyprus.

> *Othello:* I therefore beg it not
> To please the palate of my appetite,
> Nor to comply with heat, the young affects
> In me defunct, and proper satisfaction,
> But to be free and bounteous to her mind
>
> (I.3)

Shakespeare leaves us in doubt as to whether the marriage was ever consummated. In Venice Othello has "but an hour of love" for Desdemona and their nuptial night in Cyprus is interrupted by the quarrel.

Othello would never have married, had not Desdemona fallen in love with him, listening to his adventures.

> *Othello:* She wish'd she had not heard it yet she wish'd,
> That heaven had made her such a man; she thank'd me,
> And bade me, if I had a friend that lov'd her,
> I should but teach him how to tell my story,
> And that would woo her. . . .
>
> (I.3)

In the chapter on Freud, I will show that Desdemona's love for Othello is also a variant on what Freud (1914) called narcissistic love, for she loves him because he is what she would have loved to be herself.

The Moor is an interesting choice for a love object also from another point of view. To anticipate the chapter on Freud once more, Freud found that for a woman, the husband is a replacement for the father but it must be a replacement that will not evoke the incest taboo. Othello is close in years to her father but, being black, he is the opposite of an incestuous choice. Thus, two contradictory wishes to refind the father and avoid the guilt of incest can be reconciled in loving him.

Central to Othello is the strawberry handkerchief scene. The significance of the handkerchief has so far, in my opinion, not received the attention it deserves by psychoanalysts. We notice first that in Act III, Scene 3 the handkerchief fails to cure Othello's aching head. Symbolically, this indicates that she cannot satisfy his needs. When Iago obtains it, the marriage has symbolically been lost.

We note next that Othello describes the magic of the handkerchief not when he gave it to Desdemona but after she lost it.

> *Othello:* That handkerchief
> Did an Egyptian to my mother give.
> She was a charmer, and could almost read
> The thoughts of people; she told her, while she kept it

'Twould make her amiable and subdue my father
Entirely to her love; but if she lost it
Or made a gift of it, my father's eye
Should hold her loathed, and his spirits should hunt
After new fancies. She, dying, gave it me,
And bid me, when my fate would have me wived,
To give it her. I did so; and take heed on't;
Make it a darling like your precious eye;
To loose't or give't away were such perdition
And nothing else could match.

(III. 3)

We are left with the suspicion that the tale was invented after the fact. How strange that a mother would give it as a gift to a son, unless she wished to impose upon him bondage to his wife: the wife will rule him as long as she has his mother's magic handkerchief. I believe that Shakespeare has here described a case of fetishism. Othello can remain heterosexual as long as the magic of the fetish is maintained. The loss of the fetish will undo the fetishistic heterosexuality and open the gate to homosexuality and paranoia.

In the chapter on Aphrodite I indicated that few men in literature can be described as devotees of Aphrodite. Romeo is certainly one of them. The theme of jealousy, although milder, appears also in Romeo's prologue in the famous balcony scene.

*Romeo:* But soft! What light through yonder window breaks?
It is the East, and Juliet is the sun!
Arise, fair sun, and kill the envious moon,
Who is already sick and pale with grief
That thou her maid art far more fair than she.
Be not her maid, since she is envious.
Her vestal livery is but sick and green,

(II. 2)

Why should a lover be so occupied with jealousy at the point when he sees his beloved? A hint of fetishism follows the jealousy.

See how she leans her cheek upon her hand!
O, that I were a glove upon that hand,
That I might touch that cheek!

(II. 2)

Juliet's soliloquy deals with the significance of a name.

> *Juliet:* O Romeo, Romeo! Wherefore art thou Romeo?
> Deny thy father and refuse thy name;
> Or, if thou wilt not, be but sworn my loved,
> And I'll no longer be a Capulet.
> . . . Tis but thy name that is my enemy.
> Thou art thyself, though not a Montague.
> What's Montague? It is nor hand, nor foot,
> Nor arm, nor face nor any other part. O, be some other name
> Belonging to a man. O! be some other name!
> What's in a name? That which we call a rose
> By any other word smell as sweet.
> So Romeo would, were he not Romeo called,
> Retain that dear perfection which he owes
> Without that title. Romeo, doff thy name;
> And for thy name, which is no part of thee,
> Take all myself.
>
> *Romeo:* I take thee at thy word.
> Call me but love, and I'll be new baptized;
> Henceforth I never will be Romeo.
>
> (II. 2)

Romeo's response indicates that he is ready to be baptized in the name of love. The symbolic equation of love and rebirth is suggested. In this rebirth is Juliet not the new mother? Beloved and mother are symbolically equated.

Even in this most innocent scene of love, in Shakespeare's writings dark overtones are not far. Is a name really irrelevant to one's identity? What organ does Juliet have in mind when she says, "O, be some other name belonging to a man." She muses whether the taking away of a name is or is not a castration. Romeo's willingness to give up his "name" hints that he is willing to exchange identity for love.

We will also note that the two lovers have very different anxieties. Juliet's is the anxiety of losing her lover.

> *Juliet:* Dost thou love me? I know thou wilt say "Ay";
> And I will take thy word. Yet, if thou swear'st,
> Thou mayst prove false. At lovers' perjuries,
> They say Jove laughs. O gentle Romeo,
> If thou dost love, pronounce it faithfully.
> Or if thou thinkest I am too quickly won,
> I'll frown and be perverse and say thee nay,
> So thou wilt woo; but else, not for the world.

In truth, fair Montague, I am too fond,
And therefore thou mayst think my havior light;
But trust me, gentleman, I'll prove more true
Than those that have more cunning to be strange.

Romeo's anxiety is of a very different nature.

> *Romeo:* O blessed, blessed night! I am afraid
> Being in night, all this is but a dream,
> Too flattering sweet to be substantial.
>
> (II. 2)

In the chapter on Freud, I will discuss at some length why love has so
often been equated with the dream. Here, I wish to differentiate between
two anxieties frequently associated with love: the anxiety of losing the love
of the partner, experienced more frequently by women, and the anxiety
that love that sprang from unknown psychic quarters will disappear as
suddenly as it appeared.

Romeo has good reason to fear the sudden disappearance of love. Only
a day earlier, he was still in love with Rosalind. Rosalind is a familiar
figure. We have encountered her earlier on. She is the narcissist who seems
to be omnipresent in Shakespeare's work.

> *Romeo:* she'll not be hit
> With Cupid's arrow; she hath Dian's wit;
> And, in strong proof of chastity well arm'd,
> From love's weak childish bow she lives unharm'd.
> She will not stay the siege of loving terms,
> Nor bide the encounter of assailing eyes,
> Nor ope her lap to saint-seducing gold;
> O! she is rich in beauty; only poor
> That, when she dies, with beauty dies her store.
>
> (I. 1)

Although Romeo speaks of love, his metaphors are rich in aggression.
Rosalind is a siege, his eyes assail, all to no avail.

In a recently published book, MacCary (1985) examined the phenome-
nology of desire in Shakespeare's comedies; his interpretation of the comedies follows lines suggested by Freud and Lacan. MacCary reminds us that
Shakespeare's lovers in the comedies are young and therefore depict the
store of adolescent love for it is a love that often emanates from an
insecure center of identity. He finds that Shakespeare's young men go
through four stages of object choice. First, they love only themselves; then

they love mirror images of themselves. From there they go on to love
transvestized young women until they finally learn to love women in their
unique and complex virtues (p. 5).

MacCary is attempting interpretation. We will see that it has been
greatly influenced by what I will call in Chapter 14 Freud's second theory
of love. If I do not accept the interpretation, it is because it makes Shakespeare into a contemporary developmental psychologist. I do not see that
Shakespeare's younger lovers are undergoing a genuine inner growth or
resolving intrapsychic problems. Nor do I see Shakespeare himself portraying a psychic dilemma he had resolved long ago. True, comedies have a
happy ending, but the resolution, in my opinion, is never a genuine one. If
I may be allowed to paraphrase Shakespeare himself, I would say that the
ending of his comedies makes the unskilled laugh, but makes the psychologically judicious grieve.

### Narcissa in Paradise

During the Renaissance, Alberti (1404–1472), gave a radically new interpretation to the myth of Narcissus. "What is painting but the act of
embracing by means of art the surface of the pool?" (quoted in Schneider
1985: 63). Alberti's insight once more links Narcissus with Pygmalion and
makes the artist a narcissist who escapes death through his creativity. In
many paintings of the Renaissance by Titian, Tintoretto, and Velasquez,
Venus is gazing into a mirror held up to her by Cupid. To my knowledge,
art historians have not paid attention to this detail, but the message is
clear; self-love is a form of love, the form most appropriate to the goddess
of love. According to Panofsky (1969: 109) neoplatonism brought with it
a new interest in love. Panofsky states that "no period in history has
produced such a profusion of discourses 'On Love' as the first half of the
sixteenth century."*

Milton incorporated the myth of Narcissus into *Paradise Lost,* making
Eve the narcissist. This was a significant change, for heretofore, narcissistic
characters in literature were men. The transposition of the myth of Narcissus into the story of the Fall of man is surely one of the boldest attempts at

---

*During the Renaissance, curiously enough (the Jews were still isolated from the mainstream
of Western culture), a famous book on love was written by an exiled Spanish Jew, Don Juda
Abarbanel. Although a religious Jew, he was a neoplatonist philosopher. His name has come
down to us as Leone Hebreo. As a Jew he could expound platonic doctrine without fearing
reprisal from the Church at a time when such an open adherence to Plato would have been
considered dangerous for a Christian.

transposition of Greek into Hebraic culture. Milton must have seen a latent similarity between the two. Just as Narcissus, it will be remembered, could have lived longer had he not attempted to know himself, Adam could have stayed in Paradise had Eve not tempted him to eat from the tree of knowledge (and thus to know her). Eve confesses to Adam* her self love:

> I first awaked, and found myself reposed
> Under a shade of flowers, much wondering where
> And what I was, whence thither brought, and how.
> Not distant far from thence a murmuring sound
> Of waters issued from a cave and spread
> Into a liquid plain, then stood unmoved
> Pure as the expanse of Heaven; I thither went
> With unexperienc't thought, and laid me downe
> On the green bank, to look into the cleer

> Smooth Lake, that to me seemed another Sky,
> As I bent down to look, just opposite,
> A Shape within the watry gleam appeared
> Bending to look on me, I started back,
> It started back, but pleasd I soon return,
> Pleas'd it returnd as soon with answering looks
> Of sympathie and love; there I had fixed
> Mine eyes till now, and pined with vain desire,
> Had not a voice thus warnd me, What thou seest,
> What there thou seest fair Creature is thy self,
> With thee it came and goes: but follow me,
> And I will bring thee where no shadow stays
> Thy coming, and thy soft embraces, he
> Whose image thou art, him thou shall enjoy
> Inseparably thine, to him shalt beare
> Multitudes like thy self, and thence be call'd
> Mother of human Race: what could I doe,
> But follow strait, invisibly thus led?
> Till I espi'd thee, fair indeed and tall,
> Under a Platan, yet methought less fair,
> Less winning soft, less amiable mild,
> Then that smooth watry image;
>                               (Book IV, lines 455–480)

---

*It is interesting that in the gnostic literature it was Adam who lost paradise because he loved himself.

The way God persuades Eve to overcome her narcissism shows how well Milton understood the dangers of narcissism to love. First, God points out that mirror love is diurnal and disappears at night, while het-erosexual love continues into the night. He then appeals to her hermaphro-ditic aspect when he says "whose image thou art." To this God adds the symbiotic bliss of inseparability and the promise of maternity. Even so, we learn in the course of that chapter that Eve's falling in love with Adam remained incomplete; a narcissistic core was retained. This narcissistic residue will leave her open to Satan's temptation. Milton did more than transplant Narcissus into paradise; more than change the gender, he inter-preted the Fall as due to the narcissistic core that love did not conquer. In Milton's version, Satan is a projection of Eve's narcissism that did not undergo transmutation.

Before Eve meets the tempter she has a proleptic dream where she ate from the tree of interdicted knowledge. She awakens from the dream in a state of anxiety. She confesses her dream to Adam:

> Such night till this I never passed, have dreamed,
> If dreamed, not as I oft am wont, of thee
> Works of day past, or morrow's next design,
> But of offence and trouble, which my mind
> Knew never till this irksome night;
> (Book V, lines 30 ff.)

In her dream, Satan speaks the language of Greek hubris:

> Here, happy creature, fair angelic Eve,
> Partake thou also; happy though thou art,
> Happier thou mayst be, worthier canst not be:
> Taste this, and be henceforth among the gods
> Thy self a goddess, not to earth confined,
> (Book V, lines 70 ff.)

There follows an interesting discussion on the function of dreams. Adam is of the opinion that what one dreams one need not act on, that dreams are substitute for action.

> Evil into the mind of god or man
> May come and go, so unapproved, and leave
> No spot or blame behind: which gives me hope
> That what in sleep thou didst abhor to dream,
> Waking thou never wilt consent to do.
> (Book V, lines 115 ff.)

Unlike Adam, Milton knows that dreams can be prelude to action. In psychoanalytic terms, we would say that the outcome depends on the relative strength between the ego and the unconscious wish. When the ego is strong enough, dreams can usefully function as discharge for forbidden wishes, but when the wish is strong enough to overwhelm the ego, the dream becomes proleptic, leading to action.

When Eve finally encounters Satan he persuades her to eat the forbidden fruit by appealing to her narcissism which her love for Adam did not overcome. Satan flatters her by calling her

> A goddess among gods, adored and served
> By angels numberless, thy daily train.

After Eve has eaten the forbidden apple the narcissistic temptation seizes her once more. For she has become aware of her feelings of inadequacy as a woman.

> "But to Adam in what sort
> Shall I appear? Shall I to him make known
> As yet my change, and give him to partake
> Full happiness with me, or rather not,
> But keep the odds of knowledge in my power
> Without copartner? So to add what wants
> In female sex, the more to draw his love,
> And render me more equal, and perhaps,
> A thing not undesirable, sometime
> Superior; for inferior who is free?"
> This may be well: but what if God have seen,
> And death ensue? Then I shall be no more,
> And Adam wedded to another Eve,
> Shall live with her enjoying, I extinct;
> A death to think. Confirmed then I resolve,
> Adam shall share with me in bliss or woe:
> So dear I love him, that with him all deaths
> I could endure, without him live no life.
>                    (Book IX, lines 815–825)

Eve's wish to let Adam share the bliss of the tree of knowledge is a mixture of her jealousy of the Eves yet to come, jealousy of his immortality, and genuine love. After the Fall, Milton endows her with a sense of self she did not have before. Before the Fall, she was content to be the docile and charming playmate to Adam. After the Fall, she discovers that she is a person in her own right.

Adam's love for Eve is of a different kind. The juxtaposition of these two types of love enhances the significance of *Paradise Lost* as a work of art.*

> Certain my resolution is to die;
> How can I live without thee, how forgo
> The sweet converse and love so dearly joined,
> To live again in these wild woods forlorn?
> Should God create another Eve, and I
> Another rib afford, yet loss of thee
> Would never from my heart; no no, I feel
> The link of nature draw me: flesh of flesh,
> Bone of my bone thou art, and from thy state
> Mine never shall be parted bliss or woe.
>
> (Book IX, lines 908–915)

Milton knew his Plato. What he says would have been approved by Socrates. The *Symposium* comes to life in the following lines.

> Thou hast provided all things: but with me
> I see not who partakes. In solitude
> What happiness, who can enjoy alone,
> Or all enjoying, what contentment find?
>
> (Book VII, lines 360 ff.)

> Thou in thy self art perfect, and in thee
> Is no deficiency found; not so is man,
> But in degree, the cause of his desire
> By conversation with his like to help,
> Or solace his defects. No need that thou
> Shouldst propagate, already infinite;
> And through all numbers absolute, though one;
> But man by number is to manifest
> His single imperfection, and beget
> Like of his like, his image multiplied,
> In unit defective, which requires
> Collateral love, and dearest amity.
>
> (Book VII, lines 415 ff.)

If narcissism compelled Eve to eat from the tree of interdicted knowledge, symbiotic longing and an overwhelming separation anxiety made it imperative for Adam to join her. In these lines, Milton achieves a condensa-

---

*I wish to thank Dr. Slochower, who insisted that I stress the difference between a work of literature and a clinical case. (See also Slochower 1970.)

tion of psychological needs equal to any that are found in the great works of literature. Within the Greek orbit of thought, narcissism of a particular kind, under the term of hubris, was traditionally the great sin because it made man forget that he is not the equal of gods. Milton transformed the biblically prohibited wish to know into the sin of narcissism. By comparison with the Greek hubris, Eve's narcissism is poetry, she is vain and succumbs to flattery but her narcissism is that of a harmless child and not that of a defying hero.

Freud shared Milton's prejudice that narcissism is unequally distributed between the two genders.

A different course is followed in the type of female most frequently met with, which is probably the purest and truest one. With the onset of puberty, the maturing of the female sexual organs, which up till then have been in a condition of latency, seem to bring about an intensification of the original narcissism and this is unfavorable to the development of a true object-choice with its accompanying sexual overevaluation. Women especially if they grow up with good looks, develop a certain self contentment which compensates them for the social restrictions that are imposed upon them in their choice of object. Strictly speaking, it is only themselves that such women love with the intensity comparable to that of man's love for them. Nor does their need lie in the direction of loving, but in being loved; and the man who fulfills this condition is the one who finds favor with them. (Freud 1914: 88)

A contemporary reader need not agree with Milton and Freud on this point. Clinical experience has shown that narcissism is likely to be evenly distributed between the two genders.

In the long humanist tradition which I have traced in this chapter, Narcissus symbolizes a sickness of the soul, one that had to be taken seriously for it could prove fatal. In the psychiatric literature of the nineteenth century, narcissism became a form of perversion. It is in this form that Freud spoke about it in the opening paragraph of his 1914 essay "On Narcissism."

The term narcissism is derived from clinical description and was chosen by Paul Naecke in 1899 to denote the attitude of a person who treats his own body in the same way in which the body of a sexual object is ordinarily treated—who looks at it, that is to say, strokes it and fondles it till he obtains complete satisfaction through these activities. Developed to this degree, narcissism has the significance of a perversion that has absorbed the whole of the subject's sexual life, and it will consequently exhibit the characteristics which we expect to meet with in the study of all perversions. (p. 73)

Once relegated to the realm of perversion, narcissism ceased to be a universal danger. The Victorian bourgeois who read about it in Krafft-

Ebing's *Psychopathia Sexualis* could do so with a sense of confidence that it did not concern him.

The narcissistic element in the biblical image of God was commented upon by Sterba (1984). He notes how God was continuously satisfied with what he created; when he created Adam in his own image he saw that it was very good. God created man out of a lump of clay. We note that since God is conceptualized as male, the only babies he can make are anal babies. In Sterba's view, God's creativity is equivalent to the creativity of a Pygmalion. Freud made no use of the long tradition that has come down to us from Ovid, but his insights into the nature of narcissism were influenced by Heine. With keen insight, Heine recognized the narcissistic element in the story of Genesis, how self-satisfied God is with his own work, and what narcissistic pleasure it gives God to create man in his own image.

The biblical legend of creation enhanced man's pride in himself but it also made the relationship between God and man basically a narcissistic one. Heine parodied the traditional hymns of creation in seven short poems. In his mocking portrayal of Genesis, God first creates the sun and then the ox, out of the sweat of his brow. He then creates lions and in their image, pretty little cats. He creates man, and in man's image, an interesting ape. In the last of these poems, God gives away the secret of creation. It is these lines that Freud (1914) quotes:

> Illness was no doubt the final cause of the whole urge
> to create. By creating, I could recover; by creating,
> I healed myself.

On these lines, Freud commented, "a strong egoism is a protection against falling ill." But in the last resort, we must begin to love in order not to fall ill.

At this point, Freud made a "creative misreading" of Heine's verse. For Heine, creativity is the solution to narcissism, while Freud misreads this line to mean that we must love if we are to remain healthy. Love is an illness to be sure, but narcissism is an illness of greater severity and far more chronic. It was surely not based on clinical observations of narcissistic patients that Freud came to this conclusion. It was a beautiful assertion of the victory of Freud's own libido over his narcissism. It is a profound statement that reflects Freud's philosophy of life.

I have traced in this chapter some of the history and psychology of three fables that have a special bearing on love. All three were the inventions of Ovid. Narcissus was in love with himself, Pygmalion could love only what he himself created, and Hermaphroditus symbolized a type of love where the couple together stand for one bisexual person. The tree figures represent obstacles to the full capacity to love, but they also represent, as I will show in the last chapter, forms of loving.

Sterba (1984), who discusses these archetypes, suggested that a fourth be added; that of Cherubino in Mozart's *Marriage of Figaro*. Hagstrum (1980) had already noticed that Cherubino's dubious adolescent sexuality has a special appeal to women. Sterba had added that Cherubino's delicacy creates a beautiful musical contrast to the masculine eroticism of the Count and of Figaro. He notes how Cherubino is thrown into confusion by the stormy onslaught on his mind due to the hormonal influx and endocrinal changes of puberty (p. 416). Cherubino talks of love day and night, he talks to the water, to his shadow, to the mountains, and to the flowers. He also talks to the echo of his voice and all these words are put into music over the rapidly driving allegro vivace. This breathless search for an object of his feelings of love comes to a halting adagio when Cherubino notices that nobody is listening to him. Cherubino projects his love on the whole world, but he is not in love with any specific object. Contemptuously, Figaro calls him "a big butterfly in love" (*farfallone amoroso*). He also calls him a little Narcissus and a little Adonis. The cure for all this adolescent turmoil is military service. If Cherubino can be added as a fourth archetype to the three created by Ovid, he will fit well into what MacCary saw as typical of Shakespeare's adolescent lovers in the comedies.

# 12

# *Love in a Disenchanted World: From the Seventeenth to the Nineteenth Century*

One of the great books on love written during Shakespeare's and Milton's lifetime is Robert Burton's *Anatomy of Melancholy,* which appeared in 1631 when the author was forty-five years old. The final third of that book is devoted to love—and melancholy. Burton was a prodigious borrower. He insisted that, like bees that hurt nothing when they take honey from the flowers they suck, he too borrowed without stealing or destroying. On plagiarism his age was less strict than ours. It permitted quoting from memory, and often when I felt self-accused of quoting too much, his image rose before my eyes, permitting me to go on quoting.

Two thousand years separate the age of Burton from that of Greek tragedy. The two, however, have much in common. For the second time in Western history, it became permissible to inquire into the unreasonable and the pathological in human nature without attributing evil to a force like Satan, a force outside of man. Burton lived at a time when the Christian Medieval world was dying, but not yet dead. To his age, the Greek heritage was equal in significance to the teachings of the Bible. He was at home in the world of the church as well as in the world of Greek philosophy and Latin poetry. His age drew its nourishment from both the Judeo-Christian and the Hellenistic heritages. Burton sees love as a species of melancholy. He describes love as a state of flux containing the delight in the wish to possess, the pain of coveting, ending in the bliss of possession (p. 618). Burton's view of love can be contrasted with a famous statement in Goethe's *Faust:* "I stagger from desire to enjoyment and in enjoyment I languish for desire."

In Burton's world, love is ubiquitous, not yet confined to human beings alone. The moon still laments that she is impotently besotted on Endymion. Palm trees can love most fervently, trees bend their branches toward each other, stretching out their boughs as a gesture of embrace. They also kiss each other. He even quotes reports that trees were known to marry one another. Fish pine away for love and wax lean.

Burton knows not only intraspecies but also interspecies love. The myrtle and the olive embrace each other in roots and branches if they grow near each other. Between elm and vine,* vine and cabbage, and vine and olive, there is great sympathy that leads to love. Nor is love confined to the organic world, for love can also make the lodestone draw iron to it. The sun and the stars also pursue their course driven by love. Burton here echoes Dante's last line of the *Divine Comedy,* "The Love that moves the sun and the other stars."

Burton knows of dolphins who love boys—when a beloved boy dies, the dolphin leaves its aquatic habitat and perishes. Maintaining the balance between the sexes, Burton tells the story of a peacock who loved a maid so much that he killed himself when she died. When a bear loves a woman and begets sons by her, out of his loins spring northern kings. However, when women love beasts, horses, or bulls, the result of these unions is not so favorable, because from such cohabitation, monsters spring to frighten mankind.

Burton knows of a woman in Constantinople who was in love with another woman and dared an incredible thing. She went through a marriage ceremony disguised as a man (p. 653). Worse still, Burton knows that some cohabit with beautiful cadavers. Even marriage is not immune to perversions for Burton knows that "An opposite part is used from that which is lawful. Sometimes no orifice remains undefiled and is given to shameful lust."

A frequent cause of melancholy is heroical love. This is Burton's term for incestuous love. Of such love, he knows many examples. He quotes Avicenna, the medieval Persian philosopher and physician who defined passion as "a disease of melancholy, vexation, or anguish of mind, in which a man continually meditates of the beauty, gesture, manners of his

*The love between elm and vine already symbolized eternal love before Burton for Sir Philip Sidney (1554–1586), who in a nuptial poem speaks of

> The honest bridegroom and the bashful bride
> Whose love may ever abide
> Like to the elm and vine
> With mutual embraces them to twine.

mistress and troubles himself about it." He concludes that continual cogitation is not a kind of love, but a symptom of it. In anticipation of Freud, he continues, "We continually think of that which we hate and abhor as well that which we love; and many things we covet and desire without all hope of attaining" (p. 657–658).

Burton also knows happy love. It is the love of Abraham for Sarah, of Seneca for Paulina, and Orpheus for Eurydice. His description of happy love is poetic: "There is something in a woman beyond all human delight; a magnetic virtue, a charming quality, an occult and powerful motive. The husband rules her as head, but she again commands his heart, he is her servant, she his only joy and content. No happiness in life is equal unto it. No love so great as that between man and wife" (p. 54).

Shakespeare was born in 1564, Burton in 1578, and Milton in 1608. The three men were alive at the same time. Brownlee (1960) has advanced the case that Shakespeare and Burton were the same person. To prove the thesis, he has quoted parallel statements from the two authors. He has to my knowledge convinced no one, but has been admirably successful in showing that the two were breathing the same intellectual air and living in the same climate of opinion. The very concept of love-melancholy was important to both of them. Both saw the cause of this disease in excessive imagination.

Burton sees love as a special form of melancholy. This idea was very popular during the Renaissance. We find it also in Shakespeare. The root of this disease was excessive imagination.

> Lovers and madmen have such seething brains,
> Such shaping fantasies, that apprehend
> More than cool reason ever comprehends.
> The lunatic, the lover, and the poet,
> Are of the imagination all compact.
>
> One sees more devils than vast hell can hold;
> That is the madman. The lover, all as frantic,
> Sees Helen's beauty in a brow of Egypt.
>
> The poet's eye, in a fine frenzy rolling,
> Doth glance from heaven to earth, from earth to heaven;
> And as imagination bodies forth
> The forms of things unknown, the poet's pen
> Turns them to shapes, and gives to airy nothing
> A local habitation and a name.
>
> > (*A Midsummer Night's Dream*, V. 1)

The similarity between love and madness was part of the classical tradition (Plutarch's *Morals*), but to introduce the poet into this company was Shakespeare's contribution. There is no hint in Burton, as there is none in Shakespeare, that man is the only creature to know what love is, as he is also alone in knowing that he is destined to die. In the seventeenth century the belief that all nature is besotted is still held but somewhere before the nineteenth century, the break takes place. After that, only poets and lovers are permitted to feel that when they love, all nature participates in their love.

Stone (1985) found that in the late seventeenth century one of those revolutionary attitudes we have followed in the history of love took place. For increasingly from now on the demand would be made that marriage be based on love. Hagstrum (1980) assigned to Milton a central role in this "transvaluation of values." He showed that the primal pair, that is, Adam and Eve, which he had portrayed in *Paradise Lost,* became a new ideal. Now prelapserian love was an amalgam between sex and sensuality. One can hear the new ideal in Haydn's *Creation,* in Gluck's *Orfeo* and *Alceste,* as well as in Mozart's *Magic Flute.* The obverse of this point of view was that a marriage should be dissolved when the friendship between man and woman had disappeared. Love, as Milton saw it, creates marriage as the sun creates the day and when love sets it is night. It is obvious that not everyone subscribed to this view, but the Greek solution that permanently separated the realm of Aphrodite from that of Hera was no longer satisfying as an ideal for Western men and women. Psychoanalysis took over this idea in its own way and will insist that falling in love is the normal basis for the creation of enduring love relationships.

I come next to the poet Percy Bysshe Shelley (1792–1822), who not only wrote about love but embedded it in his personal biography. In every era there live outstanding men or women who for future generations exemplify the period in which they live. Not that they are in any way typical of the people of their period; on the contrary, they exemplify the age because in them and in their lives what was alive in the period has come out in a fine excess. When I think of love in the nineteenth century—lived as well as expressed—I think of the poet Percy Bysshe Shelley who died in a sea accident shortly before he reached thirty.*

In 1813, the 21-year old Shelley published privately his first long poem, *Queen Mab.* Preserved also are the notes he had written as background to this poem. Young Shelley writes about love with indignation:

*I am indebted to Mrs. Marjorie Goodman for bringing to my attention Shelley's views on love.

Not even the intercourse of the sexes is exempt from the despotism of positive institution. Law pretends even to govern the indiscilinable wanderings of passion, to put
fetters on the clearest deductions of reason, and, by appeals to the will, to subdue the
involuntary affections of our nature. Love is inevitably consequent upon the percep-
tion of loveliness. Love withers under constraint: its very essence is liberty: it is
compatible neither with obedience, jealousy, nor fear: it is there most pure, perfect,
and unlimited, where its votaries live in confidence, equality, and unreserve. . . .
   How long then ought the sexual connection to last? What law ought to specify
the extent of the grievances which should limit its duration? A husband and wife
ought to continue so long united as they love each other: any law which should
bind them to cohabitation for one moment after the decay of their affection would
be a most intolerable tyranny, and the most unworthy of toleration.

(Shelley 1952: 806)

   In no epoch in history, not even under the jurisdiction of "the court of
love" at Poitiers in the Middle Ages, was the supremacy of love over
society asserted with such an absolute claim. Under the impact of the
Enlightenment, a struggle begins to free love from the bondage to religion
and from the sin of Adam.
   In real life, Shelley's credo led to tragedy. Shelley married Harriet West-
brook, the daughter of an innkeeper when she was 16. At the time of his
marriage he was just recovering from a love for his cousin Harriet Grove,
who was alarmed by his heresies. Shelley became a father at twenty-one. A
few months after the birth of his child, he fell in love with Mary Woll-
stonecraft Godwin, the future author of *Frankenstein*. She was seventeen
when Shelley eloped with her to Switzerland. Upon returning to England,
he discovered he had a second child by Harriet. He asked Harriet to join
the two in what would have been a ménage à trois. Harriet declined and
committed suicide a year later.
   In 1818, Shelley wrote a short essay on love to be read in conjunction
with his long poem "Epipsychidion." In the essay, he defined love:

If we reason, we would be understood; if we imagine, we would that the airy
children of our brain were born anew within another's; if we feel, we would that
another's nerves should vibrate to our own, that the beams of their eyes should
kindle at once and mix and melt into our own, that lips of motionless ice should
not reply to lips quivering and burning with the heart's best blood. This is love.
This is the bond and the sanction which connects not only men with men, but with
everything which exists. We are born into the world and there is something within
us which from the instant that we live and move thirsts after likeness.

Shelley goes on to describe how:

In solitude, or in that deserted state when we are surrounded by human beings and
yet they sympathize not with us, we love the flowers, the grass and the waters and

the sky. In the motion of the very leaves of spring in the blue air there is then found a secret correspondence with our heart. There is eloquence in the tongueless wind and a melody in the flowing of brooks and the rustling of the leaves.

(Shelley 1952: XX)

The essay on love was written after Shelley finished his translation of Plato's *Symposium* and Plato's influence is palpable. It is even stronger in another statement that Shelley had made, "I think one is always in love with something or other, the error consists in seeking in a mortal image the likeness of what is perhaps eternal." In Plato's *Symposium,* Diotima could have expressed this solution to the difficulty in loving.

The feeling that nature is an active participant in human love has evoked many fine poems, of which Shelley's "Love's Philosophy" is one.

> The fountains mingle with the river
>     And the rivers with the Ocean,
> The winds of Heaven mix for ever
>     With a sweet emotion;
>
> Nothing in the world is single;
>     All things by a law divine
> In one spirit meet and mingle.
>     Why not I with thine?—
>
> See the mountains kiss high Heaven
>     And the waves clasp one another;
> No sister-flower would be forgiven
>     If it disdained its brother;
> And the sunlight clasps the earth
>     And the moonbeams kiss the sea:
> What is all this sweet work worth
>     If thou kiss not me?

In the nineteenth century, two thinkers, one a philosopher, the other a novelist, stand out as the two who have significantly enriched as well as modified our understanding of the nature of love. Neither Schopenhauer nor Stendhal could have written about love the way they did in any century before the nineteenth. Of the two, Schopenhauer had a considerable influence on Freud, and Freud had an ambivalent attitude toward him. Schopenhauer and Stendhal both stressed the uniqueness of the beloved in falling in love. For centuries, Cupid's arrows were the metaphor for the random falling in love. As long as that metaphor reigned, the uniqueness and personality of the beloved was irrelevant.

Since Plato and St. Paul, there was a tendency to separate love and sex.

In Kierkegaard's formulation, in Christianity the religious suspended the erotic. Schopenhauer stands out as the thinker before Freud who emphasized that love and sex are inseparable.

The crucial chapter for our purposes is chapter 44, volume 2, in Schopenhauer's *The World as Will and Representation,* published in 1858. The chapter opens with a traditional ambivalent hymn to the power of Eros.

> For all amorousness is rooted in the sexual impulse alone, is in fact absolutely only a more closely determined, specialized, and indeed, in the strictest sense, individualized sexual impulse, however ethereally it may deport itself. Now, keeping this in mind, we consider the important role played by sexual love in all its degrees and nuances, not merely in theatrical performances and works of fiction, but also in the world of reality. Next to the love of life, it shows itself here as the strongest and most active of all motives, and incessantly lays claim to half the powers and thoughts of the younger portion of mankind. It is the ultimate goal of almost all human effort; it has an unfavorable influence on the most important affairs, interrupts every hour the most serious occupations, and sometimes perplexes for a while even the greatest minds. It does not hesitate to intrude with its trash, and to interfere with the negotiations of statesmen and the investigations of the learned. It knows how to slip its love-notes and ringlets even into ministerial portfolios and philosophical manuscripts. Every day it brews and hatches the worst and most perplexing quarrels and disputes, destroys the most valuable relationships, and breaks the strongest bonds. It demands the sacrifice sometimes of life or health, sometimes of wealth, position, and happiness. Indeed, it robs of all conscience those who were previously honorable and upright, and makes traitors of those who have hitherto been loyal and faithful. Accordingly, it appears on the whole as a malevolent demon, striving to pervert, to confuse, and to overthrow everything. If we consider all this, we are induced to exclaim: Why all this noise and fuss? Why all the urgency, uproar, anguish, and exertion? It is merely a question of every Jack finding his Jill. Why should such a trifle play so important a role, and constantly introduce disturbance and confusion into the well-regulated life of man?

Schopenhauer proceeds to give an answer to this age-old complaint that is typical of the nineteenth century; it is almost Darwinian in outlook. No longer does a God reveal the truth; it is in the spirit of truth that speaks to the philosopher.

> To the earnest investigator, however, the spirit of truth gradually reveals the answer. It is no trifle that is here in question; on the contrary, the importance of the matter is perfectly in keeping with the earnestness and ardor of the effort. The ultimate aim of all love-affairs, whether played in sock or in buskin,* is actually more important than all other aims in man's life; and therefore it is quite worthy of the profound seriousness with which everyone pursues it. What is decided by it is

---

*Sock was a light shoe worn by comic actors in Greece; buskin was a thick-soled half-boot worn in Greek tragedies.

nothing less than the composition of the next generation. The dramatis personae who will appear when we have retired from the scene are determined, according to their existence and their disposition, by these very frivolous love-affairs. (pp. 533–534)

Coming after a long tradition that separated love from sexual lust, Schopenhauer's reunion of the two is refreshing and it supplied the broad philosophical model for Freud's ideas on love. Upon this traditional view on love, Schopenhauer grafted a typical nineteenth century view of the cunning ways of nature to assure nature's own purposes, the propagation of the species. He sees love as a delusion inflicted upon man by nature. The individual man is convinced that he pursues an individual woman out of love but nature is interested only in the propagation of the species. Love is nature's cunning device designed to assure the best selection of the coming generation. These views of Schopenhauer echo Hegel's concept of "the cunning of reason" (*Die List der Vernunft*) which is the operative force behind the flow of history. It also has to our ears a Darwinian connotation. The two were contemporaries. Darwin's trip on the HMS Beagle took place between 1831 and 1836. The results of this trip were published between 1839 and 1842. Schopenhauer could not have been acquainted with Darwin's views since his book appeared in 1858.

Schopenhauer's contribution to love constitutes a new emphasis, not to my knowledge found in the previous literature on love, on the uniqueness of the beloved.

The quite special and individual passion of two lovers is just as inexplicable as is the quite special individuality of any person, which is exclusively peculiar to him; indeed at bottom the two are one and the same; the latter is *explicite* what to the former was *implicite*. (p. 536)

Now the more perfect the mutual suitability to each other of two individuals in each of the many different respects to be considered later, the stronger will their mutual passion prove to be. As there are not two individuals exactly alike, one particular woman must correspond most perfectly to each particular man. (p. 537)

The emphasis on love as an individual experience presupposes that the lover himself has reached a high degree of individuality. What is typically nineteenth century in this view is the assumption that because we have a unique personality, we must search for a unique beloved to meet our psychological needs. Only in a culture that puts high value on individuality could Schopenhauer's definition take root. When one observes how very difficult, and at times impossible, it is for so many men and women to find the desired mate, one asks oneself whether perhaps we have carried the value of our own uniqueness to the point where finding a mate has become exceedingly difficult. But these are contemporary doubts. Schopenhauer has full confidence in the power of love to bring about the unique match between two highly individuated people.

It leads Schopenhauer to a definition of love that I consider one of the finest in the whole literature on love.

The longing of love, that the poets of all ages are forever concerned to express in innumerable forms, a subject which they do not exhaust, in fact to which they cannot do justice; this longing that closely associates the notion of an endless bliss with the possession of a definite woman, and an unutterable pain with the thought that this possession is not attainable. (p. 551)

The only thing that mars the beauty of Schopenhauer's definition for our generation is the fact that Schopenhauer, a nineteenth-century man, always regards the man as the lover and the woman as the recipient of love.

Roland Barthes (1978) says, "I encounter millions of bodies in my life; of these millions, I may desire some hundreds; but of these hundreds, I love only one. The other with whom I am in love designates for me the specialty of my desire." Barthes echoes Schopenhauer; he adds a contemporary concern with problems of identity: loving a unique person does something for the lover, it makes the lover experience his own uniqueness in a way he could not before he or she fell in love. Until we love, human sexuality has not reached the stage of individuation. In that sense at least, Plato was right. Love contributes to our feeling of being unique individuals.

## Stendhal

Under the nom de plume of Stendhal, Henry Beyle published his book *On Love* in 1842. Stendhal, it will be recalled, was the author of a very popular novel, *The Red and the Black*. Like Schopenhauer, his wish was to observe love objectively and scientifically. Stendhal introduces his book with a beguiling simplicity as an accurate and scientific treatise on a type of madness or soul sickness which is very rare in France. In the nineteenth century, to be scientific meant above all to classify the way Linnaeus would have classified species of flora. Indeed Stendhal knows of four types of love. The first is passion-love, the love identified in literature from Eloise and Abelard to Goethe's Werther. The second type of love is sympathy-love, presumably more common in the France of his day. "Whereas passion-love carries us away against our interests, sympathy-love always knows how to adjust itself to them." In sympathy-love, Stendhal informs us, a woman taking a lover takes more account of the opinion that other women have of him than the opinion she has of him herself. Singer (1984) would say that Stendhal's sympathetic love is a love of appraisal rather than of bestowal. The third is sensual-love, love that would today be classified as mere sex. The fourth is vanity-love. Here the beloved is only an instrument to enhance self-esteem.

Stendhal's contribution to the theory of love is the term crystallization. He differentiates between two stages in crystallization. Every love begins with admiration. It is followed by a feeling of bliss. Bliss gives rise to hope. It is at this stage that Stendhal advises that the woman should surrender herself to get the greatest possible sensual pleasure, for when hope is born, the eyes of even the most modest woman light up, she experiences the pleasure of hope anticipated. Love is born and the first crystallization takes place. In Stendhal's opinion, after the first crystallization, inevitably doubt is born. At this moment one feels acutely the need of a friend but, Stendhal notices perceptively, a lover at the height of love has no friends. Doubt takes different forms in men and women. Man asks himself, "Can I attract her? Will she love me?" Woman says, "Is he only amusing himself when he says he loves me? Is he reliable? Can he be sure of his sentiments not changing too quickly?" The overcoming of doubt and a sense of certainty in loving and being loved brings about the second crystallization. During this period, lovers feel that they must either be loved or perish. The second crystallization cannot take place when women surrender too quickly. But when it does take place, the lover no longer sees anything as it really is. Man belittles his own qualities and exaggerates the smallest attraction of the person he loves. To Stendhal love is primarily a matter of fantasy. Every time the woman meets her lover she takes delight not in what he actually is but in the picture that she has of him in her mind. Stendhal sees no other outcome to any love except bitter disappointment.

The book is highly perceptive in describing the process of falling in love but one looks in vain for the transformation of love into an abiding relationship. Ultimately, Stendhal's definition of love is identical to that of Schopenhauer. "With her I would experience joys which she alone in the world could give me." The true lover would rather dream of the most remote chance of attracting her in the future than receive from any ordinary woman everything she has to offer. In Stendhal's view, love can only be experienced in full ardor when it is associated with fear. Once the fear of losing the loved one is lost, confidence and sweet familiarities deaden the ardor of love. "Love is like a fever; it comes and goes without the will having any part in the process." This is particularly true of passion-love and one of the principal differences between it and sympathy-love. The women who insist that love should flatter their pride do not know what real love is. Love and vanity are incompatible.

One of Stendhal's most interesting chapters is about the contrast between Werther and Don Juan. Don Juans show bravery, resourcefulness of mind, vivacity, and coolness in the face of danger. But they have terrible moments of emptiness in their lives and a bitter old age. Don Juans renounce all duties that bind them to mankind. In the great market of life the Don Juan is a dishonest trader who always takes and never pays. What they do not see is that what they obtain, even if it is granted by the same woman, is not the same as the lover receives. The lover trembles each time he approaches his mistress. The Don Juan does not tremble, he is bored. The pleasures of love are always in proportion to the fears that love has evoked.

Unlike the Don Juans, Stendhal is perpetually in love. What he cannot tolerate is the period that follows the intensity of falling in love. His book testifies to a different malaise, one that recalls the punishment of Tantalus—to be perpetually throughout life in a permanent state of love. He is the wandering Jew of love, condemned never to come to rest. To be permanently in love Stendhal need not change partners as frequently as the Don Juans have to do, but change partners he must.

While Stendhal was collecting data on love among the aristocracies of Europe (he was employed in the French diplomatic service), changing sociological conditions were creating a new type of woman across Europe. One of the first results of the growing prosperity of the bourgeoisie was to liberate wives from the drudgery of housework and the chores of raising children. These tasks were given over to maids and nannies. Unlike women of the aristocratic classes, these bourgeois women had not been taught how to use their new-found leisure, nor did they have the guiding principles of noblesse oblige. Increasingly, these women turned to love and extramarital relations to fill the void in their lives. Religion, still powerful in their education, had little power over their conduct but was strong enough to help create an inner conflict. Flaubert's *Madame Bovary* is the great literary monument to this type of woman.

The events in the novel take place between 1827–1856. The novel itself was written between 1851 and 1856. Emma is a farmer's daughter but is sent to a boarding school for ladies of the gentry. From this school, she emerges with romantic notions derived from literature. Charles, her husband, is a health officer who is almost, but not really, a physician. His consultation room contains volumes of dictionaries on medical science but the pages are still uncut. Emma's dreamy search for love evokes genuine love in her dull and plodding husband and makes her temporarily attractive to two lovers. What Flaubert showed magnificently was how the lack of an inner core and the absence of any sense of belonging make her incapable of establishing any meaningful relationship. She can only drift into adulteries, relationships in which fantasies predominate. They bring about mounting debts and ultimately suicide. The hysterical women that consulted Breuer and Freud were better educated than Emma; their culture was Viennese and Jewish rather than Catholic and French. But the corroding acid of the nineteenth century is discernible in their sense of drift without anchor.

Love enhances sexual experience. The views of Schopenhauer and Stendhal on love represent the high point for the understanding of love in the nineteenth century. With their views as a background we should be in a better position to evaluate Freud's contribution.

Thomas Hardy's novel *The Well Beloved,* published in 1890, is a novel that interested Freud and Jung a great deal. It is a clinical study of infatuation (Werman and Jacobs 1983).

Pierston, the hero of *The Well Beloved,* meets a distant cousin, Avis Caro, and proposes marriage to her but soon afterward has misgivings. He feels that it was a mad assumption to believe that the ideal woman of his fantasy was actually Avis Caro. However, at the end of that summer, he repeats the same experience with the same adoration with another woman. The old love has vanished completely and is replaced by the new one. When this new relationship also fails, the hero in due time falls in love with Avis' daughter and later with her granddaughter.

In common usage, infatuation is customarily seen as the opposite of love, or as a fake substitute for love. As I develop my ideas on love, the reader will find that I regard infatuation as a special type of love.

The plot of *The Well Beloved* may seem clumsy and contrived to us, but the theme, as Ellenberger (1970: 708) has pointed out, was very popular in the nineteenth century. The book also influenced Jung, who derived from it "The Shadow" and "The Anima." Proust also read Hardy in 1910 and, according to Proust's biographer, Proust was greatly influenced by him (Painter 1965). In this view, we do not love a person but remain under the spell of a fleeting image of our own creation that we search for throughout our lives.

I would like to compare nineteenth-century ideas on love with those of two contemporary authors. Francesco Alberoni's book, entitled *Falling in Love* (1983), has received acclaim in the United States as well as in Europe. It is the most recent example of the genre of books on love in the Stendhal tradition. Alberoni defines falling in love as "a nascent state of collective movement involving two individuals." Ordinary sexuality, like eating and drinking, accompanies us when life proceeds uniformly. By contrast Alberoni defines love as extraordinary sexuality: "when life explores the frontiers of the possible."

Singer's (1984) book on love is based on a differentiation between appraisal and bestowal—the real estate broker appraises the market value of a house but the seller or buyer adds to this his own subjective bestowal which contains the personal meaning of the house, including what he associates with the house or remembers about it. The difference between appraisal and bestowal is crucial to Singer's understanding of love. Love consists of bestowal only. Every analyst working with a single man or woman knows the power of appraisal in this invisible market, a market in which a younger woman is more valued than an older one, where the rich are valued more than the poor, and the professionally successful more than the one who failed. Individual bestowal to a greater or lesser degree modifies in individual cases the power of the appraisal. I believe that Singer has done us all a service by drawing this distinction so sharply. However, the psychoanalyst will ask: Why do we bestow this added value? What is there about our nature that makes us so happy when we love and our love is reciprocated, and unhappy when we do not? Because the psychoanalyst works with the unconscious, he knows a territory that is all but unknown to a philosopher, even when he is open to psychoanalytic ideas. The next section will deal with psychoanalytic theories of love.

We should note a contrast between the nineteenth and twentieth centuries. Both Schopenhauer and Stendhal described love as an event that takes place within one person. It was love whether it was requited or unrequited. To Alberoni (1983) and Singer (1984) love is essentially an object relationship. It takes place between two people. In essence love belongs to group psychology, even though the group is confined to two.

I will conclude this chapter with excerpts from two letters by Freud written in 1892 shortly before his marriage. I believe that they will leave no doubt in the mind of the reader that the twenty-six-year-old Freud was at the time a typical bourgeois, a true son of the nineteenth century.

> And when you are my dear wife before all the world and bear my name we will pass our life in calm happiness for our selves and earnest work for mankind until we have to close our eyes in eternal sleep and leave to those near us a memory every one will be glad of.
>
> (August 4, 1882)

This was followed two weeks later by the following:

All we need is two or three little rooms where we can live and eat and receive a guest and a hearth where the fire for cooking does not go out. And what things there will have to be: tables and chairs, beds, a mirror, a clock to remind the happy ones of the passage of time, an armchair for an hour of agreeable day-dreaming, carpets so that the Hausfrau can easily keep the floor clean, linen tied up in fancy ribbons and stored on their shelves, clothes of the newest cut and hats with artificial flowers, pictures on the wall, glasses for the daily water and for wine on festive occasions, plates and dishes, a larder when we are suddenly overcome with hunger or a guest arrives unexpectedly, a large bunch of keys which must rattle noisily. There is so much we can enjoy: the bookcase and the sewing basket and the friendly lamp. And everything must be kept in good order, else the Hausfrau, who had divided up her heart in little bits, one for each piece of furniture, will object. And this thing must be a witness to the serious work that keeps the house together, and that thing of one's love for beauty, of dear friends of whom one is glad to be reminded, of towns one has seen, of hours one likes to recall. All of it a little world of happiness, of silent friends and emblems of honorable humanity.

(August 18, 1882; Jones 1953: 139–140)

Euphemistically, Freud described the growing domestication of his love as "passing from the lyric phase into an epic one." There is no hint in them that the author of these letters will at the turn of the twentieth century shake the foundations upon which a previous century has built its ideas of love.

# II

## *The Psychoanalytic Contribution*

# *Preamble*

The subject of love, as we have seen in the first part of this book, had been debated and illuminated for thousands of years before Freud. If psychoanalysts claim the right to be heard on this subject beside poets, novelists, philosophers, and historians it is because Freud changed our way of looking at love. A second claim that psychoanalysts can make on the subject of love is that they know of a special form of love, transference love, that has been more thoroughly studied than any other form of love.

There is still a third reason why psychoanalysts have something new to say on the subject of love: the psychoanalytic interview is perhaps the most truthful human relationship that we know. To be sure, "the basic rule," as Freud called it—the demand that the analysand say freely whatever comes into his mind, whether it seems to him to be pertinent or irrelevant, that he censor nothing—has in practice proven more difficult to follow than Freud anticipated. Eissler is of the opinion that the analysand associates freely, if ever, only at the end of the analysis when he is no longer afraid of the psychoanalyst, and no longer ashamed of anything that emerges from his unconscious. Granted these limitations, the psychoanalytic interview is unique—far closer to truth than letters, diaries, autobiographies, and other documents open to observers of love.

To a reader who is not familiar with psychoanalytic writings, I would like to offer some guidelines.

Psychoanalysis is a many-layered discipline that consists of direct observations that can usually be verified. For example, little boys express freely the idea that they will marry their mothers when they grow up. When generalized, this observation forms a clinical theory that states that both boys and girls have what Freud called oedipal wishes. During latency, that is, roughly between six to twelve years, these wishes become repressed. At this point, Freud introduced a clinical hypothesis. The boy represses his oedipal wishes because he fears castration. This hypothesis was derived from dreams and free associations of analysands and, although generally accepted by psychoanalysts, such hypotheses are not confirmable by direct observations.

A still further complication was created when Freud combined many observations into a metapsychological theory which postulated an entity called libido which undergoes development through a definite series of psychosexual phases. This hypothetical libido was conceptualized as capable of transformations, for example, from self-love to falling in love; undergoing change from narcissistic into object libido. Not all psychoanalysts today find metapsychology useful, but Freud's theories on love were stated in this language. Anyone who wishes to understand Freud's contribution to love must master his metapsychology, at least his libido theory.

Behind the new psychoanalytic view on love is a new view of man. I can state the view briefly here but will have to elaborate on it later. Men and women in this view seek not only to refind infantile love objects, as Freud thought, but to find new love objects that will heal the wounds that the parents have inflicted.

There are psychic forces that operate in the direction of growth. Many children wish ardently to be adults and have the prerogatives of their parents. This pressure, in the psychoanalytic view, fosters the reaching of the "genital position." Another force operates in the opposite direction, tenaciously maintaining the right to remain the child forever. There is a force that pushes toward individuation and there is an opposing one that operates in the direction of merging. Much has been learned in the last decades about the familial relationships that foster the strength of one or the other of these forces.

Falling in love and selecting a mate are also determined by the interaction of these forces. Love pushes toward adulthood, toward taking care of others, toward founding a family, but is also in the service of refinding lost childhood bliss, in favor of undoing the boundary that separates the self from the other.

The loss of the boundary of the self can be frightening. In mental illness it can evoke terror. It operates as a force opposing love. Mrs. P, a nearly psychotic patient of Jacobson (1971), beautifully describes this fear.

Mrs. P.—a pathetic, beautiful Ophelia clad only in a torn nightgown—pulled me down to the couch where she had seated herself. "Let us be close," she said. "I have made a great philosophical discovery. Do you know the difference between closeness, likeness, sameness, and oneness? Close is close, as with you; when you are like somebody, you are only like the other, you and he are two; sameness—you are the same as the other, but he is still he and you are you; but oneness is not two—it is one, it is one, that's horrible.—Horrible," she repeated, jumping up in sudden panic: "Don't get too close, get away from the couch, I don't want to be you," and she pushed me away and began to attack me. (pp. 253–254)

We can agree with Mrs. P. She had made a great philosophical discovery; with the clarity that often accompanies a psychotic breakdown, she has discerned the various grades of human closeness.

Since Plato, philosophers and poets, with the possible exception of Dante's Francesca and Paolo, have sung the praises of oneness. Psychoanalysts after Freud have discovered that longing for oneness co-exists with fear of merger. The dynamics of love can be seen as a struggle between these two opposing forces.

# 13

# *Freud's Indebtedness to Plato: The Problem of Sublimation*

Freud's relationship to the fable told by Aristophanes is of interest. He refered to it twice; the first time was in the *Three Essays:* "The popular view of the sexual instinct is beautifully reflected in the poetic fable which tells how the original human beings were cut up in two halfs—man and woman—and how these are always striving to unite again in love. It comes as a great surprise therefore to learn that there are men whose sexual object is man not woman, and women whose sexual object is woman and not man" (Freud 1905a: 136).

Freud's recollection of the fable must have been dim because Plato specifies that not all those who were cut in two were only heterosexual couples. It was evoked for the second time in *Beyond The Pleasure Principle* (1920). There the fable is quoted as a poetic confirmation that living substance was torn apart into small particles and endeavors through the sexual act to be reunited.

As a young man, Freud used the fable to express love to his fiancée. He wrote:

I am really only half a person in the sense of the old platonic fable which you are sure to know, and the moment that I am not active my cut hurts me. After all, we already belong to each other. (August 28, 1883)

Freud must have had the platonic fable in mind when he said in 1930:

When a love relationship is at its height there is no room left for any interest in the environment; a pair of lovers are sufficient to themselves, and do not even need the child they have in common to make them happy. In no other case does Eros so clearly betray the core of his being, his purpose of making one out of more than one; but when he had achieved this in the proverbial way through the love of two human beings he refuses to go further. (p. 108)

Earlier, Freud (1921) showed that Eros can bind larger groups, particularly crowds, when it appears as religious zealotry or patriotism.

That Freud's concept of the libido has much in common with Plato's Eros has been noted by Nachmanson (1915), Pfister (1921), and recently by Simon (1978). Nachmanson noticed that the term "libido" is the Latin translation of the Greek "Eros." He deplores this Latinization for had Freud retained the original Greek term, the historical connection between Plato and Freud would have been preserved. Prior to 1920, Freud used the term Eros only in his *Leonardo* (1910) when he said: "So resolutely do they [Leonardo's drawings] shun everything sexual that it would seem as if Eros alone the preserver of all living things was not worthy material for the investigator in his pursuit of knowledge" (p. 70).

Strachey remarks that the designation of Eros as the preserver of all living things here antedates Freud's use of the term in *Beyond The Pleasure Principle* by ten years. After 1920, Freud no longer used the term libido and Eros as synonymous.*

The term Eros Freud now conceptualized as a life force that combines organic substances into ever larger units (1920: 42–43).** This new view of Freud would have been congenial to the revelers of the *Symposium*. Historically speaking, Freud's 1920 dual instinct theory is an astonishing revival in the twentieth century of tenets prevalent in Greek philosophy.

Plato's *Phaedrus* contains the well-known allegory of the charioteer. Each soul is divided into three parts: two horses and a charioteer. The right horse is white, with a lofty neck and aquiline nose. He loves honor, modesty, and temperance. He needs no touch of the whip, being guided by admonition only. His companion is dark, with short neck and flat face, a crooked and lumbering animal, a mate of insolence and pride, hardly yielding to the whip. When the charioteer beholds the vision of love, his soul is full of desire. The obedient steed under the government of shame holds back, while the other plunges forward. The opposing disposition of the horses forces the charioteer to lose control. For a while the dark horse wins. Eventually the wild horse is tamed. From now on, the soul of the lover follows the beloved in modesty and holy fear.

Freud did not refer to Plato when he used the rider and the horse as a metaphor for the ego and the id. However, Plato's allegory bears such a

---

*I am indebted to Dr. Harold Blum for drawing my attention to this distinction.
**In rare moments one can even feel a libidinal tie to all of mankind as for example in the Ninth Symphony when Beethoven puts to music Schiller's words "Be embraced ye millions." Gagarin, the first astronaut and the first man to be separated from the globe, reported that he experienced earth longings on his flight.

striking similarity to the tripartite division of the personality into superego, ego, and id that Plato's influence must be assumed.

Plato visualized the conflict as taking place between the rational (*logistikon*) part of the personality and the appetitive (*epithumetikon*). Of the two the appetitive is the older. It is the part that remains awake when we are asleep or dreaming. This description of the appetitive part of the personality also bears a striking similarity to Freud's concept of the primary processes.

Simon (1978) notes another similarity between the two. Both used "person within a person" language: that is, both described intrapsychic struggle as if it were a debate between two persons. Simon also notes that for Plato sickness of the psyche is a manifestation of the wild primitive part of the mind, expressing its claims loudly (p. 205). What is striking in this observation is not so much that Freud's view is the more complex, but that Freud's first formulation of the nature of neurosis being the result of repression of unacceptable wishes replicated Plato.

Plato was among the first to understand the dream not as a message from God but as an intrapsychic event. Plato should therefore be credited with the achievement of a momentous step in the history of culture: the internalization of the dream. The dream as a message is part of the mythological point of view. The understanding of the dream as reflecting the inner world of men belongs to the postmythological view of the world (Bergmann 1966).

When Freud summarized his understanding of love with the epigram "all finding is refinding" he was again echoing platonic doctrine. However, what was to Plato the refinding of the prenatal bliss of the soul became to Freud the refinding the early love object of infancy in adult love (Freud 1905b: 202). On one significant point the two differed markedly. Plato regarded homosexuality as belonging to the higher part of the psyche while heterosexuality he saw as the mere expression of the appetitive part. To Freud homosexuality was the earlier and the more primitive form of the two sexual organizations.

## The Problem of Sublimation

Sublimation refers to a process where something is made sublime. We have already seen that Plato advocated the deflection of sexual love into contemplation of higher things. The word has an interesting history; it is derived from the Latin *sublimare*. The word was used by alchemists during the Middle Ages to mean raising into vapor in order to purify. The term already acquired a metaphorical meaning in the Middle Ages for any activity that elevates and purifies. In the eighteenth century it was used by Goethe in the sense that human feelings and events cannot be portrayed on the stage in their original state of naturalness but must be presented in a sublimated form (Kaufman, 1950). The first to assign to sublimation a central psychological function was Nietzsche. He speaks of good actions and sublimated bad ones. He also speaks of the artist sublimating sexual wishes. Nietzsche even spoke the language of psychoanalytic metapsychology when he said: "One brings about a dislocation of one's quanta of strength by diverting one's thoughts and play of physical forces into other channels" (Kaufman 1950: 192). Nietzsche was mainly concerned with the sublimation of the will to power—in psychoanalytic language, the sublimation of the aggressive drive—rather than the sublimation of the sexual drive.

In Freud's writings, the term sublimation appeared for the first time in 1905(a) in the *Three Essays on Sexuality:*

What is it that goes to the making of these constructions which are so important for the growth of a civilized and normal individual? They probably emerge at the cost of the infantile sexual impulses themselves. Thus the activity of those impulses does not cease even during this period of latency, though their energy is diverted, wholly or in great part, from their sexual use and directed to other ends. Historians of civilization appear to be at one in assuming that powerful components are acquired for every kind of cultural achievement by this diversion of sexual instinctual forces from sexual aims and their direction to new ones—a process which deserves the name of sublimation. (p. 178)

One is at a loss to ascertain who these historians of civilization might be, until one recalls that it was Plato who derived gymnastics, agriculture, pottery, archery, and poetry, as well as the arts of the smith, directly from Eros. In a humorous vein, Rabelais' Pantagruel adds that Eros can instruct brutes in arts which are against their nature. He can make poets out of ravens, jackdaws, and chattering jays, parrots, and starlings: he even can make poetesses out of magpies.

Surprising as it may seem, the observation that the sexual drive lends itself to sublimation, was, as we learn from Sulloway (1979: 283), a generally accepted idea in the psychiatric literature before Freud. These psychiatrists and sexologists were in turn influenced by Schopenhauer and Nietzsche, who saw sexuality as the basis upon which culture is built.

In the Dora case (1905) Freud says:

The sexual life of each of us extends to a slight degree now in this direction, now in that—beyond the narrow lines imposed as the standards of normality. The perversions are neither bestial, nor degenerate in the emotional sense of the word. They are developments of germs, all of which are contained in the undifferentiated sexual disposition of the child, and which by being suppressed or by being diverted to a higher, asexual aim—by being sublimated—are destined to provide the energy for a great number of our cultural achievements. (p. 50)

Such ideas were expressed by Henry Maudsley in 1872 and were transmitted to Freud through Krafft-Ebing's *Psychopathia Sexualis* which appeared in 1866 and went through numerous editions. The sexologists of Freud's generation held the belief that sexual life is the primary basis of ethics, aesthetics, poetry, and religious feelings. Krafft-Ebing also stressed the connection between certain religious practices such as asceticism and self-flagellation as socially sanctioned forms of perversion.

That the sexual life of many normal people contains a measure of perversion was, according to Sulloway, also not original to Freud (p. 298); it was stressed earlier by Binet in 1898. Even the statement that the child has an undifferentiated sexual disposition has been asserted before Freud by Dessoir in 1888. What was new with Freud was the assertion that sublimation draws its energy from pregenital sexuality.

The fate of the pregenital impulses was of great interest to Freud. If they retain their dominant position they lead to perversion. If they are repressed, they lead to an inhibited sexual life; if the repression fails, it may lead to neurosis. One of the tasks of love according to Freud is to free us from pregenital inhibitions and unite the pregenital with the genital. "The inclination to take the man's sexual organ into the mouth and suck on it, which in respectable society is considered a loathsome sexual perversion, in a state of being in love it appears completely to lose its repulsive character" (Freud 1910: 86).

By contrast to Freud, Eissler (1961: 189) believes that the genius sublimates genital impulses. Genital impulses, in his view, are harder to sublimate than pregenital ones. The biographies of both Leonardo and Goethe are cited as examples.

Freud spoke of another form of sublimation—transformation into character. "It is therefore plausible to suppose that these character-traits of orderliness, parsimony and obstinacy, which are so often prominent in people who were formerly anal erotics, are to be regarded as the first and most constant results of the sublimation of anal erotism" (Freud 1908c: 171).

The passage is of historical significance; for the first time, Freud linked a psychosexual fixation with character. No less significant, however, was Freud's decision to see character as a form of sublimation of the psychosexual fixations. This paper was the first of a series written by both Freud and Abraham to associate character traits with sublimation of psychosexual fixations.

One of the surprising conclusions to which I came in the course of this study was the realization that in his clinical work, apart from the connection between character and fixation, Freud made little use of the concept of sublimation. He was interested in sublimation primarily as a philosopher of culture and as a biographer of great men.

In the paper "Civilized Sexual Morality and Modern Nervous Illness" (1908), Freud was concerned with the damage that sexual abstinence might cause young people.

The relationship between the amount of sublimation possible and the amount of sexual activity necessary, naturally varies very much from person to person and even from one calling to another. An abstinent artist is hardly conceivable but an abstinent young savant is certainly no rarity. The latter can, by his self-restraint, liberate forces for his studies while the former probably finds his artistic achievement powerfully stimulated by his sexual experience. (p. 197)

Why artistic sublimation is enhanced by sexual activity while scientific sublimation should be enhanced by abstinence was not explored by Freud. (There is an interesting discussion of views about abstinence by various artists from Durer to Van Gogh in Eissler 1961, chapter 6.)

In no other work was Freud as occupied with the problem of sublimation as when he wrote about Leonardo da Vinci (1910). At that time Freud was interested in the fate of a period he called infantile sexual researches: the intense preoccupation of the young child with the problem of where babies come from. Typically, latency brings out only a repression of sexual wishes, but the cessation of curiosity and inhibition of thought also sets in. In another group, the period of infantile research turns into brooding. Thinking itself becomes associated with pleasure and anxiety. Investion becomes a sexual activity; explaining replaces sexual satisfaction. Finally, in rare cases, repression of infantile sexuality does not take place and the full strength of the sexual drive is sublimated. The only area that must be excluded from research is the sexual one (p. 79–80).

In the chapter on Freud, I will discuss the concept of "refinding" which in Freud's thinking was at the basis of all falling in love. In *Leonardo* he applied the same theory to sublimation. In Freud's view, Leonardo refound the smile of his mother while he painted the Mona Lisa. An ordinary mortal under such conditions would fall in love with the model. Leonardo, however, could not part with the Mona Lisa and in his subsequent paintings recreated the same smile (Eissler 1961).

Leonardo transferred his love from the memory of the mother to the canvas. One can see Leonardo as the obverse of Pygmalion. A special form of sublimation goes from memory of love for an animate, to love of the inanimate.

In 1937, Freud wrote to Princess Bonaparte that both instincts, love and aggression, participate in sublimation. They have to go together for the sublimation to be successful. Curiosity, the impulse to investigate, is a sublimation of the destructive drive (Jones 3: 64).

The artist was seen as having "a strong capacity for sublimation and a certain degree of laxity in repression" (Freud 1916–1917: 376). Otto Rank (1907), one of Freud's early followers, embraced this doctrine with enthusiasm. He proclaimed that the artist is the very opposite of the neurotic. By his capacity to sublimate the artist can evade neurosis. This credo belongs to the youthful era of psychoanalysis.

Young Freud, like Rank, believed that sublimation is a protection against neurosis. In subsequent developments, when artists entered psychoanalysis and biographies of artists were studied with greater detail, it became clear that works of art and literature do not protect their creators from neurosis. By that time, psychoanalytic theory itself had changed and Freud no longer regarded repression as the main pathogenic agent. It is possible to be a great artist, to be highly capable of sublimation, and to be mentally ill at the same time.

For reasons that are not easily understandable, Freud was particularly impressed with the capacity of homosexuals to sublimate. In the Schreber case (1911) Freud said: "It is not irrelevant to note that it is precisely manifest homosexuals, and among them again precisely those that set themselves against an indulgence in sensual acts, who are distinguished by taking a particularly active share in the general interests of humanity— interests which have themselves sprung from a sublimation of erotic instincts" (Freud 1911: 61).

Only once, to my knowledge, did Freud deal with sublimation on a clinical level. That was in the analysis of the Wolf Man (Freud 1918a). In this work, Freud describes a religious sublimation that took place in the four-and-a-half year old boy. The Wolf Man was a victim of insomnia because he feared the return of the nightmare that gave the case its name. His mother, Freud reported, was "determined to make him acquainted with the Bible story in the hope of distracting and elevating him" (p. 61). The result was that the phobic state gave way to an obsessional neurosis, which manifested itself in ritualistic reciting of prayers, kissing holy pictures, and making innumerable signs of the cross before going to sleep.

These obsessive rituals did cure the insomnia. The Wolf Man, however, was hardly a good Christian, for even as a child he became critical of God's behavior during the Crucifixion and rejected the doctrine of turning the other cheek. He also ruminated over the question of whether Christ had a behind. This rumination Freud interpreted as a displacement of the intrapsychic conflict over homosexual impulses directed toward his father and displaced onto the figure of Christ. Freud went on to describe three sexual trends discernible in the Wolf Man: "In his unconscious he was homosexual and in his neurosis he was at the level of cannibalism; while the earlier masochistic attitude remained the dominant one" (p. 64). What Freud meant is not easy to understand. I interpret the statement to mean that the masochistic attitude toward his father was the least repressed; that the cannibalistic wishes in a disguised form were reflected in the fear of being eaten by the wolves, and finally that homosexuality took the form of doubting whether Christ had an anus. At this juncture Freud introduces the concept of sublimation: "His knowledge of the sacred story now gave him a chance of sublimating his predominantly masochistic attitude toward his father. He became Christ" (p. 64). In spite of the obsessional symptoms that accomplished and accompanied the religious conversion, Freud considered the sublimation an educational success.

It may be said that in the present case religion achieved all the aims for the sake of which it is included in the education of the individual. It put a restraint on his sexual impulsions by affording them a sublimation and a safe mooring; it lowered the importance of his family relationships, and thus protected him from the threat of isolation by giving him access to the great community of mankind. The untamed and fear-ridden child became social, well-behaved, and amenable to education.

As Christ, he could love his father, who was now called God, with a fervor which had sought in vain to discharge itself so long as his father had been a mortal. The means by which he could bear witness to this love were laid down by religion, and they were not haunted by that sense of guilt from which his individual feelings of love could not set themselves free. In this way it was still possible for him to drain off his deepest sexual current, which had already been precipitated in the form of unconscious homosexuality; and at the same time his more superficial masochistic impulse found an incomparable sublimation, without much renunciation, in the story of the Passion of Christ, who, at the behest of his divine Father and in his honour, had let himself be ill-treated and sacrificed. So it was that religion did its work for the hard-pressed child—by the combination which it afforded the believer of satisfaction of sublimation, of diversion from sensual processes to purely spiritual ones, and of access to social relationships. (pp. 114–115)

This was a far cry from the early optimistic view of sublimation as an alternative to repression and neurosis. All that the sublimation in the case of the Wolf Man achieved was the transformation of a phobic state into a compulsion neurosis. The step was viewed positively by Freud because the compulsion neurosis had a more acceptable social character. Since the Wolf Man's case was published, a number of cases were reported where psychoanalysis achieved not a resolution of the neurotic conflict but a transformation of the form the neurosis takes (Bornstein 1949).

The religious conversion did not protect the Wolf Man from developing a very severe neurosis as a young adult. When he came to Freud as an adult before World War I he was an incapacitated man. Repeated attempts to analyze him met only with partial success. Psychoanalysis accomplished something analogous to what religion had achieved. It gave him a new sense of identity. As a child he was Christ. As an adult he remained Freud's famous patient. As the Wolf Man he introduced himself to the Russian officer who arrested him in Vienna during the occupation. His haughty demeanor struck the officer as so odd that he was thought to be unbalanced (Gardiner 1971; Blum 1974).

Until 1923, sublimation was seen by Freud essentially as a displacement of sexual energy. With the advent of ego psychology in *The Ego and the Id,* Freud speculated that all sublimation takes place through the medium of the ego. Sublimation becomes possible when the ego changes object libido (attachment to another person) into narcissistic libido. The ego may use the newly acquired narcissistic libido to build up its own character. For character, Freud now emphasized, is formed on the basis of abandoned object relationships. That is, one becomes in time more like the person one has lost or abandoned. The ego, so to speak, says to the id, "love me for I am like the parent you loved earlier" (p. 30). Or it may use the newly acquired narcissistic libido for new sublimations. For example, a disappointment in love can be an impetus to new creativity. Freud postulated a displaceable energy, neutral in itself, which can be added to erotic as well as destructive impulses (p. 44). Desexualized libido can also be described as sublimated libido because the main purpose of eros, that of uniting and binding, has been retained (p. 45). This remark, not central to Freud's thinking, was the starting point for Hartmann's ego psychology, destined to play a dominant role in American psychoanalysis.

Under Hartmann's influence Kris (1955) differentiated between neutralization and sublimation. The term *neutralization,* he suggested, should be applied when there is evidence of energy transformation; *sublimation* should be applied when there was a displacement of a goal. Mystics and poets sublimate, they do not employ neutralized energy. Eissler (1963: 1411ff.) suggested that no passionate interest operates with neutralized energy. He called neutralized energy the energy of inhibited ego functions.

Difficulties with the concept of sublimation were recognized early in psychoanalytic history. Already in 1922 Bernfeld was critical of the cultural bias in Freud's use of the term sublimation. He recommended that sublimation be used neutrally for all instances where sexual wishes are diverted to serve the aims of the ego without regard to whether they serve important cultural purposes.

Melanie Klein saw sublimation as derived from feelings of enjoyment and gratitude experienced at the breast. Gratitude results in a wish to return the pleasure received. She saw sublimation as an act of reparation (1957: 19).

I found an unusual case of sublimation in Jane Van Lawick-Goodall, the noted observer of chimpanzee behavior, in her book *In The Shadow of Man* (1971). I quote from that book: "Perhaps it had begun in my earliest childhood. When I was just over one year old my mother gave me a toy chimpanzee, a large hairy model celebrating the birth of the first chimpanzee infant ever born in the London zoo. Most of my mother's friends were horrified and predicted that the ghastly creature would give a small child nightmares; but Jubilee (as the celebrated infant itself was named) was my most loved possession and accompanied me in all my childhood travels. I still have the worn old toy (p. 3)." With a wonderful intuition, Jane Goodall is tracing her unusual interest in the chimpanzee and the amazing patience that she was able to show in long hours of observing them back to what analysts call transitional objects. Her case, unusual as far as my knowledge goes, is an example of the sublimation or the transitional object.

Psychoanalytic experience has demonstrated the vulnerability of sublimation to resexualization of reaggressivization. An interesting example of the undoing of sublimation through resexualization has been reported by Kohut (1977: 200–1), which I here paraphrase:

Mr. X sought psychoanalysis when he could not realize his occupational goal of either becoming a minister or being accepted by the Peace Corps. Mr. X's mother had idealized him and supported openly his display of grandiosity. He had identified himself with the boy Jesus who confounds the doctors in the temple (Luke 2;41:52). He felt obliged to give up the ministry when the Holy Communion entered into his masturbation fantasy. At the moment of receiving the host, he visualized his penis and that of the officiating priest making a cross. This fantasy brought about ejaculation.

Gross and Rubin (1973) drew attention to the fact that when a psychosis is threatening, sublimation can become a desperate attempt to maintain a tie to reality. They found that frenzied sublimatory activity can be observed just before the onset of the psychotic break. They point to the frenzied painting activity by Van Gogh that preceded his psychotic break. Gross and Rubin also cite the case of Mishima, who suicided on the day he completed his tetralogy. A few months earlier he is reported to have said, "Once he had finished his new novel into which he had poured all his skill and experience he would have nothing left to do." The authors cite this case in support of their idea that sublimation protected Mishima against his suicidal wishes. As I see it, another dynamic constellation can also be discerned: many artists have felt that their creation has absorbed all that they have; they felt exhausted and depressed after the completion of the artistic endeavor. But in Mishima's case, the relationship between the artistic product and the self showed a deeper pathology. Like some severe superegos of melancholics, he projected on his artistic work the demand that he sacrifice himself to it not only metaphorically but literally. His work seems to have turned upon its creator, demanding his death.

I will conclude with a clinical example of my own: some years ago, I was consulted by a highly gifted European engineer who presented the following problem. For fifteen years he had a happy love relationship with a woman twenty years his senior. With her he experienced happiness and she also inspired him to develop many of his intellectual capacities. When he reached middle age, he found himself attracted to younger women. A dormant urge to become a father asserted itself. He felt intense guilt feelings toward his now aging friend. A new love made the conflict acute. Torn by this conflict, he sought psychoanalytic help. It so happened that in the course of our work, he told me about an invention he had made. He was in charge of a plant where the old machinery began to deteriorate. Should the company scrap the machinery that was making too many errors and overhaul the whole plant? At this point my patient found a creative solution. By accelerating some of the defects of the old machinery, a new product could be produced. Thus, the old machinery did not have to be discarded. New machinery was ordered and both were producing together, to the delight and profit of the company.

I stressed earlier that my patient was a highly intelligent man, and yet he was entirely unaware of the connection between his personal dilemma and his brilliant technical solution. What he could not solve in his personal life, he solved in his professional work. Important and gratifying as it was, it contributed nothing to the solution of his personal problem. It seems probable that the problem that occupied him personally exerted pressure against discarding the old machinery and thus led to a technical solution.

A historical question remains: why was it necessary for Freud to develop the cryptoamnesia for his debt to Plato, and repeat the same amnesia with the work of Schopenhauer and Nietzsche? It became fashionable in psychoanalytic circles to describe Plato as a forerunner of Freud, denying the direct influence that Plato had on Freud's thinking. A number of possible explanations come to mind.

Freud had the highest respect for artists and their capacity to sublimate. Toward philosophers, however, he was less charitable. He accused them of clinging to the illusion of "being able to present a picture of the universe which is without gaps." He felt that philosophers were overestimating the epistemological value of logical operation (1933: 160–161). The publication of Freud's letters to his adolescent friend Silberstein (Stanesau 1971) goes some way toward explaining Freud's animosity for philosophy. We know now that under Brentano's influence, Freud himself had considered becoming a philosopher. The choice of medicine as a profession was based on the need to make a living and was achieved with neutralized energy. Freud remained throughout his life ambivalent toward medicine. After the battle for the recognition of psychoanalysis was wrested from medicine, Freud returned to the interests of his youth. But a bias against those who pursued what he passionately wished to pursue remained.

Freud wished to be associated with the great discoverers, those whom he felt disturbed the narcissistic sleep of mankind: Copernicus, who deprived us of our pride in the centrality of the earth; Darwin, who forced us to recognize that the gulf between man and animal was not as absolute as we would wish. Freud saw himself as a discoverer who forced us to realize that we do not exert dominion even over our own unconscious. He did not wish to be remembered as a disciple of Plato, Schopenhauer, and Nietzsche. The climate of opinion in which psychoanalysis developed as a branch of medicine militated against the acknowledgment of its philosophical debt. There were enough people who scoffed at psychoanalysis without the addition of another charge that psychoanalysis is no more than a latter-day, warmed-up platonic philosophy. But now that the battle for recognition has been won and Freud's place in history is secure, psychoanalysis can only gain by acknowledging its own humanistic origins. A significant difference between Freud and Plato remains. Plato sought to sublimate the love for beautiful boys. Freud put the emphasis on the sublimation of the sexual drive.

# 14

# *What Freud Discovered*
# *About Love*

I t can be stated with reasonable certainty that no aspect of Freud's life
work has been as little understood, and so misunderstood, as his contribution to the understanding of love. Some of the difficulty lies with Freud
himself. For his manifold contributions to love never reached the same
degree of theoretical cohesion as his theories of sexuality, or his dream
theory. It requires some effort to bring Freud's observations on love into a
coherent structure. In this chapter I will attempt to do so.

Dream theory was a triumph. With a mixture of exultation and incredu-
lity, Freud playfully asked Fliess whether he believed that a commemora-
tive plaque would ever be erected stating that: "On the 24th day of July
1895 the secret of the dream revealed itself here to Dr. Sigmund Freud"
(Freud 1950; letter No. 137, December 6, 1906). There is no equivalent
moment in Freud's life where he believed that the mystery of love had
revealed itself to him. Love was a topic associated with conflict: insights
came one at a time, without evoking the exultation that comes with conquest. When in 1910 Freud discovered "the necessary conditions for loving" he apologized for wresting the territory of love from the poets. He
argued that science must reluctantly enter the field of love "though her
touch must be clumsier and the yield of pleasure less." Psychoanalysis, he
argued, must do so because "the poets do not reproduce the stuff of reality
unchanged, and moreover, show only slight interest in the origin of mental
states" (Freud 1910:165).

In Freud's correspondence with Jung, one can discern a reluctance on
Freud's part to decipher the secrets of normal love, a reluctance reminiscent of Freud's attitude toward art. On January 13, 1910, when he was
absorbed in drafting his first theory of love, Freud wrote to Jung: "I do

not think that our psychoanalytic flag ought to be raised over the territory of normal love."

Gould (1963), who ranks Freud with Plato and St. Paul as one of the three men in the history of the Western world who have created encompassing theories of love, nevertheless goes on to say: "As for Freudians, their life must be even bleaker than that of the Christians and the Platonists. To confuse love with mere sexual need is almost the worst mistake a person can make. Sexual need is a tension which is easily satisfied and vanishes with the satisfaction; love is exclusive, unpredictable, ever demanding and grows rather than dies when it is fulfilled."

What Professor Gould has said about love is poetic; what he says about Freud is mistaken. Nowhere in his writing did Freud confuse love with sex. What he did do is follow Schopenhauer and look upon love, a human emotion, from the point of view of the sexual drive. Yet many, including psychoanalysts, have made similar mistakes. Even Theodore Reik, an early collaborator and a close personal friend of Freud, wrote at a time when he was rebelling against his master: "But Freud? Did not psychoanalysis deal fully and penetratingly with love? It did not, it dealt with sex, but this is something quite different" (1944:11).

The view expressed by Reik is widespread. Dicks et al. (1967), who have made important contributions to the understanding of love, write:

Though Freud certainly conceived the *libido* as object-seeking, this powerful drive was nonetheless visualized as essentially an effect of impersonal neurophysiological or hormonal activity seeking to discharge its tensions and manipulating the ego to do its bidding. His was a physiological psychology of "impulse gratification." This might have sufficed for the study of the development of sexual attractions between two people leading to successful intercourse. But we know that however strong the operation of the sexual drive, this is not adequate to explain or even describe the range of phenomena involved in marriage. (p. 6)

Generalizations such as this one ignore Freud's manifold contributions to love. In a less critical vein, Altman (1977) also stated that Freud had more to say about sex than about love. Because Freud has stressed sexuality and instincts it became a prevalent opinion to assume that he knew little or nothing about love. That this was not so is the argument of this chapter.

### Infantile Origins of Love: Freud's First Theory

Freud's first theory of love was the byproduct of his discovery of infantile sexuality; appropriately therefore it appears in his *Three Essays on the Theory of Sexuality* (Freud: 1905a).

In my opinion, *The Interpretation of Dreams* (1900) and this book contain the most significant ingredients of psychoanalysis. Without these two books there would have been no psychoanalysis; what followed was significant but not as fundamental. In the *Three Essays* Freud postulated that human beings, unlike animals, have a biphasic sexual development which is the direct result of man's prolonged infancy. The first phase is that of infantile sexuality. It is usually pregenital in form and centered around sexual zones like the mouth or anus; only rarely does it reach the stage where the aim of the sexual drive is the union of the genitals. Infantile sexuality reaches its peak in the Oedipus complex when one of the parents is usually desired and there is a wish to murder the other. During the oedipal phase, the relationship to both parents is ambivalent. The rival parent is also loved and homosexual wishes compete with heterosexual ones. The heterosexual parent, the object of love, is also hated, because it belongs to the other parent. At this point latency sets in and infantile sexuality becomes repressed. An amnesia ensues. During adolescence the libido makes a fresh start, searching for a new and nonincestuous love object, but the new love object must nevertheless in some way remain reminiscent of the old. Freud's favorite metaphor, to understand the "flow of the libido," was to see it as a current.

Freud made significant discoveries never made before about love because he looked for love in a place only a few observers before him had thought of looking: in the years of infancy. Before Freud, sexuality was synonymous with genitality and therefore began with puberty. The study of neurotic symptoms and dreams led Freud to conclude that sexuality in the broader sense begins with infancy; that nursing at the breast not only fulfills the need of nourishment but is also a source of pleasure, destined in time to become sexual pleasure, which persists into adulthood in the form of kissing, oral sex, and other forms of foreplay. Foreplay in turn has the function of increasing genital satisfaction. Once Freud had recognized that the root of sexuality goes back to infancy, it was only one further step to his recognition that love, too, has its origins in the same years of infancy.

The discovery of transference (a subject I will deal with later at greater length) was the second reason why Freud could decipher some of love's secrets. As Freud struggled to master the transference, he learned much that was new about love in general. For transference love can be seen as an artificial "hothouse" type of love, which appears regularly in psychoanalysis and is carefully nurtured in the course of treatment. At first the appearance of transference posed a difficult problem. As Freud (1905) learned to master the role of transference, his understanding of love also deepened. It was in the Dora case (Freud 1905) that Freud began to appreciate the role that transference plays in treatment. During the same year he also discovered that love has its origins in infantile prototypes (1905a).

The *Three Essays on Sexuality* (1905a) already contained a theory of love. This theory stated that in the early years of life, the sexual desires of the infant are directed toward one or the other parent. The mother, or her substitute, becomes both the first love and the first sexual object.

I will quote a passage of particular significance within the context of this book. It happens to be one of Freud's enigmatic passages.

At a time at which the first beginnings of sexual satisfaction are still linked with the taking of nourishment, the sexual instinct has a sexual object outside the infant's own body in the shape of his mother's breast. It is only later that the instinct loses that object, just at the time, perhaps, when the child is able to form a total idea of the person to whom the organ that is giving him satisfaction belongs. As a rule the sexual instinct them becomes auto-erotic, and not until the period of latency has been passed through is the original relation restored. There are thus good reasons why a child sucking at his mother's breast has become the prototype of every relation of love. The finding of an object is in fact a refinding of it. (p. 222)

I regard Freud's statement that "the finding of an object is in fact a refinding of it" as Freud's most profound contribution to love. One must admit, however, that it is embedded in a problematic paragraph. If indeed Freud means, as Kleinians have reaffirmed, that the mother's breast is the child's first love object, then it would be only a part-object that the future adult refinds. It would not enable a person to differentiate between one woman and another. Subsequent findings have confirmed that the infant before latency retains much more of the mother than her breast. Even though Freud tended at times to see that what is refound is a single characteristic of the mother, such as her smile, or the color of her eyes, he was right in his assertion that all finding is refinding.

During latency, the current that carries both affection and direct sexual impulses is split into two. The sexual current undergoes repression, while the affectionate one remains conscious. This is the normal way for the oedipus complex to undergo repression. In adolescence, the sexual current breaks loose from the connection to the incestuous object and can now be directed toward a new nonincestuous love. The newly selected person must in some way resemble the old, but must not awaken the guilt feelings associated with the incestuous oedipal object. Thus in adolescence, under favorable conditions, the two currents that were split during latency become united once more. The similarity between the old love in infancy and the newly discovered love prompted Freud to echo Plato: "The finding of an object is in fact the refinding of it." But unlike Plato Freud added, "The child sucking at its mother's breast becomes the prototype of love." Under favorable conditions, "What is left over from the sexual relation to the first object helps to prepare for the choice of an object and thus to restore the happiness that has been lost" (1905:222).

In 1909, accompanied by Jung and Ferenczi, Freud undertook his first trip to the United States, where he delivered the Clark University Lectures. The event is important in the history of psychoanalysis for it marks the first academic recognition of Freud's work. There Freud added: "It is inevitable and perfectly normal that a child should take his parents as the first object of his love. But his libido should not remain fixated to these first objects; later on, it should merely take them as a model, and should make a gradual transition from them on to extraneous people when the time for a final choice for an object arrives" (Freud 1910b:48).

We should pause to note the language in these two passages. For hidden behind a technical, neutral language lies the mystery of happy love as Freud deciphered it. Love is the restoration of a happiness that was lost: intrapsychically the parental figures that were once love objects remain important (cathected) but the attachment to them should not be so strong as to veto the choice of a new object. Subdued, they help to prepare the adolescent to choose a new love object.

In 1905, Freud assumed that the mother was the first love object for the boy, the father for the girl. Freud had not yet discovered the preoedipal love of the girl for her mother, or the negative oedipus complex of both sexes—that is, the love for the parent of the same sex. These discoveries came later (1931a).

For Freud, happy love (or normal love, a term Freud would use more often) was love free from neurosis. One of the reasons why this theory of love was overlooked was because it was overshadowed by Freud's emphasis on neurotic love. Freud was, after all, a professional healer—not like Stendhal, an explorer of love as a puzzling emotion.

What happens in neurotic love is the opposite of what occurs in happy love. "Should these currents fail to converge," Freud said, "the focusing of all desire upon a single object will be unattainable" (1905a:200). The failure to combine the two currents gives rise to neurotic symptoms. This was summarized by Freud in a succinct sentence: "Where they love they do not desire, and where they desire they cannot love" (Freud 1912:183). A further consequence of the inability to fuse the two currents is the need to debase the sexual partner and continue to overvalue the loved person with whom no sexual relationship is possible. We should note the change: the differentiation between divine Aphrodite and her earthly counterpart, which philosophers since Plato held dear, is to Freud a symptom of neurosis.

This insight explained why some men and women can experience full sexual pleasure only with partners that belong to other nationalities, other races, or different economic classes than themselves. Abraham (1913), one of Freud's earliest adherents, called this need "neurotic exogamy." Such men avoid women who remind them of their mothers or their sisters and turn to women who are as dissimilar and therefore as distant as possible from their own family. However, the attempt to solve the incest problem through such a flight is seldom satisfactory. Once the relationship has been established, the similarity to the incestuous love object becomes reestablished and a new partner has to be sought.

To Freud the crucial point is the remingling of the two currents of the libido in adolescence. But why do some succeed while others fail? In 1905 the culprit in Freud's view was the seductive parent or another adult who prematurely awakens the child's genital wishes. The normal child enters latency in a pregenital state. The sexually overstimulated child reaches premature genitality and therefore has a greater tendency to remain fixated upon the parent. In this form, remnants of the early seduction theory survived even after Freud eliminated seduction as the principal cause of neurosis.

Freud noticed another danger. There are men and women who after adolescence fall in love, but when this new love is not requited their libido returns to the earlier point of fixation. A typical example would be a woman who loved once, was rejected, and ever after devotes herself to taking care of her parents, converting the oedipus complex into duty rather than resolving it.

We must accustom ourselves to a dynamic way of thinking. When pregenital impulses are too strong, the result is perversion; when they are repressed, the result is neurosis. When they are beneficially subdued by the genital impulses, they so to speak work for the master and contribute to sexual pleasure. Similarly, when the attachment to the original parent is too strong, fixation will result in neurosis. When the attachment is moderate it will help prepare the ground for adult love.

At this point we may stop to consider how Freud constructed psychoanalysis as a mental therapy on the basis of the theory I have recapitulated. Since the libido was conceptualized as a flowing current, it was also seen as a current whose further flow can be inhibited by obstacles. These obstacles were conceptualized by Freud as fixations. Essentially there were two types. In the first, the libido clings to the parental images and, as it were, refuses to become detached from them; therefore new love objects cannot be found. In the second, a person remains fixated on earlier forms of libidinal development, oral, anal, or phallic stages. Usually, the two types of fixation go together. The oedipus complex is merely the last fixation point on a line of pregenital fixations.

In psychoanalysis, one finds oral fixations that manifest themselves in inhibitions against cannibalistic impulses, anal fixations that survive in the preference for the anus as the organ of sexuality, phallic fixations that manifest themselves as castration anxiety or penis envy, oedipal fixations that manifest themselves in sexual inhibitions in adulthood because the new object is only a displacement for the old incestuous one. Psychoanalysts are specialists in recognizing these fixation points. They make them conscious, thus facilitating the capacity of the libido to renew its forward flow toward genitality and toward nonincestuous love objects. Psychoanalysts therefore are first of all surveyors: they learn from the analysand's biography and from descriptions of his current sexual life the highways and byways of the analysand's libidinal development. What has been distorted or missed in the understanding of the biography will appear in transference in the form of libidinal wishes toward the psychoanalyst. Transference analysis gives the psychoanalyst a second chance to understand the analysand. The need to repeat in transference the vulnerable points of fixation draws attention to these difficulties and highlights them in a way that could not be understood in the mere telling of the biography. In transference, the earlier battles that were fought and lost by the ego are now refought with the help of the psychoanalyst, with a better chance of favorable results.

Long before Freud the connection between infantile and adult sexuality was surmised by poets. John Donne (1572–1671) wrote in the "Good Morrow":

> I wonder by my troth, what thou and I
> Did, till we lov'd? Were we not wean'd till then?
> But suck'd on country pleasures, childishly?
> Or snorted we in the seven sleepers den?
> 'Twas so; But this, all pleasures fancies be.
> If ever any beauty I did see,
> Which I desir'd, and got, t'was but a dream of thee.

Now that "our eyes have been opened" by Freud's recognition of the close affinity between adult love and infancy, we can admire the poet's intuitive

capacity to establish this connection by the use of metaphor and by eliminating the time that passed between being in the womb (the sleepers den),
nursing (sucking on country pleasures), and falling in love. Once the connection has been hinted at, the love the poet feels, the love of the beloved
toward him, becomes anchored in the past and becomes stronger. The poet
achieves a similar result for generations of readers of his poetry who, when
in love, read this poem to each other. (I shall pursue this subject further in
a later chapter.) Only in one respect did Donne fail to tell his love the
whole truth. The last two lines are experientially true when one loves, but
historically the beloved was not prefigured in earlier loves but refound.

The poet can speak in symbols: "sucking on country pleasures, childishly" or "snoring in the seven sleepers den." The use of symbols leaves
the reader to choose how much of the transmitted message he chooses to
interpret or even note. By comparison, the psychoanalyst must be brutal,
for the psychoanalytic equivalent of this poem states, "Before you fell in
love you were in the womb and then you nursed at your mother's breast.
Your love is a wish to refind these childhood pleasures." Furthermore, the
poet is licensed to make the beloved come first. All that preceded her "was
just a dream of thee." The psychoanalyst must reverse the order and give
priority to the mother and at times finds that the beloved is little more
than a dream of the past.

Freud told Jung that it is not desirable for the connection between the
old and the new love to become conscious. For then it may reawaken the
incest taboo. The poet did well to evoke the associations to childhood and
then proceed to reassure himself as well as his love that all his previous
loves were mere prefigurations. Great psychologists uncover the whole
truth. Great poets intuitively recognize profound psychological truths but
mercifully convey to their readers only a part of them.

The difficulty of overcoming the incest taboo led Freud to another discovery: certain neurotic men and women have a rigid precondition for
loving. Some men can fall in love only with women who belong to other
men, others only with promiscuous women. Still others require that the
woman be in need of rescue or at least appear to be so. Freud demonstrated that all such preconditions are techniques by which the primary
processes* convert the woman into a mother-substitute. They are "consequences of the fixation on the mother" (Freud 1910). The examples Freud
chose applied only to males, but they are applicable to women. Some

---

*One of Freud's great discoveries was the differentiation between logical thinking which he
called secondary process, and the kind of logic that governs dreams and neurotic beliefs
which he called primary process.

women can love only married men, older men, or men for whom they feel contempt.

Preconditions for loving, or even for the arousal of sexual wishes, are highly specific. In analyzing the Wolf Man (Freud 1918a) found a highly specific precondition for loving. It will be recalled that in the paper Freud reconstructed that the Wolf Man at the age of one-and-a-half observed his parents in sexual intercourse from behind. At the age of two-and-a-half the Wolf Man saw a nursemaid scrubbing the floor in a similar position. When he saw her he remembered urinating. Freud interpreted this memory as a masculine identification with the father. As an adult the Wolf Man used to fall in love with peasant girls in a kneeling position. "He fell in love with the girl instantly and with irresistable violence although he had not yet been able to get even a glimpse of her face." In each case it was the position of the woman that evoked his love.

I had the opportunity to observe a woman who was sexually aroused only by members of the police force. The policeman stood for law and order, and was therefore a representative of the superego. For her to have a sexual relationship with a policeman meant to be absolved of guilt, as well as to triumph over the law. However, since this woman felt the same excitement with any policeman, I consider this a precondition for sexual gratification and not a precondition for loving.

Deutsch (1930) described the case of a woman whose prerequisite for falling in love was that the man should be a widower still mourning for his dead wife. As Deutsch described it, the widower's mourning affected her patient like a love potion; she wished to be loved like the dead woman had been loved. The fact that the rival was dead had, for this woman, the advantage that it was not necessary for her to become a murderess. Even so, the defensive fantasy that the rival was no longer alive failed to protect the woman from a sense of guilt and every widower eventually had to be renounced.

One may differentiate successful from unsuccessful preconditions for loving. When a precondition fails to resolve the intrapsychic conflict, it leads to the creation of a fate neurosis. To fall in love with one widower is a simple precondition for loving; to fall in love repeatedly and then have to renounce the widowers becomes an example of a fate neurosis. Freud's concept of refinding implies that in the absence of neurosis, the adult love object always recalls the infantile one, but the person is free to select from a large number of traits of the infantile love object. The traits that the two have in common form the bridge that facilitates the transfer of the libido. The term "precondition," on the other hand, suggests that neurosis has severely curtailed freedom of choice, leaving only one avenue open.

Schafer (1977) interprets Freud's preconditions for loving more broadly. Everyone chooses the love partner according to certain unconscious rules. When these rules are discovered in the course of a psychoanalysis, the infantile prototypes of loving are invariably uncovered. In that sense, everyone has his or her own preconditions for loving. In my opinion, Freud reserved the term for a neurotic narrowing of the range of choices.

## Case Example: Refinding with a Precondition for Loving

In my own practice, I have encountered a case of refinding that is of particular interest. Until his third year of life, Mr. A was reared exclusively by a nurse, who, with the advent of a war, had to flee the country without even saying goodbye to him. The nurse seemed to have been a cold, demanding, and meticulous person. She dressed the child carefully, and kept him clean, quiet, and away from the company of other children. When the patient came to treatment as an adult, he was meticulously dressed and made a well-scrubbed impression. To himself, as well as to his family, he was a puzzle. He was devoid of ambition, he seldom worked, he had cronies but no friends. There was nothing that he could tell one person that he could not just as easily communicate to another. He lacked the capacity for intimacy. Sexuality was limited to compulsive masturbation, and he had to prove to himself time and again that he was not injured by this practice. As one would expect, his relationship to the therapist was positive, but lacked discernible intensity. He enjoyed coming and talking, but claimed that the analysis only helped him to fill empty hours. During summer vacations, he insisted that he never missed the analyst or gave the analysis any thought. His character structure and behavior in the analysis fitted well into the category that Gitelson (1958) described as ego defects. I attributed his incapacity to establish intimacy to the coldness of the nurse, as well as to her sudden disappearance, and I repeatedly made this interpretation.

During treatment, a cousin was born. Almost immediately, the patient identified with the cousin, and the relationship with the baby was the first in which I could discern any warmth. He displayed an unusual interest in the baby's welfare. He babysat, played with him, and even invented stories for him. When the boy reached the age at which Mr. A's nurse had left him, he fell in love with the boy's nurse, and thus established his first heterosexual relationship.

Perhaps because the disturbance was so great, the refinding process in this case had to take a concrete form. It seems probable that a period of identification with the infant had to precede the renewal of the capacity to find the lost nurse. It is not easy to determine whether treatment here facilitated this refinding, or whether the great similarity between the infantile and adult situations by itself was sufficient to have created the preconditions for loving. When the situation determines the choice of the love object, the personal characteristic of the refound love object cannot play a significant role.

Many couples reenact refinding. After a love affair, they separate, chance brings them together, and they discover their love with an intensity they earlier did not have. Couples may also marry, divorce, and remarry. In the same unconscious realm, the popularly known "same place next year" encounters represent another form of refinding. Not all refindings are successful. Not infrequently older people try to meet a sweetheart they had known a generation ago but the old flame cannot be rekindled.

Some philosophical observations on love appear at the end of Freud's 1912 essay on love. The tone and the dark conclusions prefigure the ideas that were to find expression in *Civilization and Its Discontents* (1930). Freud argues that we must reckon with the possibility that something in the nature of the sexual instinct itself is unfavorable to the realization of complete satisfaction. He suggests that the biphasic onset of object choice,* the incest barrier, and finally the fact that the adult love object is not the original one, but merely a surrogate, accounts for the inherent state of dissatisfaction in loving (p. 139).

It was not long before Freud's idea of refinding made its way into fiction. Thomas Mann's *The Magic Mountain,* published in 1924, may be the first novel to include a psychoanalyst among its characters. We meet Dr. Kowalsky lecturing to a group of tubercular patients in the sanitarium, explaining to them how sexual deprivation is converted into disease. Hans Castorp's declaration of love to Madame Chauchat shows that the author has eaten from the psychoanalytic tree of knowledge. Hans Castorp tells Madame Chauchat something that few lovers would have been conscious of before Freud, namely, that she, the new love, reminds him of a youthful friend with whom he was homosexually in love during his adolescence. The young man had asked him for a pencil the same way he had asked Madame Chauchat earlier in the evening. The episode described is an example of both refinding and the transfer of the libido from a homosexual fixation back to a heterosexual choice, to a woman who by age and experience stands for the mother.

*By biphasic Freud meant infantile and adolescent sexuality.

In *The Magic Mountain,* Freud's theories found artistic rendering. Freud was of the opinion that such a transfer of the libido can only take place unconsciously. In *The Magic Mountain,* the linkage is described as taking place consciously.

## Love and Narcissism: Freud's Second Theory

There is a painting of Dido and Aeneas attributed to Poussin in the Toledo Museum of Art that can serve as an introduction to this section. It portrays the moment Aeneas is falling in love; we know this because Cupid is aiming his arrow at him. Enraptured Aeneas looks at Dido. She, however, is entirely absorbed in gazing into the mirror while attendants are assisting in her toilet. To fall in love with a woman absorbed in her own image is a pictorial representation of Freud's idea that narcissism in another person is conducive to falling in love (for a different interpretation of this painting, see Hagstrum 1980).

The discovery of narcissism is the second milestone in Freud's exploration of love. The implications of this theory go far and deep. At the center of the stage during this phase is "his majesty the baby," the child that has not as yet lost the feeling of omnipotence, not yet discovered death, and is not yet aware of the limitations gender identity will impose. In the fantasy of every child, there is only one sexual organ, the phallus; castration anxiety and penis envy are as yet unknown. This majestic baby lives in a state of narcissistic self-sufficiency. In subsequent developments, this view will be shattered, the baby will be dethroned when he discovers that he depends on mother's comings and goings and realizes how vulnerable he is to her loving him. If the baby is a girl, she will discover that she lacks an organ boys have. If the baby is a boy, he will fear that the precious organ is endangered and can be cut off, just as he assumes it was cut off in the girls he meets. The discovery of the differences between the sexes will at first be denied but later the child will create various fantasies to account for these differences (Freud 1908a). Other childhood misfortunes, such as birth of siblings, illnesses, and absence of parents, will all add to the narcissistic wound. To varying degrees, depression and anxiety will indicate that the paradise of infancy has been lost.

Ellenberger (1970) reports that the myth of Narcissus became popular in Neo-Romantic literature, which flourished between 1895 and 1900, the years in which Freud published the *Studies on Hysteria* and *The Interpretation of Dreams.*

In 1901, long before Freud coined the term narcissism, he observed:

there thus runs through my thoughts a continuous current of "personal reference," of which I generally have no inkling, but which betrays itself by such instances of my forgetting names. It is as if I were obliged to compare everything I hear about other people with myself; as if my personal complexes were put on the alert whenever another person is brought to my notice. This cannot possibly be an individual peculiarity of my own: it must rather contain an indication of the way in which we understand "something other than ourself" in general. (p. 24)

Sterba (1984) observed that what Strachey translated as "personal reference" appears in German as a word especially coined by Freud, "Eigenbeziehung." It connotes a new psychic territory in which Freud found that we remain attached to ourselves inwardly, even though outwardly we are engaged in an activity in the outside world. In time, this freshly coined German word will become the familiar term "narcissism."

The term narcissism was introduced into psychiatric literature by Naecke and Havelock Ellis to describe a perversion, characterized by excessive self-love and inability to love another. It is the first example, to my knowledge, of a mental condition named after a mythical personage. Later, the term oedipus complex was coined by Freud on an analogous basis.

Sadger's presentation to the Vienna Psychoanalytic Society on November 10, 1909 was the stimulus to Freud's first recorded formulation of narcissism.

Being enamored of oneself (of one's own genitals) is an indispensable stage of development. From there one passes over to similar objects. In general, man has two primary sexual objects, and his future existence depends on which of these objects he remains fixated on. These two objects are for every man the woman (the mother, nurse, etc.) and his own person; and it follows from this that (the question) is to become free from both and not to linger on too long with either. (Nunberg & Federn 1967:312)

Two fixation points threaten the love of every human being: the incestuous fixation and the narcissistic one. In 1914 Freud called the first type of love anaclitic and the second narcissistic. In the published writings, the first reference to the concept of narcissism appears in a modest footnote added in 1910 to the *Three Essays* (1905a), where' Freud discussed object choice of homosexuals:

In all the cases we have examined we have established the fact that the future inverts, in the earliest years of their childhoods, pass through a phase of very intense but short-lived fixation to a woman (usually their mother), and that, after leaving this behind, they identify themselves with a woman and take *themselves* as their sexual object. That is to say, they proceed from a narcissistic basis, and look for a young man who resembles themselves and whom *they* love as their mothers loved *them*. (p. 145)

The two statements taken together illustrate the logic of Freud's position; homosexuality is a variant of normal development. In the essay on narcissism (1914) Freud emphasized that it was in the psychoanalysis of homosexuals that he discovered the type of love that we shall call "mirroring love." Within the context of this book, the passage just quoted is of special significance beyond the problem of homosexuality. Here Freud discovered that identification plays a crucial role in falling in love. Love appears as a sudden reorganization of the inner dramatis personae. The homosexual who falls in love becomes, psychologically speaking, his mother. Another man stands for his former self. A hitherto unsuspected fluidity between self and object representations is the intrapsychic basis for this kind of falling in love.

The narcissistic choice that Freud postulates here for homosexuality is secondary narcissism, because the narcissistic object choice follows upon a disappointment in the primary love object. In the Schreber case, Freud (1911) observed that megalomania is never so vehemently suppressed as when a person is in the grip of an overwhelming love. Freud quotes the Persian mystic poet Rumi (Jalal Al Din) who lived in the twelfth century:

> For when the flames of love arise
> The self the gloomy tyrant dies. (1911:65)

In megalomania, all libidinal cathexes are concentrated on the self, while in love everything is centered on the love object. Megalomania is the sexual overvaluation of the self and parallels the overvaluation of the love object. These observations foreshadow the theory of narcissism published in 1914.

Few passages in Freud's writing are as well known or have been as influential as his 1914 classification of the ways of loving.

> A person may love:
> (1) According to the narcissistic type:
>     (a) what he himself is (i.e. himself),
>     (b) what he himself was,
>     (c) what he himself would like to be,
>     (d) someone who was once part of himself.
> (2) According to the anaclitic (attachment) type:
>     (a) the woman who feeds him,
>     (b) the man who protects him.
>                             (Freud 1914:90)

Typically, homosexual men choose their love object on the narcissistic model while heterosexual men choose on the anaclitic one. While these categories are stated for men, they are applicable to women. A wealth of data is condensed in these lines, particularly if we keep in mind that a love relationship in real life will seldom be confined to only one of the categories enumerated, but will represent a unique blending of a number of these types.

Category I(a), "what he himself is." Here the lover represents little more than the image in the mirror.

Category I(b), "what he himself was," is represented in the narcissistic love of the old for the young. The love of the Eronemus for the Erastes belongs to this category, as does also Shakespeare's young lover in the Sonnets, typical of the way narcissistic parents love their children.

Category I(c), "what he himself would like to be." Here the sexual object has replaced the ego ideal. The bliss of this love is due to the fact that if love is returned, the ego ideal once more loves the person. When this happens, the tension between the ego and the ego ideal is, for the time being, eliminated.

Freud postulated three stages in the development of narcissistic libido: During the first stage, the self (then called "the ego") is the recipient of the total libido; parental criticism and the growing awareness of one's own shortcomings inaugurate the second stage, forcing the transfer of the libido from the self to the ego ideal. At this phase, the child ceases to love himself and directs his love to what he aspires to be. During the third stage the ego ideal is projected and thus becomes what Freud calls the sexual ideal. A person will then love "what possesses the excellence that he never had" (1914:101).

Expressed in current psychoanalytic vocabulary, Freud discovered that it is not only the libido with which object representations are cathected that can be displaced on new objects, but also the libido with which the self and wishful images of the self are cathected can be projected.

Category I(d), "someone who was once part of himself." In this type one loves what had to be repressed in one's self. Freud's example was the love of men who had given up their narcissism for women who have remained narcissistic, the formula being: "I love you because you are as narcissistic as I was before I had to repress my narcissism or I love you because you are as narcissistic as I never dared to be."

Anaclitic love is also vulnerable. I am familiar with the case of a man who first "fell in love" with a woman who resembled his mother. The transfer was successful, but since the original mother was more hated than loved, her replica shared the same fate. He then fell in love with another woman who reminded him of his father, whom he loved dearly. But in this case too he was disappointed every time the woman he loved did not conform in her behavior to the image of the father.

The discovery of narcissistic love ranks among Freud's important discoveries. Traditionally (as I've shown in chapter 4), self-love was contrasted with the love for the other. Now Freud added a third category, that of narcissistic love. It is a love for another human being modeled on the love of the self. The analyses which I have made in chapter 4 of the myth of Narcissus and Shakespeare's sonnets could never have been made were it not for Freud's discovery of narcissistic love.

Freud now formulated an antithesis between ego libido and object libido: excess object libido depletes narcissism. The highest form of development of which object libido is capable is in the state of being in love. Then the subject is ready to sacrifice his own personality in favor of a love object (p. 76).

From the storehouse of narcissistic libido, Freud derived the overestimation of the love object characteristic of many who are in love. Neurotic people in particular are in danger of impoverishing the self by excessive object cathexis.

A massive transfer of libido, Freud thought, is not without dangers. Falling in love can impoverish the ego to the point where self-esteem is catastrophically lowered. The fortunate lover has self-esteem restored by having his love reciprocated by the idealized love object. In extreme cases, "The object has so to speak consumed the ego" (Freud 1921:113). From 1914 on, Freud spoke of love increasingly in economic (quantitative) terms:

The difference between an ordinary erotic object cathexis* and the state of being in love is that in the latter, incomparably more cathexis passes over to the object and that the ego empties itself as if it were in favor of the object. (1927:164–165)

Freud could now enlarge upon what happens intrapsychically when one falls in love. Normally, there is a state of tension between ego and ego ideal, with the ego ideal demanding more than the ego can accomplish. The tension between ego and ego ideal has beneficial as well as detrimental effects. It spurs toward achievement but it can also create feelings of dissatisfaction and despair. In a state of love, the ego ideal is projected on the partner. This projection is possible because, in childhood, the parents were idealized by the child before the ego ideal was formed. The lover,

---

*The term cathexis belongs to Freud's metapsychological language. It refers to a concentration of hypothetical quantities of love or hate on one particular person.

becoming childish, regresses to this state. When this happens the beloved will receive the same idealization as did the parents. When the ego ideal is projected, the tension between ego and ego ideal is temporarily abolished—the same mechanism accounts also for manic states. When love is reciprocated it is as if the self were suddenly loved by the ego ideal; this is experienced as the proverbial bliss, what Proust called "filling me with precious essence," and popularly known as "living on cloud nine." Exchange between ego ideal and the beloved takes place unconsciously, the experience of bliss alone becomes conscious.

If the idealization is strong and the lovers cannot imagine their love being reciprocated, they may consider themselves too unworthy of the idealized beloved and refrain from wooing. Freud (1921) stressed the similarity between love and the behavior of a crowd toward its leader. In both cases the ego ideal has been projected. Annie Reich (1940) observed the phenomenon of women who were not themselves capable of criminal behavior, who became criminals when they loved such men. These women take over their lover's ego ideal.

Freud's first theory was essentially genetic in orientation, emphasizing the past. The second was economic in nature, emphasizing the transfer of hypothetical quantities of libido from the self to the object. In Freud's conceptualization, falling in love occurs at the moment in which narcissistic libido is being transformed into object libido. This was a significant new insight. We may not be aware of it, but normally, that is, when we are not in love, we experience discomfort due to too much self-involvement. We know that this self-involvement was a burden only after we experience the exhilarating feeling of love. Lovers experience themselves as infinitely richer than they had previously felt themselves to be. They feel free both from envy and hostility. We recall how Romeo refused to fight Tybalt, Juliet's cousin and his enemy, because his love for Juliet made him love the whole Capulet clan. Romeo's refusal to fight, in turn, led to Mercutio's death, an act that doomed the lovers. Shakespeare's play can be read as a cautionary tale that shows the danger of repressing all hostility in the state of being in love.

How love achieves a reconciliation between ego ideal and ego, eliminating feelings of inadequacy and envy, was described by Shakespeare in Sonnet No. 29.

> When in disgrace with Fortune and men's eyes,
> I all alone beweep my outcast state
> And trouble deaf heaven with my bootless cries,
> And look upon myself and curse my fate,

Wishing me like to one more rich in hope,
Featured like him, like him with friends possessed,
Desiring this man's art, and that man's scope,
With what I most enjoy contented least;
Yet in these thoughts myself almost despising,
Haply I think on thee, and then my state,
Like to the lark at break of day arising
From sullen earth, sings hymns at heaven's gate;
For thy sweet love remembered such wealth brings,
That then I scorn to change my state with kings.

Many lovers have reported that one of the greatest rewards in love is the sudden freedom from jealousy and envy. "No one has more than I, and I need envy no other man or woman," lovers frequently exclaim.

A link may exist between the discovery of narcissism and the literature of the time. Two years prior to the appearance of Freud's theory of narcissism, Thomas Mann published *Death in Venice*. Never to my knowledge has narcissistic love for what one was and no longer is been sketched so sharply as in the love of the aging Aschenbach for the adolescent Tadzio.

The relationship between Freud and Thomas Mann has interested a number of psychoanalytic writers; usually Mann's indebtedness to Freud has been investigated. In describing *Death in Venice*, Mann wrote in 1925, "Without Freud I would never have thought of dealing with this erotic material or I would certainly have treated it differently" (Lehmann 1970:202). On the other hand, there is nothing in Freud's writing prior to 1914 that could have given Mann the specific idea for *Death in Venice*. Freud, who described himself as one of Mann's oldest readers and admirers, may well have read *Death in Venice* before he wrote the paper on narcissism. Freud's paper and Mann's novella breathe the same air.

## Freud's Third Theory

Freud's third theory on love is found in the paper *Instincts and their Vicissitudes* (1915a). It was the reading and possibly the misreading of this paper that was responsible for the widespread belief cited earlier that Freud confused love with sex. It happens to be one of Freud's most difficult essays and it is difficult precisely because Freud himself is in inner conflict.* Freud tries to stay within the confines of instinct theory, but

---

*My teacher, Paul Federn, one of Freud's early associates, observed that Freud is a pleasure to read except when he is struggling against himself. Another example of a work written in a state of inner struggle is *Inhibition, Symptom and Anxiety* (1926).

reluctantly he recognizes that love cannot be explained on the basis of instinct alone. For the first time, the term ego appears in connection with love.

Many psychoanalytic writers and particularly Lacan (1978) have regarded this paper as the one containing Freud's most important contribution to the understanding of love.

Freud observed in 1915: "The object of the instinct is what is most variable about the instinct, and not originally connected with it but becomes assigned to it by consequence of being peculiarly fitted to make satisfaction possible" (1915a:122).

I have already shown earlier that Freud attributed this view to the Greeks. In passages such as these Freud deemphasized the role of the beloved. This is so contrary to what lovers feel, namely that it is the excellence of the beloved that is the reason for their love, that it was easy to assume that Freud understood little about love.

The theory I will now discuss was formulated only one year after the essay on narcissism. Freud confronted the problem that many of his critics had contended that he never faced, namely how the drive for sex becomes love. The problem was never entirely resolved. Nevertheless Freud made some pertinent observations and what he said in that paper had a great influence on subsequent psychoanalytic developments.

The case of love and hate acquires a special interest from the circumstance that it refuses to be fitted into our scheme of the instincts. It is impossible to doubt that there is the most intimate relation between these two opposite feelings and sexual life, but we are naturally unwilling to think of love as being some kind of special component instinct of sexuality in the same way as the others we have been discussing. We should prefer to regard loving as the expression of the whole sexual current of feeling; but this idea does not clear up our difficulties, and we cannot see what meaning to attach to an opposite content of this current.

Loving admits not merely of one, but of three opposites. In addition to the antithesis "loving—hating", there is the other one of "loving—being loved"; and, in addition to these, loving and hating taken together are the opposite of the condition of unconcern or indifference. (1915a:133)

In passages such as these, Freud invites the reader to share his groping for a solution which he has not as yet found.

If we follow Freud's inner struggle, we will observe that he attempts to understand love as the whole current of sexual feelings, but then he becomes dissatisfied with this view. In my opinion, we should not drop the idea so hastily, for the concept "the whole current of sexual feeling" is entirely novel. It is not to be equated with mere sex, but rather connotes that all the sexual wishes have become centered on one person. No other sexual objects are desired, nor is there a yearning for other sexual practices than those that have found expression in the relationship. This may not be a sufficient definition of love but it is much more than an ordinary sexual attraction. We recall that, in Freud's view, the sexual drive originally consisted of component instincts, each one seeking its own outlet. The concentration of all the sexual components on one person is an important aspect of love, one that has never been noticed before. In the next chapter I will show that when Freud wrote *Gradiva* (1907), this was his definition of love. In the passage quoted above, he recognizes that this formulation leads to fresh difficulties.

The quote further illustrates that Freud recognized the existence of a contradiction between his theory of sexuality and his theory of love. Love and hate are no longer seen as simple manifestations of instincts. They have become emotions, and an emotion is characterized by the fact that the person toward whom the emotion is felt is not easily interchangeable as is the case with the object of drives.

Finally, in the passage quoted, Freud suggests that we attempt to understand the nature of love by observing its three antitheses: (1) loving as opposed to being loved, (2) loving as opposed to feeling indifferent, and (3) loving as opposed to hating. The first antithesis was exploited by Shakespeare: narcissists love only because they mistakenly believe that they are loved.

The second category, where love turns to indifference, tells us little about the fate of the libido. We know that love can be displaced to another person, even to another gender. It can also regress back to self-love, or terminate in a depression when the hate of the superego is turned on the ego.

As to the third category, the dichotomy loving-hating, we frequently have the chance to observe in the course of treatment how after some estrangement, love turns into anger and hate. Those who undergo this change of feeling are convinced that they are no longer in love. However, as long as the emotion, be it love or hate, is strong, the relationship persists, although it now bears a negative sign. Some loves that turn into a hate that never heals make new love impossible and require psychoanalytic help.

A few pages later in the same paper, Freud made a fresh attempt to understand love.

Love and hate cannot be made use of for the relations of *instincts* to their objects, but are reserved for the relations of the *total ego* to objects. (p. 137)

The fact that we are not in the habit of saying of a single sexual instinct that it loves its object, but regard the relation of the ego to its sexual object as the most appropriate case in which to employ the word "love"—this fact teaches us that the word can only begin to be applied in this relation after there has been a synthesis of all the component instincts of sexuality under the primacy of the genitals and in the service of the reproductive function. (p. 138)

The language is still clumsy but a new idea is in the process of being formulated. Love is not an instinct; it is the ego or the total ego that loves its objects. Libido and love are no longer synonymous. The sexual instinct as such cannot explain the nature of love. This was a very important reformulation, for now love, being an emotion, belongs to the sphere of the ego.

Once Freud shifted emphasis from instinct to ego, he needed a developmental theory to explain the capacity to love. This is how he conceptualized the process: the nascent ego finds satisfaction of his instinctual impulses autoerotically, that is, in sucking and in early forms of masturbation. Gradually, the child learns that it is dependent on objects. The ego now tries to incorporate into itself the pleasurable aspects of the caretaker. It becomes a "pleasure ego"; whatever is pleasurable becomes part of the self, while what is unpleasurable is regarded with indifference and remains outside the self. During these developmental stages, the polarities are ego-external world and love-indifference. This dichotomy can be maintained as long as narcissism prevails. Freud put it thus: "Love is derived from the capacity of the ego to satisfy some of its instinctual impulses auto-erotically by obtaining organ-pleasure. It is originally narcissistic, then passes over on to objects, which have been incorporated into the extended ego" (p. 138).

Once the existence of objects outside the self can no longer be denied and these external objects become sources of pleasure, the third dichotomy, ego and love object, emerges. Freud postulated that because these objects give pleasure, they are loved. The realization that pleasure depends on objects existing outside of the self is followed by the recognition that one is at the mercy of these objects. Everyday experience confirms that love can turn into hate. Theoretically this was not easily explained, for Freud had difficulty in accepting the idea that one drive can turn into another.

Love itself is not transformed into hate. "Not until the genital organization is established, does love become the opposite of hate" (p. 139). When it seems that love turned into hate, what actually happens is a regression from the genital position to a pregenital one.

If a love-relation with a given object is broken off, hate not infrequently emerges in its place, so that we get the impression of a transformation of love into hate. This account of what happens leads on to the view that the hate . . . is here reinforced by a regression of the love to the sadistic preliminary stage; so that the hate acquires an erotic character and the continuity of a love-relation is ensured. (p. 139)

When the formerly loved person is now hated, the relationship itself has not been given up.

In 1921 Freud summarized his third theory of love.

Libido is an expression taken from the theory of the emotions. We call by that name the energy regarded as a quantitative magnitude (though not at present actually measurable), of those instincts which have to do with all that may be comprised under the word "love." The nucleus of what we mean by love naturally consists (and this is what is commonly called love, and what the poets sing of) of sexual love with sexual union as its aim. But we do not separate from this—what in any case has a share in the name "love"—on the one hand, self-love, and on the other, love for parents and children, friendship and love for humanity in general, and also devotion to concrete objects and to abstract ideas. (Freud 1921:90)

Libido is the energy, and love once more becomes an instinct, an instinct that attaches itself to a wide variety of objects. A clarification that was reached in 1915 that linked love with ego and separated it from instinct is no longer in evidence. More confusing still was the idea that libido is not a concept—an abstraction through which certain clinical observations can be explained—but is a quantity of energy which, in time, will become, like electricity, measurable.

It is evident from this discussion that what mattered most to Freud was that the link between love and sex should not be lost.

In the same essay, Freud once more returned to the theory of the two currents, but now used it to differentiate between love and lust.

In one class of cases being in love is nothing more than object-cathexis on the part of the sexual instincts with a view to direct sexual satisfaction, a cathexis which expires, moreover, when this aim has been reached. (Freud 1921:111)

More often, however, the adolescent succeeds in bringing about a certain degree of synthesis between the unsensual, heavenly love and the sensual, earthly love, and his relation to his sexual object is characterized by the interaction of uninhibited instincts and of instincts uninhibited in their aim. The depth to which anyone is in love, as contrasted with his purely sensual desire, may be measured by the size of the share taken by the aim-inhibited instincts of affection. (Freud 1921:112)

Although at first reading, this paragraph seems no more than a repetition of "the two-current theory" of 1905, there are significant differences. We note first the platonic vocabulary differentiating heavenly from earthly love. Freud is closer here to Plato than he was in 1905. Of greater significance is the derivation of love, not from the confluence of the two currents, but directly from the tender one. Freud, it seems to me, has retracted much of what he said earlier. The tender current as distinct from the sexual is no longer a phenomenon of latency, but follows an independent course, through the life cycle. Since I have suggested that love arises at the point of the confluence of the two currents, I see Freud's later formulation as a retreat to those ideas on love that were current before Freud. By abandoning the idea of confluence of the tender and the sexual drive which he had developed in 1905, Freud diminished a uniquely creative contribution that he had made earlier.

In the postscript to *Group Psychology* (1921), Freud commented:

Those sexual instincts which are inhibited in their aims have a great functional advantage over those which are uninhibited. Since they are not capable of really complete satisfaction, they are especially adapted to create permanent ties; while those instincts which are directly sexual incur a loss of energy each time they are satisfied, and must wait to be renewed by a fresh accumulation of sexual libido, so that meanwhile the object may have been changed. (p. 139)

Freud goes on to say:

On the other hand, it is also very usual for directly sexual impulses, short-lived in themselves, to be transformed into a lasting and purely affectionate tie; and the consolidation of a passionate love marriage rests to a large extent upon this process. (Ibid.)

Freud reiterated his belief in the permanence of aim-inhibited ties in 1923, when he compared "the affectionate relationships between parents and children, which were originally fully sexual" with "the emotionalities in a marriage" of long duration, which also had their origins in sexual attractions" (p. 258). Implicit in these formulations is the idea that what happened during latency repeats itself once more in relationships of long duration.

Freud reiterated his mistrust of sexual passion as a binding force ten years later: "First marriages of young women which they have entered into when they were most passionately in love" come to grief from unavoidable disappointment while second marriages, presumably less passionate, "turn out better" (Freud 1931:234).

These ideas expressed by Freud after 1920 hardly fall into the image that most people have of him, as the liberator of human sexuality. They show that Freud did not believe that sexual striving can be integrated into a matrix of an enduring human relationship. The human being in this view must either sacrifice stability and permanence in his most basic relationship, or sacrifice the full capacity for sexual pleasure. Once more Freud asserted his belief that "aim-inhibited" and "aim-deflected" strivings are the basis for sublimation and therefore more reliable for the building of an enduring relationship (see also Hartmann 1955:223). These last pessimistic appraisals by Freud went unnoticed. Psychoanalysts assumed that if the two currents could be united in the course of a psychoanalysis, potency and capacity to love could be combined in the relationship to one person.

Freud's ideas on love were formulated within the topographic model. By analogy to dream theory, the instigator of love is the prohibited oedipal wish. The person one actually falls in love with is modeled after the day residue of the dream that awakens the dormant wish. The fact that the similarity between the new love object and the old is not known to the lover testifies to the success of a force analogous to the dream work.* Dreaming and falling in love take place in a state of benign regression; normally, we expect no structural change to occur as a result of either dreams or love.

The topographic model was particularly well-suited to explain love at first sight, when the individuality and complex character of the love object play only an insignificant role. In falling in love at first sight, reality testing is excluded in a way that is reminiscent of dreams. The dreamlike quality that is typical of falling in love is due to the absence or the greatly diminished participation of the ego. The equation of dream and love is a familiar theme in poetry; for example in "The Dream," John Donne wrote:

> Deare love, for nothing lesse than thee
> Would I have broke this happy dreame,
>     It was a theame
> for reason, much too strong for phantasie,
> Therefore thou wak'dst me wisely; yet
> My dream thou brok'st not, but continued'st it,
> Thou art so thruth, that thoughts of thee suffice,
> To make dreames thruths; and fables histories;
> Enter these arms, for since thou thought'st it best,
> Not to dreame all my dreame, let's act the rest.

---

*Freud's dream theory assumes that the dream is a compromise formation between three psychic forces: the awakened unconscious wish which is censored in the daytime, the event that happened during the day which gave rise to this awakening called the day residue, and the wish of the person to sleep which in turn forces the unconscious wish to undergo distortion so that awakening is not necessary.

When in 1923 Freud added the structural point of view with its emphasis on ego, id, and superego to the topographical model, he did not return to illuminate love from the structural point of view. This transition was accomplished by other analysts and will be discussed in chapter 19. Here I wish only to add that the topographic point of view with its emphasis on the unconscious and the past tends to make love only a replica. The ego, on the other hand, is conceptualized as less bound to the past and capable of finding new solutions to old problems. Therefore, under the impact of the structural point of view the ideas on love were bound to change.

If we look backwards from Freud to Schopenhauer and Stendhal (as the two who have expressed the knowledge about love in the nineteenth century), Freud's achievement is striking.

Summarizing the chapter, I conclude that Freud's three theories of love were addressed to different aspects of loving. The first emphasized the unconscious dependency of the adult love choice on infantile prototypes. It also explained why some have difficulty in combining love with sexual desire. The second theory described from a metapsychological point of view what happens intrapsychically when one falls in love: how love of the self is converted into the love of the other by the projection of the ego ideal. The third theory dealt with the process of maturation that leads to the capacity to have an enduring relationship free from a too-destructive ambivalence. Here Freud affirmed that love is more than a manifestation of the sexual instinct, because the whole ego is involved. Such a love, Freud thought, becomes possible only when the genital level of libidinal development has been reached. Freud thus affirmed that the state of being in love need not be identical with the capacity to love over a long period of time.

# 15

# *Biographical Notes to Freud's Discoveries on Love*

The reader who followed my effort to trace the historical evolution of Freud's ideas on love may well have become curious about what is known about Freud's own loves. Fortunately, in a disguised form Freud left us an account of his first adolescent love in his paper of 1899 on screen memories. There Freud disguised himself as "a man of university education, aged 38, who has taken an interest in psychological questions ever since I [Freud] was able to relieve him of a slight phobia by means of psychoanalysis." That this was no other than Freud himself was discovered by Bernfeld (1949). Indeed, Freud's self-analysis did result in the cure of a train phobia as well as a phobia of visiting Rome.

The young woman, Gisela Fluss, whom Freud fell in love with, was the sister of his close friend. It took place when Freud was sixteen years old. The occasion was a visit to the town of his birth and early infancy. Following Freud's discoveries of preconditions for loving, one can say that the reencounter with the world of his childhood must have contributed to this falling in love. Because she was the sister of his best friend, we may also assume that the love represented a transfer of homosexual feelings from brother to sister. Eissler believed that this falling in love was traumatic for Freud, that he felt helpless against the sudden onrush of passion. The love soon turned into scorn. Freud therefore knew that love can turn into its opposite from a personal experience. For years afterward Freud was the scientist uninterested in women in a way reminiscent of the archeologist in *Gradiva* whom I will discuss later.

Eissler discovered an astonishing detail. Gisela's nickname was Ichtyosaura (an aquatic reptile of dinosaurus proportions). As research assistant, Freud was dissecting eels, descendants of Ichtyosaurus, whose bisexuality Freud was studying. The screen memory itself deals with two boys suddenly attacking a girl and taking away from her by force the flowers she had picked. In the memory Freud recognized the theme of defloration. He was, however, puzzled by how one man could assist another in defloration. Today this presents no problem, for we are familiar with so-called "gang bangs" taking place in fraternities and two boys visiting a prostitute together to encourage each other. The homosexual component also plays a role in such events. In 1899 Freud's self-analysis was not sufficiently well advanced to understand such a homosexual component.

Fortunately Freud's capacity to love was not permanently damaged. We are in possession of many love letters to his betrothed, Martha Bernays. One must note, however, that these love letters were not continued after the wedding. It is possible that this was the biographical fact behind Freud's belief that sexual love is short-lived while inhibited love relationships are more reliable.

In the previous chapter I outlined the developments of Freud's ideas on love as they appear in his published writings. As I was working over this material, I came upon some hitherto unnoticed biographical data that throw light on the way some of these discoveries were made. My material deals with the first phase of his theorizing, between 1905 and 1912.*

During these years Freud had a lively exchange of letters with C. G. Jung (McGuire 1974). We also have the minutes of the meetings of the Vienna Psychoanalytic Society (Nunberg and Federn 1962–1975), where Freud expressed himself more freely than in his published writings.

In the previous chapter I described three theories of love by Freud. The second period of Freud's theorizing on love (1914) was ushered in by Jung's defection and the challenge his ideas presented to Freud. The third period of his writings on love grew out of close collaboration with Abraham and the influence of Abraham's ideas on Freud is discernible.

Jung had developed a father transference to Freud and this transference took a negative turn. Freud's relationship with Jung can, in my opinion, best be characterized as a desexualized love relationship. In intensity, Freud's feelings for Jung were close to the feelings Freud previously held for Fliess. If Fleiss was the idealized father and brother, then Jung was the idealized son and "heir apparent." Abraham was close to Freud and his

---

*Beyond what I have said above, I will not deal in this chapter with what is known about Freud's love life. An interested reader should consult the idealized biography by Jones (1953) as well as Fromm's *Critical Comments* (1959). For an interesting controversy about Freud's adolescent love, see Gedo & Pollock (1976:72–77).

lifelong disciple, but Abraham never evoked the personal feeling in Freud that Jung did. The minutes of the meetings and his correspondence with Jung show that what appears as an effortless creation of Freud's genius in his printed works was actually achieved through an inner struggle.

On November 28, 1906, Freud reported to the Vienna Society that he was planning "a study of man's love life." In a more personal vein he wrote to Jung from Rome on September 19, 1907: "When I have totally overcome my libido (in the common sense), I shall undertake to write a love life of mankind" (McGuire, 1974:89). This is indeed a strange sentence to come from the man who impressed upon the world the ubiquity and power of the sexual drive. It represents, however, an old idea that has come down from Plato. In the first book of the *Republic*, Plato says:

"How do you feel about love, Sophocles? are you still capable of it?" to which he replied, "Hush! if you please: to my great delight I have escaped from it, and feel as if I had escaped from a frantic and savage master." I thought then, as I do now, that he spoke wisely. For unquestionably old age brings us profound repose and freedom from this and other passions. When the appetites have abated, and their force is diminished, the description of Sophocles is perfectly realized. It is like being delivered from a multitude of furious masters.

Freud's book on the love life of mankind did not materialize; only three papers appeared which may have constituted aspects of the book he had in mind (Freud 1910a; 1912; 1918). A fourth paper, "The Theme of the Three Caskets" (1913a), which I will discuss, belongs in the series, but it was not so designated by Freud. It seems plausible that Freud thought that love would become a topic beyond the confines of psychopathology, to be illuminated by psychoanalysis.

At the same November 28 meeting of the Vienna Society, Freud was further quoted as saying:

"In the final analysis, the treatment accorded the child is decisive for his love life. People in love, for example, use for each other pet names by which they were called during childhood. Man becomes childish when he is in love . . . Love is said to be irrational, but its irrational aspect can be traced back to an infantile source: the compulsion in love is infantile. Such a condition of love found a very beautiful expression in Goethe's *Werther* when young Werther enters the room and immediately falls in love with the maiden. He sees her buttering slices of bread and is reminded of his mother" (Nunberg and Federn: I, 66).

The passage is of great interest because there is nothing like it in any of Freud's published writings. In the published writings of the same period Freud mentions the selection of the new love object on the model of the parent, but he does not suggest, as he does so clearly here, that love itself is a regression to infancy. It was Balint who, as we shall see, stressed this aspect of love. Nor did Freud call love a compulsion although many have seen it as such. The allusion to *Werther,* in the passage quoted above, is significant. As Eissler (1971:467) has pointed out, Freud derived important clinical findings from works of literature and, later, confirmed or refound them in his work with patients.

The scene in which Werther falls in love is richer in symbols than Freud's summary would suggest. There is no hint that Werther is reminded of his mother; it is Freud who discovers that the woman one falls in love with reminds one of one's mother, and he attributes his discovery to Goethe. Werther comes upon the young woman dressed in white, holding a knife and a loaf of black bread. What impresses young Werther is the justice with which she distributes the evening bread to the children according to their size and appetite. Significant, too, is her remark that the children will accept their evening meal from nobody else. She wields the "phallic" knife, belongs to another, is pure, and is a feeder who plays no favorites. No substitute for her is acceptable—all of which are a powerful combination conducive to falling in love. Great writers usually take care to motivate the moment of falling in love, as Goethe did. For example, Anna Karenina is open to falling in love on her visit to St. Petersburg because this is the first time she is separated from her son, who no longer needs her.

If we apply Freud's ideas on psychic determinism to the Werther scene, we will note the similarity with Freud's (1899) own screen memory. Freud, too, fell in love at first sight. In Freud's case, also, the color of the girl's dress played a role, as did the fresh-tasting country bread and the woman (a nurse) who wielded the knife. It seems probable that Freud had not yet discovered the mother-figure behind his adolescent love when he analyzed his own screen memory, but completed the self-analysis when he came upon the scene of Werther's falling in love and attributed his own discovery to the idealized Goethe. The same fatal knife appeared again when Freud fell in love with his future wife, Martha. According to Jones (1953), "on this occasion, [Freud] was arrested by the sight of a merry maiden peeling an apple and chatting gaily at the family table ... That very first glimpse was a fatal one" (p. 103).

The correspondence with Jung further demonstrates that Freud frequently drew upon literature to enrich his insight into the nature of love. "Our love objects form series (he told Jung), one is a recurrence of another (*The Master of Palmyra*) and each one is a reactivation of an unconscious infantile love, but this love must remain unconscious; as soon as it is aroused to consciousness, it holds the libido fast instead of guiding it onward, and a new love becomes impossible" (McGuire 1974:100).

*The Master of Palmyra* mentioned in Freud's letter to Jung is a five-act play by Adolf von Wilbrandt, published in 1889. All but forgotten today, the play was well known to Freud's generation. It is a sentimental variant on the theme of Faust. The hero, a general of Palmyra living at the end of the Roman pagan era, is granted immortality. A woman companion is given the opportunity to return in every generation in a new disguise and becomes each time the beloved of the immortal hero. As his life continues, he finds himself alone in the increasingly strange Christian world and, in contrast to his earlier wish for immortality, he longs for death. The same woman appears for the last time and in her arms he finds the wished-for death.

I believe that *The Master of Palmyra* provided the stimulus not only for Freud's idea that love objects come in series but, probably, also for "The Theme of the Three Caskets" which Freud took from Shakespeare's *The Merchant of Venice*. There Freud (1913a) said: "the three forms taken by the figure are ... the mother herself, the beloved one who is chosen after her pattern, and lastly the Mother Earth who receives him once more. But it is in vain that an old man yearns for the love of woman as he had it first from his mother; the third of the Fates alone, the silent Goddess of Death, will take him into her arms" (p. 301).

If my reconstruction is correct, "The Three Caskets" paper, by its content as well as publication date, belongs to the series of papers on love and may represent Freud's more personal feelings. The idea that a man reencounters in his love the same woman from infancy to death is so logically rooted in the oedipus complex that one could easily believe that it was original to Freud. However, Ellenberger (1970) showed that it was a prevalent belief in the nineteenth century before Freud. He cited Nietzsche's aphorism: "Every man keeps in himself an image of the woman deriving from that of his mother, and according to the image he will be prone to respect or despise women" (p. 708).

The unconscious equation of death and womb has a long tradition. Schopenhauer (1858) stated: "If the universal mother carelessly sends forth her children without protection to a thousand threatening dangers, this can be only because she knows that, when they fall, they fall back into her womb where they are safe and secure" (p. 473).

Freud's 1910 paper on love was discussed on May 19, 1909 at the meeting of the Vienna Psychoanalytic Society. A striking difference between the printed version and the oral presentation aroused my interest. The published paper opens with an apology for encroaching upon the territory of the creative writer in depicting the necessary conditions for loving. In the *Minutes,* a writer who was Freud's inspiration is cited:

Another case of more deep-going prerequisite for love was recently related by Paul Lindau in a feuilleton in the *Neue Freie Presse:* a man, writing to his friend, tells him the story of his love affair, which he himself finds completely puzzling. The man, who, since his mother's death, had led an altogether solitary life, one day became engaged to a young girl, who was lovable in every respect. Accompanying her is a plain-looking girl, a close relative of hers, to whom he does not pay the slightest attention. One day, the young man rescues this (other) girl from the sea and when she, almost benumbed, is restored to life, he falls in love with her and (ultimately) *marries her.* To the psychoanalyst, there is nothing at all to question about this affair; for this man, the prerequisite for love is a (dead) body that one can love; in the man's introductory remarks, there is already the intimation that this refers to the dead mother. (Nunberg and Federn 1962–1975:238)

The *feuilleton,* entitled "The Resurrected One," appeared in the *Neue Freie Presse* in two installments on October 22 and 23, 1908—eight months before Freud's presentations to the Vienna Psychoanalytic Society. Its author, Lindau, complains in the prologue that he had never before experienced the inadequacy of psychology as strongly. "Our knowledge," he continued, "of the human psyche has not outgrown its baby shoes." (*"Niemals habe ich das Unzulaengliche unserer Psychologie so empfunden wie jetzt. Unsere ganze Seelenkunde steckt noch in den Kinderschuhen".*) It is easy to imagine how forcibly this sentence must have struck Freud. The author then describes his engagement to a worthy woman for whom he felt a great deal of sympathy but little passion. When he rescued the poor and plain-looking relative, he did not marry her as Freud's summary states, but rather, for reasons he could not explain, broke off his earlier engagement. There is no reference to a "dead mother." If the rescued woman represented the mother, as Freud postulates, her representative vetoed the marriage to another woman; although she herself did not meet the necessary precondition for loving, Lindau's account makes it clear that the original choice lacked the passion of love. Even before the rescue, the reporter was ambivalent. The *feuilleton* does not illustrate Freud's preconditions for loving. Once more, as in the case of Werther, Freud credited another man with his discovery. In this instance, he could do so only through a memory distortion.

## Freud's Analysis of Gradiva Revisited

Freud's (1907) analysis of Jensen's novella *Gradiva* is seldom read and no longer quoted in the psychoanalytic literature. There was a time when this work ranked higher in the estimation of psychoanalysts, when it was customary to have a copy of the Vatican relief, around which the story of Gradiva has been woven, adorning the consultation room. As a historical document of Freud's evolving ideas on love the *Gradiva* is of great interest.

It might be useful to summarize the plot of Jensen's novel.

A young archaeologist, Norbert Hanold, lives immersed in Greco-Roman antiquities. He has become indifferent toward women and at a party fails to recognize his childhood sweetheart, Zoe Bertgang. In the Vatican museum he comes across a relief of a young beauty lifting her hemline and revealing a raised ankle. He falls in love with the relief and fantasies that she lived in Pompeii and perished in the eruption of Mount Vesuvius. He now "becomes engrossed in an experiment." He compares her gait with the walk of women in his native northern city. While engaged in this experiment he chances upon his childhood love and nearly "discovers" the same beautiful gait. Interest in the movement of women's legs revives his sexual wishes. The libido, as Freud puts it, long repressed, now begins to return from repression. A dream that he meets the girl in Pompeii draws him to that city. He is now fully in love with the phantom and calls her Gradiva, the girl of splendid walk . . . He is oblivious of the connection between the Latin "Gradiva" and the German "Bertgang," which contains the word "gang," meaning stepping. He is also unaware of the transformation of her first name, Zoe, meaning "life" in Greek, into a woman dead for two thousand years. On the way to Pompeii, he is annoyed by honeymoon couples, also attracted to the city. He first mistakes them for brothers and sisters. It was this mistake that gave Freud the idea that Jensen had a sister. When he cannot help overhear their love-making he dreams that the famous Apollo Belvedere (in the Vatican museum) is carrying away the Venus (in the Capitoline Museum). Within the context of the evolving story, the dream is well-placed. Jensen shows how the young archaeologist is displacing sexually disturbing impressions into the classical past. Conversely, it also shows us how the statues of antiquity are awakened in his dreams to sexual life. Here too, the inanimate crosses the threshold into the animate.

The childhood lovers meet in Pompeii, and Hanold is convinced that she is Gradiva revenant. Zoe grasps the nature of his delusion, and in a few brilliantly conducted meetings, cures the delusion and reawakens Hanold's love for her.

When first published, Freud was happy with his analysis of *Gradiva* for he wrote to Jung: "this little book was written on sunny days and I myself derived great pleasure from it. True, it says nothing that is new to us, but I believe it enables us to enjoy our riches" (McGuire 1974:51). Jones, in his biography of Freud (1955) praises it as one of the three writings to which the word charming can most fittingly be applied; the other two are *Leonardo* (1910) and "The Theme of the Three Caskets" (1913a) (Jones, p. 341).

Eissler (1971) found the *Gradiva* to be a perfect specimen of endopoetic research. Where the analytic interpretation does not go beyond the literary work, it draws all the inferences from the work itself and therefore does not utilize the biography of the writer as a source of insight. Eissler expressed admiration for the fact that while the dreams of Norbert Hanold, the hero of the novel, were "artificial dreams" created by the novelist, they could be interpreted by the application of the technique developed in Freud's *Interpretation of Dreams* (1900), a work unknown to Jensen. If I do not quite follow Eissler here, it is because, as I have pointed out elsewhere (Bergmann 1966), dreams in literature, unlike dreams in real life, have to be understood by the reader. They are therefore richer in what I called the communicative function of the dream and much less a resistance to interpretations than dreams of analysands.

Now that we have the Freud-Jung correspondence available (McGuire 1974) it is evident that Freud and Jung read Jensen's other novels and speculated about the biographical roots of Gradiva. Freud made the following biographical construction:

But now what do you think of the following bold construction? His little sister had always been ailing, she had a horse-hoof foot and limped, later she had died of tuberculosis. This pathological element had to be excluded from the embellishing fantasy. But one day, the grieving author came across the relief and saw that this deformity, the horse-hoof foot, could be refashioned into a mark of beauty. Gradiva was now complete—a new triumph of wish fulfilling fantasy.

(pp. 100–101)

It should be kept in mind that during this period, Freud was convinced that works of literature arose directly from daydreams. It turned out that Jensen had no sister; the relationship between biography and the work was, therefore, more complex than Freud thought at that time.

The hero's cure comes through the insight that Gradiva was nothing but a translation into Latin of the German name of the girl he once loved. This enables Freud to comment that in psychoanalysis too, explanation coincides with cure. This is followed by an astonishing statement on the relations between love and cure:

The process of cure is accomplished in a relapse into love, if we combine all the many components of the sexual instinct under the term "love"; and such a relapse is indispensable, for the symptoms on account of which the treatment has been undertaken are nothing other than precipitates of earlier struggles connected with repression or the return of the repressed, and they can only be resolved and washed away by a fresh high tide of the same passions. Every psychoanalytic treatment is an attempt at liberating repressed love which has found a meagre outlet in the compromise of a symptom. Indeed, the agreement between such treatments and the process of cure described by the author of *Gradiva* reaches its climax in the further fact that in analytic psychotherapy too the re-awakened passion, whether it is love or hate, invariably chooses as its object the figure of the doctor. (p. 90)

Freud goes on to say:

It is here that the differences begin, which made the case of Gradiva an ideal one which medical technique cannot attain. Gradiva was able to return the love which was making its way from the unconscious into consciousness, but the doctor cannot. Gradiva had herself been the object of the earlier, repressed love; her figure at once offered the liberated current of love a desirable aim. The doctor has been a stranger, and must endeavor to become a stranger once more after the cure; he is often at a loss what advice to give the patients he has cured as to how in real life they can use their recovered capacity to love. (p. 90)

Freud here candidly admits that it is easier to evoke the transference than to resolve it and make the analysand capable of finding a love object in the real world. I will return to this subject in a later chapter.

Freud's statement is of interest from many points of view. Love is defined as the synthesis of all of the components of the sexual instinct, the very definition he will reject as inadequate in 1915. Nor has Freud elsewhere stated so boldly that cure takes place in a state of relapse into love. (In the original, Freud coined a new term, *Liebesrezidiv*. The term *rezidiv* has a stronger medical connotation of a return of the illness.)

It seems likely that Freud was so enthusiastic about *Gradiva* and overvalued it as a work of art because he was ready to decipher the novella. The primary process by which an earlier repressed love is displaced on a new person was never described as well before.

Her father had nothing left over for her: all his interest was engrossed by the objects of his science. So she was obliged to cast her eyes around upon other people, and became especially attached to her young playmate. When he too ceased to have any eyes for her, her love was not shaken by it but rather increased, for he had become like her father, was, like him, absorbed by science and held apart by it from life and from Zoe. Thus it was made possible for her to remain faithful in her unfaithfulness—to find her father once more in her loved one, to include both of them with the same emotion, or, as we may say, to identify both of them in her feeling. What is our justification for this piece of psychological analysis, which might well seem arbitrary? The author has presented us with it in a single, but highly characteristic detail. When Zoe described the transformation of her former playmate which had so greatly disturbed her, she abused him by comparing him to an archaeopteryx, the bird-like monstrosity which belongs to the archaeology of zoology. In that way she found a single concrete expression of the identity of the two figures. Her complaint applies with the same word to the man she loved and to her father. (p. 33)

The passage is the best description we have of what Freud meant by refinding. Zoe and, by implication, all lovers who transfer their libido are "faithful in their unfaithfulness." It is identification that makes love possible. The one stems from the other and the same emotion envelops both. The bird, an archaeopteryx, is Jensen's wonderful creation. Like the dreams reported, it is rich in communicative function. No one before Freud would have deciphered the meaning of this term the way Freud did, but many who read and laughed at the term preconsciously understood the meaning. We can here understand the difference between novelist and psychologist. The novelist can create the condensation, aware of the connection it contains between archaeology and zoology. But the broader implication of the transfer of libido from father to lover remained for Freud to discover. Behind this beautiful and illuminating description lies a paradox that Freud glossed over. The father who had no time for Zoe must have inflicted much pain on this lovely girl. Why did she then choose to repeat the painful event when she chose a man who had no time for her? To be sure, in the case of the father, she had to suffer the pain passively, but with her lover she could actively wean him away from the obsession of his science. Unbeknownst to Freud, a mechanism of undoing a childhood trauma is crucial to adult falling in love.

That all this should have taken place in Pompeii must have pleased Freud. It should be noted that at the turn of the century these excavations were still going on. In the same year that *Gradiva* was written, Freud told the Rat Man:

I then made some short observations upon *the psychological differences between the conscious and the unconscious,* and upon the fact that everything conscious was subject to a process of wearing away, while what was unconscious was relatively unchangeable; and I illustrated my remarks by pointing to the antiques standing about in my room. They were, in fact, I said, only objects found in a tomb, and their burial had been their preservation: the destruction of Pompeii was only beginning now that it had been dug up.* (1919a:176)

*I am indebted to Dr. Mark Kanzer for drawing my attention to this parallel. What mattered most to Freud when he wrote the *Gradiva* was to stress the affinity between poet and clinician. "The author has expressly renounced the portrayal of reality by calling his story a phantasy. We have found, however, that all his descriptions are so faithfully copied from reality that we should not object if *Gradiva* were described not as a phantasy but as a psychiatric study" (p. 14). "Thus the creative writer cannot evade the psychiatrist nor the psychiatrist the creative writer, and the poetic treatment of a psychiatric theme can turn out to be correct without any sacrifice of its beauty" (p. 44).

The problem of diagnosis of the archaeologist's mental illness is interesting. Freud first suggested "fetishistic erotomania as a special case of paranoia." Finding no evidence of paranoia, he suggested in a footnote that the diagnosis should be hysterical delusion (p. 44). The diagnosis of fetishism was based on his being in love with a piece of sculpture and his interest in women's ankles. This raises the interesting question: what was known to Freud about fetishism in 1907? The major contribution to the understanding of fetishism did not come until 1927, when Freud said: "It [the fetish] is the token of triumph over the dread of castration and protection against it" (p. 154). He went on to add that the fetishist, by making the woman into a phallic woman, protects himself against his homosexual impulses. In the *Three Essays* (1905a) this was not yet clear. Freud followed Binet in the belief that a fetish is an aftereffect of some impression usually received in early childhood. Incidentally, it is of interest to note that *DSM-III** has incorporated Binet's view: "The fetish is often associated with someone with whom the individual was intimately involved during childhood, most often a caretaker" (p. 268).

Other sexual pathologies like homosexuality, sadism, or masochism were in Binet's view also determined by chance events. He stressed that some degree of fetishism is present in every one. "Normal fetishism" is the preference for a certain color of hair or eyes. Love itself Binet thought was a form of fetishism—"a harmonious symphony of fixed obsessions about the beloved" (quoted from Sulloway 1979:286). Even in 1905, Freud went a step beyond Binet to point out that a fetish may be determined not just by an aftereffect but also through a symbolic connection to the love object (p. 155). In general, Freud, like Binet, believed that a certain amount of fetishism is part of normal love. In those cases where a normal sexual aim is unattainable, the fetish becomes pathological only when it has replaced the normal aim. In light of these considerations we may assume that the archaeologist's fetishism would have been regarded by Freud as fully within the boundaries of normal life.

The two diagnoses given by Freud are problematic. The dictionary defines erotomania as "a mental disorder caused or characterized by excessive or irrational love." In this sense, the archaeologist's falling in love with a plaster cast can be described as irrational love. However, in all the cases of erotomania known to me, the delusional belief consists in the conviction that one is pursued by an imaginary lover. There is no hint that

*_Diagnostical and Statistical Manual of Mental Disorders,_ third edition (New York: American Psychiatric Association, 1980).

Hanold entertained such a belief; on the contrary, Gradiva seemed to him absorbed in her own life, unaware of his interests.

As to hysterical delusion, the term does not appear in any of Freud's writings on hysteria except in this footnote, nor was I able to find it in the psychiatric literature of the time. The closest I could come was Bleuler's description of hysterical twilight states where the patients find themselves in a different environment, desert or heaven, where they relive states of bliss. Hanold finds himself in a different world, but he does not relive a state of bliss but rather an excited anxiety state. Ellenberger (1970) states that the archaeologist's condition would have been familiar to psychiatrists of the previous century as an example of "ecstatic vision" when vivid daydreams and events in normal life are perfectly blended.

The question of diagnosis is significant, for if my hypothesis is correct, there is no mental illness in real life that corresponds to the archaeologist's illness. Why then did Freud accept the illness as real, and why did subsequent writers echo his belief? Stanley Hall, in his 1917 preface to the translation of *Gravida,* followed Freud and stated: "The young archaeologist suffered from a very characteristic mental disorder and was gradually but effectively cured by a kind of naive psychotherapy inherent in all of us."

My own reconstruction of *Gravida* runs as follows: Jensen does not describe a psychiatric case study but rather gives a thinly disguised piece of autobiography. He describes the significant moment when falling in love and the reawakening of sexual desire was made possible by the undoing of sexual repression with the aid of a fetish. Gradiva, by revealing her ankle, becomes a phallic woman and thus simultaneously becomes a defense against castration anxiety, and homosexuality. While Hanold was engrossed in studying the gait of women, he succeeded in deflecting his attention from the genital to the foot. We may call this period the period of fetish formation. Indeed, when Zoe for the first time crosses the street in Pompeii, no longer disguised as Gradiva, she makes sure to lift her skirt and demonstrate the existence of the indispensable ankle. Had Freud known the secret of the fetish in 1907 he would not have had to assume that Jensen's sister had a deformed foot.

During the process of self-cure, Hanold projected his own sexual deadness on the dead Gradiva, and as the discovery of the fetish revived his sexuality, Gradiva herself returned to life. He can love once more when he is assured that the beloved has a symbolic phallus.

The formation of the fetish enables the archaeologist to transfer latent homosexual libido into a heterosexual one. I have alluded to a latent homosexual motif, when Hanold transformed Homer's Mars Gradivus, the light-stepping god of war, into the feminine Gradiva, but a more explicit homosexual motif is present in Freud's interpretation of Hanold's lizard dream.

In Hanold's dream, Gradiva, rather than her zoologist father, is catching lizards. His actions and words are transferred from masculine to feminine. Freud deciphers the meaning of the transposition when he says: "Gradiva catches lizards like the old man. She is skilled in lizard-catching, just as he is" (p. 74). Hanold himself is the prized lizard. The father stands behind the daughter.

Freud ignored the homosexual component in the dream, but it adds evidence to the fetishistic solution of the archaeologist's struggle against repression.

There is still another point in which Freud, as I see it, succumbed to the illusory web woven by Jensen. I believe that only when the infantile love object is a substitute for the oedipally forbidden mother can a childhood love undergo such repression. It follows that if the illness is oedipal, then the woman whose love is the cause cannot effectively minister to the disease. Freud taught us that our first love toward the mother, or her substitute, must undergo repression. Only another woman who resembles the first, but is not subject to the incest taboo, can be the object of an adult love. The substitution of a playmate for the mother makes it possible for Jensen to beguile his readers, including Freud, into believing that we can as adults refind the childhood love object we had to give up as a price for the mastery of the oedipus complex. This substitution gave the *Gradiva* its fairy-tale quality. Had Freud seen *Gradiva* as I do, as a piece of self-cure through the formation of a fetish, the work would have had to be seen as more tragic, depicting symptom formation rather than an almost miraculous cure. Had this connection been deciphered, the book inevitably would have lost its beguiling charm.

The cure of the archaeologist follows the model of Glover's (1931) "inexact interpretation," that is, a cure brought about by the creation of new symptoms and new defenses.

*Gradiva* attempts a solution to the problem of love during infancy where in fact there is none. It therefore offers only illusory pleasure. Freud in this instance did lay down the critical arms of psychoanalysis before a work of fiction.

The biographical significance of *Gradiva* has evoked interest in a number of psychoanalysts. Friedman (1966) suggested that the *Gradiva* can be linked to Freud's own screen memory (1899). Both Freud and Norbert

Hanold were so preoccupied in their adolescence and young adulthood with their work that they repressed early childhood loves. Furthermore, Freud liked to compare psychoanalysis with archaeology (Bernfeld 1949). Friedman called attention to the fact that during Freud's first eight years of life his mother was pregnant six times. Gradiva can stand for Gravida, the pregnant mother.

Schur (1972) believed that Freud was attracted to *Gradiva* because it dealt with the theme of immortality and revenant themes that were of special interest to him. Slochower (1970) drew attention to the fact that *Gradiva* was written two years after Freud's visit to the Acropolis. He connected *Gradiva* to this visit. The Acropolis has evoked in Freud a feeling of depersonalization which Slochower interpreted as a memory of the sight of a nude mother. In the *Gradiva,* Freud could deal with the same topic a step removed. Therefore, instead of evoking anxiety in Freud, the *Gradiva* gave him a sense of pleasure.

Jensen's *Gradiva* contained two of the most important discoveries that Freud had made during this period. It showed very concretely how falling in love is in fact refinding. It also showed what Lindau's story did not: that falling in love is dependent upon an unconscious precondition, in this case the raised ankle. There was more to Gradiva than merely "enjoying one's riches." Zoe, who symbolizes a nonneurotic person, shows that one can fall in love simply by identifying the lover with the father. It is therefore a genuine case of refinding. Norbert's path to love is more complex. He can refind his capacity to love only through a symbolic act of bringing to life and through the compromise of a fetish. In his case love signaled the return of heterosexuality from repression as well as a shift from homosexuality to heterosexuality. For the full recognition of the significance of such a complex precondition for loving Freud was not yet ready in 1907.

# 16

# *Love and Genitality: The History of a Controversy in Psychoanalysis*

In a previous chapter, I have traced Freud's three successive theories on love. What supplied the glue which held the three theories together is the libido theory. In Freud's third theory, love becomes possible when the last psychosexual phase called the genital phase is reached. The relationship between love and genitality has an interesting history of its own. It begins with Freud but it already belongs to an era of psychoanalysis after Freud.

In the last decade of his life, Freud no longer developed new theories of love. He became increasingly interested in philosophical issues. In the essay *Civilization and Its Discontents* (1930) Freud discussed the relationship between love and human happiness. As Freud saw it, to raise the question about the purpose of life is already a sign of depression, but if we look at the behavior of men and women, the answer is not difficult to find. Men and women strive after happiness. Some exert all their energy merely to avoid pain. Others seek to experience strong feelings of pleasure. Happiness, however, Freud suggested, was not included in the plan of creation. We can experience happiness only when we obtain a sudden satisfaction of needs that have been dammed up for a long time (p. 76). By its very nature happiness is only an episodic phenomenon. If the situation is prolonged, happiness at best turns into mild contentment. In a poignant passage, Freud said:

I am, of course, speaking of the way of life which makes love the centre of everything, which looks for all satisfaction in loving and being loved. A psychical attitude of this sort comes naturally enough to all of us; one of the forms in which love manifests itself—sexual love—has given us our most intense experience of an overwhelming sensation of pleasure and has thus furnished us with a pattern for our search for happiness. What is more natural than that we should persist in looking for happiness along the path on which we first encountered it? The weak side of this technique of living is easy to see; otherwise no human being would have thought of abandoning this path to happiness for any other. It is that we are never so defenseless against suffering as when we love, never so helplessly unhappy as when we have lost our loved object or its love. (Freud 1930:82)

A year later Freud took up the relationship between libido and character in a short paper entitled "Libidinal Types" (1931). The psychoanalytic libido theory, Freud suggested, can be used as a basis for a description of major psychological types. He differentiated the three types: the erotic, the narcissistic, and the obsessional. By themselves, all three types are normal; no type need necessarily be neurotic and all three can succumb to neurosis if there is a conflict between the major psychological structures, ego, id, and superego; or when there is a conflict between homosexual and heterosexual impulses; and finally if there is a conflict between libido and aggression.

For the erotic type, loving, and above all being loved, are the most important psychic events. When persons of the erotic type become neurotic they live in a continuous fear of losing love. Because they fear loss of love, the erotic types are usually dependent on the other types. The narcissistic types are mostly concerned with self-preservation. They have a large amount of aggression at their disposal. Such persons strike us as independent and prefer loving to being loved. The narcissistic types often impress others as charismatic. The obsessional types are distinguished by the extraordinary role that the superego plays in their lives. They are dominated by the fear of conscience rather than the loss of love. Those who belong to this type are usually conservative in disposition. In real life, we often find various mixtures of the three types.

In "Libidinal Types," Freud ventures outside of the clinical realm to make observations on humanity as a whole. Erotic types are in danger of loving whoever loves them. Narcissistic types are typically pursued by those who have lost their own narcissism, and the obsessive types once they fall in love have a capacity to stay in love for long periods of time. Typically, they are also immune to other sexual temptations.

One may also ask whether the three types described by Freud exist in real life or whether they merely represent pure types, not found in the real world except in various mixtures. This question occurs every time psychoanalysts describe a type. Psychoanalysis here echoes the old debate between Plato and Aristotle as to whether the idea of things exists outside of their representation in the real world as Plato thought, or whether the idea or ideal is to be found only within the actual representation in the real world as Aristotle taught. This problem presents itself whenever an attempt is made to generalize from the clinical data.

Few subjects have evoked as much controversy as the differences between men and women in the way they love. Freud regarded women as more narcissistic than men. He thought they valued being loved more than loving. If women love on the anaclitic model, Freud thought this was due to the masculine component of their libido. He also thought that bisexuality was stronger in women than in men (1931a).

In the course of normal development, every child experiences three inevitable shocks: (1) the shock that one is not part of one's mother, (2) the shock of gender difference, (3) the shock of the inevitability of death. The two sexes react differently to the shock of gender difference. The boy responds with castration anxiety. He fears that, like the girl, he may lose his penis. The castration anxiety causes him to repress his oedipal wishes. The girl responds to the discovery that she and her mother have no penis with penis envy and the turning in the search of love from the mother to the father. Freud also thought that since the woman already feels castrated, she has less of a need to develop her own superego.

Jacobson (1937) constructed the history of feminine love differently. At first, the girl experiences strong oral-sadistic wishes to incorporate the penis of the father. For these aggressive wishes, she feels guilty. More or less reluctantly, the girl accepts the fact that she can receive the penis only temporarily in the sexual act. The vagina becomes erotized. Narcissism gives way to object love. Loss of love replaces the original castration anxiety. Women, therefore, remain throughout their lives more dependent on the man in love than do men. Love is more central to the lives of women than it is usually to the lives of men. Chasseguet-Smirgel (1970) stressed that women idealize love more than men. As a result they live in a romantic dream like Madame Bovary. Idealization is necessary so that the original aggressive wishes toward the penis remain repressed.

## The Contribution of Karl Abraham

Karl Abraham, one of Freud's earliest and most gifted disciples, followed in his footsteps and delineated the oral character by analogy to Freud's delineation of the anal character (Abraham 1916 and 1924a).

In Abraham's hands the psychosexual phases were coordinated into a diagnostic and developmental theory that was to dominate psychoanalytic thinking until after World War II. Abraham differentiated the following developmental stages: the sucking stage, the biting and cannibalistic stage, early and late anal sadistic stages, the phallic stage and finally, the genital stage. Every stage was correlated to a special kind of love. These included autoerotic love, narcissism (self-love), partial love (love of certain parts of the body rather than the person as a whole), and finally on the genital level, postambivalent love.

Abraham's classification is still at the core of Fenichel's classic of 1945 (p. 101). Many psychoanalysts, particularly Kleinians and other European analysts, still use Abraham's classification as the basis of their diagnostic thinking (for example, see Grunberger's 1971 book on narcissism). In American psychoanalytic thinking, Anna Freud's concept of developmental lines* has replaced Abraham's classification based on psychosexual phases of development.

In his paper on "Character Formation on a Genital Level" (1925) Abraham argued that character is the sum of a person's instinctive reactions toward his social environment. A person's character can only be complete when his or her libido has reached the stage of the highest organization, the achievement of the capacity for object love. To reach this stage, the person must first overcome his or her destructive, hostile impulses, mistrust, and avarice. (In keeping with psychoanalytic thinking at that time, Abraham derived these impulses from the anal phase.) Furthermore, the oedipus complex must be subdued, original narcissism overcome, and the dominance of the pleasure principle broken. Feelings of ambivalence toward the genital organs of the heterosexual partner also have to give way to the capacity to enjoy sexual intercourse without inhibition.

In Abraham's description, the genital character absorbs the best from the pregenital phases. From orality, enterprise and energy; from the anal phase, perseverence; and the sadism associated with the anal phase of the genital character transforms into life-enhancing constructive energy. The genital character is free from hostility toward the mate and directs productive hostility to those who in the real world block his or her progress (p. 415). The genital character does not disavow instincts but has them under control.

Much that later psychoanalysts will assign to the ego is here assigned to the libido. Unlike the ego, the libido, if it is not interfered with by neurosis, runs a normal predictable course toward genitality. The reason why frigidity and impotence were considered so detrimental was because they dammed up the libido, preventing the unfolding of the genital character.

*The concept of developmental lines is more sophisticated than Abraham's libidinal phases since it assumes the different parts of the personality have different rates of development. Thus a person may be fixated on an early psychosexual level and yet have a much sterner sense of morality.

Within the context of this book it is significant that Freud in his essay on libidinal types gave no space to Abraham's genital character. We may take this to mean that Freud believed that the genital character is an idealization not to be found in real life. Fenichel (1945) stated explicitly that the genital character formulated by Abraham and popularized by Wilhelm Reich did not represent a real entity. A significant difference between Freud and Abraham should not be allowed to escape us. In Freud's view, genitality enables a person to separate love from hate. To Abraham it meant much more and had an almost utopian connotation.

The impact of Abraham's theory on psychoanalytic thinking on love was great. The capacity to love was no longer viewed merely in quantitative terms of transferring the libido from incestuous parental objects to new ones free from incestuous encumbrances, as Freud's first theory of love had postulated. Nor was love merely the result of transferring narcissistic libido into object libido and transferring aspects of the ego ideal on the beloved as the second theory had postulated. Finally, the capacity to love was no longer conceptualized as present from infancy on. It could be reached only after a long process of development. One could love only after one had overcome one's own bisexuality, one's own narcissism, and one's hostility toward and fear of the opposite sex. Genitality became the prerequisite for the capacity to love. By definition, as it were, all perversions were now seen as devoid of the capacity to love. Eventually a reaction against the idealization of genitality began to set in. As we shall see, this happened after World War II.

## Wilhelm Reich

Reich gave the genital character a radical interpretation. In a paper written in 1929, entitled significantly "The Genital Character and The Neurotic Character," Reich saw character as "chronic alterations of the ego reducing psychic mobility, making a person rigid." He created the term "character armor." In his view, it is the repression of the instinctual demands that gives rise to character formation. Once a character trait has been established, the instincts need no longer be repressed. For the character trait has so modified the person's attitude toward this instinct that no further energy need be expended on repression. A character trait develops whenever a previously meaningful relationship leads to disappointment and is given up. Character is achieved by the conversion of object libido into narcissistic libido. (The very opposite process, according to Freud, leads to falling in love.) This approach led Reich to emphasize character analysis before the analyst can hope to liberate the repressed instinctual wishes of his analysand. This character becomes manifest in treatment in the form of a special character resistance to free associations. It consists of pregenital fixations, dammed-up libido which can find no outlet, and reaction formations against the instinctual demands. By contrast, the genital character has a superego that encourages sexuality and the libido flows freely into the sexual relationship.

A quote from Reich's 1929 paper* will enable the reader to capture the climate of opinion in that epoch.

In no respect is the individual possessing a genital character stiff or rigid; nor are the forms of his sexuality. Since he is capable of gratification, he is capable of monogamy without compulsion or repression; but he is also capable, if a reasonable motive is given, of changing the object without suffering any injury. He does not adhere to his sexual object out of guilt feelings or out of moral considerations, but is faithful out of a healthy desire for pleasure: because it gratifies him. He can master polygamous desires if they are in conflict with his relations to the loved object without repression; but he is able also to yield to them if they overly disturb him. The resulting actual conflict he will solve in a realistic manner. There are hardly any neurotic feelings of guilt. His sociality is based on not repressed but on sublimated aggression and upon his adjustment to reality. This does not mean, however, that he always bows to reality; on the contrary, more than any other he is capable of criticizing and changing his environment for the reason that his character structure is the opposite of that of the neurotic, our civilization being entirely obsessional-neurotic (anal and sadistic); his lack of fear of life makes it unnecessary for him to make those concessions to the environment that would be in conflict with his convictions. (Reich 1929:161)

It is hardly surprising that such a utopian view exerted an appeal on the younger generation of psychoanalysts. The genital character appeared to be capable of solving all problems of sexuality and loyalty without any inner struggle.

Two years earlier, in 1927, Reich published a book under the title, *The Function of the Orgasm.* There he introduced the concept of orgastic potency, a further elaboration of Abraham's genital character. The orgastically potent man enjoys his erection but he does not admire it as the narcissist does; it is naturally associated with the urge to penetrate. In the sexual act the man is spontaneously gentle without the need to cover sadistic impulses during sexual intercourse; as excitement mounts, the urge to penetrate very deeply increases. This takes place without sadistic im-

---

*Reich's book on character analysis has been often revised to accommodate his later views. What Reich's views were when he was a psychoanalyst can be found in Fliess (1948), in the section on characterology (see Reich 1929).

pulses disturbing coitus. There is no mental concentration on the sexual pleasure, there are no distracting thoughts, and there is no need to resort to fantasies during the sexual act. When the stage of orgasm is reached, the involuntary contraction of the muscles is deeply gratifying. Clouding of consciousness occurs; the sexual excitation takes over the whole person. After orgasm, excitation tapers off gradually and the proverbial feeling of sadness so often discussed in the literature does not take place (pp. 72–87).

As to object relationships, Reich believed in a genuine transference from the original incestuous object to the new one. When this takes place, the partner corresponds in his or her essential traits to the object of the fantasy. When there is no genuine transfer of libido, one feels that the sexual relationship is insincere or faked, and there is a disillusionment after intercourse. Fantasizing during intercourse about other sexual relationships indicates that a genuine transfer of the libido has not taken place. When this happens, a false excessive idealization may defend against the breakdown of the illusion that one has found a genuinely new and satisfying partner (pp. 86–87).

Reich's discussion of the masochistic character is important within the context of this book. A person with a masochistic character, as distinguished from masochism as a perversion, is self-deprecating and self-damaging. They complain continuously and torture others with their unhappiness. Behind the provocations is a deep disappointment in love. The masochistic character has an inordinately high need to be loved that makes real gratification impossible. To his partner or the analyst, the masochistic character says in behavior even more than in words, "Look how miserable I am, please love me . . . You must love me . . . I am going to force you to love me."

It will be recalled that one of the cardinal rules of the court of love in the Middle Ages was that love can only be given freely. Reich showed that love can also be demanded. We may add that one of the cardinal features of neurosis is to demand love. To demand love is to destroy the very soil in which love can grow. Nevertheless, many people spend their lives demanding love.

Fenichel (1945) quotes Reich's view with approval. Fenichel's definition of love is a modest one. "One can speak of love only when consideration for the object goes so far that one's own satisfaction is impossible without satisfying the object too" (p. 85). "In love there must be a partial or temporary identification for empathic purposes" (p. 84).

Reich's and to a lesser extent Fenichel's emphasis on sexual orgasm as the antidote to neurosis was more radical than what Freud envisioned, but not as much of a departure from the views of the young Freud as is generally assumed. In 1905 Freud wrote: "Most psychoneurotics only fall ill after the age of puberty as a result of the demands made upon them by normal sexual life" (Freud 1905a:170).

Elsewhere in his book (p. 496), Fenichel defined the genital character in terms taken directly from Reich, except that he recognizes what Reich did not, that the genital character is an ideal concept, not one found in real life. Reich implied that genitality is the real goal of every analysis; Fenichel saw it only as an ideal to be approximated. Unlike Reich, Fenichel's authority remained high. It is therefore not an exaggeration to say that for a generation after Freud the attainment of genitality was the implicit goal of psychoanalysis.

## Michael Balint

In 1947, the stage shifts from Reich to Balint. In his paper "On Genital Love" (1947), without referring to Abraham or Reich by name, Balint observed that in psychoanalysis, genitality has been defined essentially in negative terms: absence of oral greed, no wish to humiliate or devour the partner, absence of castrating wishes toward the partner, no feelings of disgust for the sexual organs of the partner, no feelings of shame that one's penis is too small or that one's breasts are either too small or too large, or that one's sexual organs are inferior to those of the partner. Balint defined genitality as the overcoming of all sexual inhibition and inadequacies that are part of the neurotic heritage from childhood. In contrast to Abraham and Reich's genital theory, Balint drew attention to narcissistic personalities who are capable of genital orgasm but devoid of the capacity to love.

In another paper written in 1956, Balint emphasized that in perversions, particularly among fetishists and transvestites, one finds a preference for orgasm with the aid of inanimate objects rather than with another person. They do so because the inanimate fetish is always available, never needs to be taken into consideration, and makes no demands. Voyeurism and exhibitionism require the presence of other human beings but not their cooperation, a subtle but important difference. Furthermore, the objects in these perversions are exchangeable. The more primitive and infantile the psychosexual phase, the less are the needs of objects taken into account. By contrast to the more infantile forms of sexuality, genitality depends to a high degree on the willingness and the cooperative attitude of the partner. Genitality assures the capacity of maximum sexual pleasure but, to Balint, it is not synonymous with genital love. Genital love, according to Balint, becomes possible when genitality is associated with idealization, tenderness, and a special form of identification.

The differentiation between genitality and genital love led Balint to draw a radical conclusion: genital love is a regressive phenomenon, it is our prolonged childhood that makes us susceptible to genital love and unhappy with loveless genitality.

Balint saw genital love as a fusion of two nonharmonious elements: genital satisfaction and pregenital tenderness, reviving Freud's two current theories: "The reward for bearing the strain of this fusion is [to Balint] the possibility of regressing periodically for some happy moments to a really infantile stage of no reality testing, to the short-lived reestablishment of the complete union." For Balint, love is not a natural emotion; it has to be taught. Culture compels the individual to fuse sex with love. Freud's ideas expressed in *Civilization and its Discontents* are applied by Balint to love itself. Balint suggested that man be looked upon as a retarded animal who, even in his mature years, remains under the power of an infantile form of sexuality. Love to Balint is the mark of human immaturity. Genital love he saw as a latecomer in evolution and permanently unstable. Although Freud himself emphasized the origins of love in the years of infancy, he did not in his published writings go so far as to call love a symptom of retardation in the human species. Informally in a meeting of the Vienna Psychoanalytic Society he did express a similar attitude.

All the ingredients of Freud's thinking are found in Balint, but while Freud in 1905 thought that the remingling of the tender and the sexual currents make happy genital love possible, Balint, like the late Freud, assumed that they forever remain in an uneasy alliance. The longing for infantile fusion was seen by Balint as a persistent danger to adult sexuality. Balint introduced into psychoanalysis a negative attitude toward love, which he saw as a useless remnant of childhood that can never be refound in adulthood. Love was to him essentially an emotion that handicaps men and women in the pursuit of sexual pleasure. Balint's voice, although influential, was for a long time a lonely one. The equation of sexual orgasm with the capacity to love would dominate psychoanalytic thinking for another twenty years. Novey (1955) criticized the concept of genital character because it failed to take into account the vicissitudes of the aggressive drive. Man is social, Novey argued, precisely because his own sense of self remains impaired. Handelsman (1965) showed that men and women who are borderline or psychotic are also capable of orgasm. He pointed out that, contrary to Reich's assumption, impotence and frigidity take place when there is a higher and more developed intrapsychic structure and there is conflict between superego, ego, and id.

In 1968, at a meeting of the American Psychoanalytic Association, a symposium was held on "The Theory of Genital Primacy in the Light of Ego Psychology" (Berezin 1969; Ross 1970). In this symposium, Ross took the lead in questioning the connection between postambivalent object relations and the attainment of sexual orgasm. This was a significant turning point in the psychoanalytic understanding of love. Not that Freud had been entirely wrong; he was right in assuming that frigidity and impotence are caused by inhibitions in loving. But the reverse, however, was not true. Freedom from sexual malfunctioning was not necessarily a sign of the capacity to love. In a historical perspective, one has to admit that neither Handelsman nor Ross studied the orgasm with the detailed attention that Reich gave to it. In the history of psychoanalytic writing on love after World War II, Balint emerges as the most important modifier of Freud's views on love. Many of the changes that other psychoanalysts introduced go back to Balint.

I wish to stress the contradiction that Balint discovered in the genital character. On one hand, genitality must be reached for the sexual relationship to acquire depth and to be free from hostility and envy. Therefore, genitality is prerequisite for love. On the other hand, the maturity of the genital character, the greater distance from childish needs, and the higher degree of separateness or independence should make love unnecessary. Neither Balint nor Reich could find good reason why two genital people should stay together in a prolonged or even life-long relationship. It seems that the riddle of love slipped out of the net into which the psychoanalytic writers on genitality hoped to capture it. Genitality remains a significant prerequisite for a happy love but it failed to solve the puzzle of love.

The next milestone in psychoanalytic conceptualization on genitality and love was a paper by Binstock (1973), who emphasized that in a happy heterosexual relationship each partner experiences vicariously the other gender in the act of love. The distinction between the genders is not lost but heightened. At the same time remnants of bisexual needs are continuously projected on the partner, heightening one's own sense of gender identity. A similar identification cannot take place in homosexual love and therefore the danger of confusion between self and object is greater for the homosexual. In Binstock's view, the person who feels that life without the partner is unthinkable, who prefers death to separation, has regressed to the state where boundaries of the self are lost. The celebrated *Liebestod* is not a sign of true love but a sign of regression. Such relationships usually improve when the analysand recaptures in analysis the capacity to imagine that he or she will survive without the partner.

Binstock differentiates between love and infatuation. Being in love enhances gender identity. This is not experienced in an infatuation. When bisexuality is too strong, falling in love is not possible. Love makes men feel masculine and women feminine. Psychoanalysis discovered the bisexual nature of human beings. As a technique of therapy, it has a dual purpose, first to uncover the repressed "countergender wishes" and then to increase the tolerance, especially of the superego, to accept the masculine wishes in women and the feminine wishes in men. Paradoxically, when this has been achieved, falling in love becomes easier and love enables each partner to project countergender wishes on the other. Within the historical frame of reference that I have been pursuing in this book, it is significant that Binstock's views are dramatically opposed to those of Plato. Plato thought that our search for a lost bisexuality makes us fall in love, while Binstock finds that love rids us of the encumbrance of residual bisexuality.

The connection between love and genitality proved more complex than Freud and Abraham anticipated. Genitality is a psychosexual phase. It is not identical with genital love, which is a heterosexual love relationship in which the feminine wishes of a man and the masculine wishes of a woman are projected on the partner so that the man feels more strongly his masculinity and the woman her femininity. Genitality is a form of sexual gratification. It is independent of the emotion of love that one person feels for another. A genital relationship need not be a love relationship, and a love relationship need not be based on genitality.

# 17

# *Love and Homosexuality*

In a previous chapter we found that the Western attitude toward homosexuality, as toward love in general, had its origins in the Bible and in Greek thinking. The Bible condemned homosexuality as an abomination against God's will. Greek culture showed tolerance at least toward some forms of homosexuality, primarily between men and adolescent boys. The Greeks also honored Sappho's poetry, which contained many lesbian poems. In this way, too, they showed a greater tolerance towards homosexuality.

The genesis of the term perversion was far from neutral. *The Oxford English Dictionary* defines perversion as the action of turning aside from truth and from what is right, or as a diversion to an improper use. The term was originally used to designate turning away from the true, religious belief. It was only later adapted to designate sexual deviations.

The single most influential work on the subject of perversions was Freud's first essay in the *Three Essays on Sexuality* (Freud 1905a). This book together with *The Interpretation of Dreams* are in my view Freud's greatest works. The first essay is entitled "The Sexual Aberrations." Upon first acquaintance this chapter is not likely to capture the enthusiasm of a contemporary reader. The numerous editions of this book have burdened it with footnotes. Too many authors are cited and the essay gives the impression of a patchwork hastily put together. But if the reader is willing to dig deeper he or she will find that the essay is one of the most original ever written by Freud; for nobody before him thought of approaching the subject of sexuality in general through the perversions. By doing so, Freud overcame the then current prejudice that perversions are either a sign of degeneracy or insanity. As a result, a new way of looking at human sexuality became accessible.

Calling the sexual drive "the most unruly of all instincts" (p. 161),

Freud emphasized that people can be sick in the sphere of sexual life without showing any signs of abnormality in other spheres. Freud further found that the sexual drive consists of many components. These components become unified under the supremacy of the genital phase. In perversions the components come apart once more (p. 162). Freud assumed a universal predisposition toward bisexuality in both men and women. Whether one or the other predominates in adulthood, Freud thought, is determined by many factors, including traumatic events of childhood. In the 1910 edition Freud added a footnote where he described such a typical event. Future homosexuals have a very strong relationship with their mothers. At one point in their development, their love turns into identification. They then look for young men who resemble themselves and love them as they were loved (p. 145 footnote). In 1922, Freud amplified and significantly changed this description by introducing the element of jealousy. The mothers of the future homosexuals prefer other young men; identification with the mother is an emergency device to deal with the jealousy. The future homosexuals love their formal rivals.

As to the definition of perversion, Freud felt that any sexual activity that is preparatory to the union of the genitals which helps enhance the sexual excitement and leads to genital orgasm is not a perversion. Only when some other sexual activity has replaced more or less permanently the genital union, do we speak of perversions.

Neuroses were seen by Freud as the negative of perversions. All neurotics show strong homosexual tendencies but censor these tendencies. For many neurotics, disgust is evoked not only for pregenital forms of sexuality but also for the sexual organs themselves. Neurotics handle the conflict between the demands of the drive and the antisexual psychic forces by evasion, that is, by transforming the sexual impulses into symptoms so that the symptoms constitute the sexual life of neurotics.

Following Freud, psychoanalysis employed the term perversion to designate situations where coitus takes place with other than the opposite sex (homosexuality, paedophilia, and bestiality), or when an organ other than the genital is sought as the main organ for sexual gratification (oral and anal sex), or when sexual orgasm depends on certain extrinsic conditions (fetishism, voyeurism, exhibitionism, transvestitism) (Laplanche and Pontalis 1967). Strictly speaking, there is nothing psychoanalytic about this definition. It only states where psychoanalysts draw the line of demarcation for perversions.

Freud brought about a transformation of the term perversion when he equated perversion with earlier infantile forms of sexuality. Thus in psychoanalytic thinking, perversions are normal in the sense that they correspond to early forms of sexuality but not optimal since the genital stage has not been reached. When society condemns and punishes perversion, it is trying to force a person to behave sexually above the psychosexual level the person has reached. From a psychoanalytic point of view, what the libido has failed to reach, society or the superego demands. To demand that a person reach a later psychosexual phase is morally unjustified and futile. These observations constitute the significant definition of perversion from a psychoanalytic point of view.

In a letter to a mother of a homosexual written in 1935, Freud said:

> Homosexuality is assuredly no advantage, but it is nothing to be ashamed of, no vice, no degradation; it cannot be classified as an illness; we consider it to be a variation of the sexual function, produced by a certain arrest of sexual development. Many highly respectable individuals of ancient and modern times have been homosexuals, several of the greatest men among them (Plato, Michelangelo, Leonardo da Vinci, etc.). It is a great injustice to persecute homosexuality as a crime—and a cruelty, too. . . . By asking me if I can help, you mean, I suppose, if I can abolish homosexuality and make normal heterosexuality take its place. The answer is, in a general way we cannot promise to achieve it. In a certain number of cases we succeed in developing the blighted germs of heterosexual tendencies, which are present in every homosexual; in the majority of cases it is no more possible. . . . What analysis can do for your son runs in a different line. If he is unhappy, neurotic, torn by conflicts, inhibited in his social life, analysis may bring him harmony, peace of mind, full efficiency, whether he remains homosexual or gets changed. (E. Freud:1960:423–424)

The letter implies that psychoanalysis can achieve a great deal for the homosexual—perhaps all that it achieves for a heterosexual, without changing the homosexuality.

Schafer (1974) showed that Freud's and Abraham's psychosexual phases, culminating in the genital phase, were based on an evolutionary model that required a teleological view of propagation. In this view, anything short of genital sexuality is a sign of arrest, unnatural, defective, or abnormal; pregenital pleasures being nonprocreative belong at best to foreplay if not to the realm of perversion.

There is an implicit but powerful value system in this view. At the same time and in partial contradiction to this view, genital heterosexuality remained in Freud's view a precarious achievement. Society has to exercise considerable pressure to repress feminine wishes in men and masculine wishes in women. Parents and educators do not leave the reaching of gender identity to the child but intervene when boys play with dolls and girls prefer baseball. Deviant education can masculinize daughters and effeminize sons. By deviant education, Schafer means the need of some parents to treat a son as if he were a daughter or a daughter as if she were a son. Such parents dress up boys in skirts or teach a daughter masculine sports as if she were a son. Because we are not firmly rooted in our gender identity, and because we need to project our own bisexual wishes on others, an attitude of society toward sexual deviations was traditionally a harsh one.

Are homosexuals capable of loving? On this question, crucial within the context of this book, there is no unanimity. Perhaps the most influential view is that of Anna Freud (1952). She concluded that psychoanalysis can restore for male homosexuals their lost masculinity, the masculinity that was often sacrificed to the oedipal mother. These men become phallic but this change is not sufficient to cathect a woman as a true love object. They regain heterosexual potency but not the emotional potency necessary for love. They cathect narcissitically their own refound penis but not the women. Psychoanalysis can restore what they lost but fails to help them attain the genital phase. As Anna Freud put it, "Psychoanalysis makes them once more like five-year-olds but five-year-olds are not very good lovers." I am puzzled by Anna Freud's statement, for in my experience, male homosexuals have if anything hypercathected their penises. They may feel that their penis is less adequate than that of other men, but heterosexual men often share this fear. Khan (1979) finds that in homosexual relationships the partner is not experienced as another person. As a result, the partner is not represented intrapsychically as separate from the self. In his view, homosexual relationships are relationships with a fantasy figure devoid of real human characteristics. Socarides (1978) cites cases that also demonstrate the homosexual's incapacity to love. Isay (1985) found that while psychoanalysis modifies sexual behavior of homosexuals the results are not lasting ones: "the patients remained homosexual in that their sexual orientation, as expressed by the predominance of homosexual fantasy, remained unchanged. When I treated them, they either previously or currently had the additional difficult social and personal complication of a family" (p. 246).

In the last few years, two Freudian psychoanalysts, Janine Chasseguet-Smirgel (1983) and Joyce McDougall (1980), developed a model for the understanding of perversions that is very different from that held by Freud. Their point of departure is the writing of the Marquis de Sade, whom they regard as the spokesman for the perverse point of view. Sade accepts no restrictions on the sexual wishes. Everything usually forbidden is cultivated with a vengeance. Incest is accepted, there are no generational boundaries and no gender differences.

In their view, the pervert-to-be did not go through a latency period and hence had no chance to develop the "tender current" that Freud spoke about. Perverted sexuality like pornography knows no tenderness. The future perverts were exposed to the primal scene, sexual relations between the parents, and often also to sexual activities of one or both parents with others. They reacted with rage and envy to these experiences like other children but they developed defensively an ideology that regards infantile sexuality as superior to adult sexuality. They use others to reenact an inner script which they feel compelled to perform. Gunther Grass's *The Tin Drum* is a graphic representation of such a clinical case.

A structural analysis led Kernberg to differentiate three types of homosexuals and therefore also three types of love (Kernberg 1975:329). In the first group, Kernberg finds that homosexuality resulted from the renunciation of heterosexuality in order to retain the love of the father. This type corresponds in essence to the acting out of the constellation of the negative oedipus complex. Such homosexuals are capable of love and fidelity to one person. In the second group, Kernberg placed those homosexuals whose homosexuality is based on the exchange of roles between self and object. Such homosexuals identify themselves with their mother and the homosexual love object represents what they have been as children. They see in their love object the representation of their own infantile self. (This type of homosexual object selection was described by Freud.) Love on this basis can be called narcissistic because the homosexual love object stands for the self. By reversing roles, such homosexuals can love. Their motherly concern for their partner contains elements of identification with the parents, therefore their love is not purely a narcissistic one. Such homosexuals, Kernberg believes, "are able to love deeply, if neurotically." The third group is the most disturbed, for here the other does not stand for another person but, psychologically speaking, only for the grandiose self. Such a love is devoid of genuine object relationship and rests only on a projection of aspects of the grandiose self. They cannot love but function well in the outside world.

McDougall (1980) reported cases where a homosexual relationship was a healing one. Women who mutilated their bodies in adolescence stopped doing so when they could love another woman's body. The partners lavish on each other the caresses, minute explorations, and tender care that they themselves would have wanted to receive. Then, if the partner responds to these signals and returns them, they receive back what they wished to receive but could not verbalize. Almost literally, the partner first learns and then gives back what the mother originally failed to give. McDougall cites the case of a lesbian woman who lived in dread that she would be deserted if she ever vomited. When this happened, the partner took the vomit into her hand and kissed it. The gesture was a healing one for it meant total acceptance. McDougall's data are unfortunately incomplete about the long-term effects of this reparative love. Lesbian relationships are modeled more closely on the mother-child relationship than other types of love. Like all loves, they offer a second chance. The extent to which an adult can internalize this love and undo the trauma of childhood is crucial in this as in many other love relationships. McDougall believes that lesbians can love but their love is primarily in the service of reparation of the earliest relationship between mother and daughter.

Should the term perversion include group sex, wife-swapping, or triangular relationships? Should couples who use pornographic films as techniques for sexual arousal be classified as perverts? The variations on this theme are infinite. On one side, we find a woman who shows to her would-be lovers limited editions of expensively printed erotic books that evoke images of mysterious sexual relations in distant lands; on the other side, we find the man who, prior to intercourse, looks at pornographic films which make him angry and then has intercourse associated with sadistic or masochistic fantasies. The line between normal and pervert, as Freud already recognized, is a fluid one. But this much is clear: in all such cases, the love object has lost some of its unique capacity to be the sole arouser and gratifier. The deviations from the accepted dyadic norm need not signal the end of love, but they do imply that a compromise had to be sought between love and other psychic needs.

My psychoanalytic experience has shown that couples who engage in group practices seldom forgive each other after the event even when both have consented. Each partner blames the other for his or her inability to maintain the sense of uniqueness in their sexual relationship. I have also had the opportunity to observe a woman who before her marriage was told that the husband expected her to participate in triangular relationships. She did not wish to lose him and consented but was unable to forgive. To cite an example of the opposite, an analysand met a woman in a so-called orgy. He fell in love with her and, within this group, increasingly wanted to be only with her. After a number of meetings, he asked her for her last name and her telephone number, and although she too preferred him within the setting of group sex, she rebuffed him when he asked for a personal relationship. This analysand taught me that love can take root even in rather unpromising soil.

Any reader who followed the chapters dealing with Plato's ideas on love or Shakespeare's love for the young man will entertain no doubt that some homosexuals can love. That this is doubted by psychoanalysts was, as I showed in the previous chapter, based on the mistaken equation of love and genitality. Homosexual love takes a different route than heterosexual love. It may well be more narcissistic but it is a love just the same. Lesbian love, on the other hand, is probably the most anaclitic form of love since most homosexual women seek to refind in their partner the loving mother they never had.

The fact that the recovery of infantile amnesia does not as a rule lead to a change from homosexuality to heterosexuality suggests that more than a libidinal fixation is involved in homosexuality. Heterosexual love makes it possible for the partners to project on each other their respective counter-gender wishes. This relief is not open in homosexual love. Homosexual love still presents a puzzle for psychoanalytic theory.

# 18

# *Transference Love and Love in Real Life*

For centuries men and women have searched for mandrake roots and other substances from which a love potion could be brewed. And then at the turn of the century, a Jewish Viennese physician uncovered love's secret. There is indeed a way in which one human being can make another fall in love, and the prescription is astonishingly simple: (1) keep the environment as constant as possible. Let the person whose love you wish to elicit speak freely about everything that comes to his or her mind; (2) intrude as little as possible into the evolving feelings and memories and above all do not disturb the flow of childhood memories; (3) be particularly attentive to the recall of forgotten or repressed past loves. Give these repressed love feelings a chance to emerge from repression and to be re-experienced; (4) show the person whose love you wish to elicit that after every disappointment he or she has developed defense mechanisms against future love. Illustrate how frustration of the wish to love and be loved has been transformed into undesirable character traits and symptoms and how these have been used to maintain a barrier of suspicion and mistrust to loving. If this method is followed over some period of time, sooner or later transference love will turn toward the person who listened to the recital, particularly if the person also has been engaged in digging up the repressed feelings of infantile love.

The discovery of transference as a potent psychic force, which can be mobilized in the course of psychoanalytic treatment, and harnessed in order to explore the analysand's childhood, ranks among Freud's most original contributions to the psychological understanding of human be-

A modified version of this chapter appeared in the *International Journal of Psycho-Analytic Psycho-Therapy*, 11:1985.

ings.* It is in transference that infantile prototypes reemerge and are experienced with a strong sensation of immediacy. Transference is, therefore, the process through which unconscious wishes and hitherto unconscious fears become actualized (Laplanche and Pontalis 1967:455). The emotional life of most people is spare, and so the number of associations that occur spontaneously is generally limited. Most people will not associate for long before they begin to repeat themselves. Left to their own devices, most people will begin to "go in circles," continually returning to subjects already familiar. It is the task of the psychoanalyst's interpretations to break this circle and help the analysand gain insight into deeper, hitherto unconscious wishes, fears, and fantasies. Among the interpretations, transference interpretations are of particular significance.

Why does transference inevitably develop during a psychoanalysis? On this issue, psychoanalysts' opinions differ. I shall cite the work of two, representing two extreme positions. MacAlpine (1950) stressed that it is the psychoanalytic situation itself that creates an infantile setting to which the analysand—if he or she is analyzable at all—adapts himself or herself by means of regression. It is within this artificially created regressive situation that transference flourishes. In MacAlpine's opinion, this reggression is brought about by a complex set of factors. The psychoanalyst reduces the stimuli from the external world; the environment is constant; the same room, the same hour, the same analyst, and the same facial expression greet the patient at each session. The analysand and his or her world alone are the subject matter. Only rarely does the outside world break into the hermetically closed circle that is created between the analyst and the analysand. The emphasis on free association liberates unconscious fantasy from conscious control. Under these conditions the analyst's authority replaces the parent's authority. The analyst's attitude, consisting of a combination of sympathetic listening and the frustration of gratification, also enhances the development of the transference. "To have created such an instrument of investigation may well be the most important stroke of Freud's genius" (p. 526) is MacAlpine's summary of her analysis of the psychoanalytic situation.

In sharp contrast with MacAlpine, Brenner (1982) believes that although it is true that in the analytic situation the wishes and conflicts of early childhood are transferred to the analyst, it is not true that there is

*To my knowledge, two psychoanalytic studies dealt with the relationship between transference and love in real life. One was written by Jekels and Bergler (1934), who believe that in love only the ego ideal is projected whereas in transference both ego ideal and superego are projected. Their conclusion differs from my own clinical findings. The other study is by Schafer (1977).

anything unique or special about such a transference. In his view, transference is ubiquitous, every object relation is a new edition of the early object relationships of childhood: the transference is a typical rather than an exceptional state. In life transferences are re-enacted, their nature remains unconscious. Physicians are transference figures to their patients, teachers to their pupils. Physicians utilize transference to cure their patients, teachers use it to evoke a love for learning. What is unique to psychoanalysis is not the evocation but rather the way in which the transference is handled. It is the analyst's response to the analysand's communication that represents the unique feature of psychoanalysis. The analyst analyzes the transference reactions instead of responding to them. Brenner maintains that Freud saw transference as a pathological phenomenon, properly subsumed under the heading of the return of the repressed, whereas Brenner believes that transference is a normal, ubiquitous phenomenon (p. 194–196). The two attitudes of MacAlpine and Brenner are nevertheless compatible. There is something ubiquitous in the appearance of transference reactions in every sphere of life, as Brenner maintains, but it is equally true, as MacAlpine suggested, that the psychoanalytic situation is designed to exploit, deepen, concentrate, and focus whatever potential for transference the analysand harbors. This focusing is brought about by how the analyst responds to the analysand's transference manifestation, and also by the special setting of the psychoanalytic situation.

The very existence of transference love was to Freud (1915a:196) proof that an unimpaired object cathexis exists in the unconscious and may last a lifetime. For example, under suitable conditions, most people will form a father or mother transference toward people who fulfill a role in their lives equivalent to that of their father or mother, such as a teacher, physician, superior officer, or any person in whose power one happens to be. From this inexhaustable storage, transference love draws.

In 1912, Freud pointed out that only some of the sexual impulses undergo development and find gratification in reality (1912a:100). Another portion of the erotic strivings is repressed. The impulses that are not satisfied by reality create what Freud called "libidinal anticipatory ideas." During psychoanalysis, the wishes that have not been gratified fuel the transference.

Earlier, I advanced the idea that every form of falling in love draws upon hitherto repressed wishes and early loves, but what in life is left to accident becomes in psychoanalysis a deliberate technique. By systematically uncovering repressed impulses, fresh capacities for love are unearthed. Liberated, these go to enrich the analysand's current sexual and love life, or they may also become the source of transference love. The discovery of transference love in turn leads to two questions of particular significance within the current context. First, is transference love essentially similar to love in real life, or is it fundamentally different? Second, if it is different, can it be seen as a transitory form of love that will enable the analysand to transfer to a new object significantly better than he or she would have been able to achieve had psychoanalysis not intervened? I shall deal with both questions.

## A Brief History of Transference Love

It is of historical interest that in 1895 when Freud first noticed the presence of transference, he saw it only as a disturber of the rational relationship between the patient and analyst. He called it "an external obstacle and not one inherent in the material" and "a false connection and a misalliance." As an example of such a misalliance, Freud presented the following case:

In one of my patients the origin of a particular hysterical symptom lay in a wish, which she had had many years earlier and had at once relegated to the unconscious, that the man she was talking to at the time might boldly take the initiative and give her a kiss. On one occasion, at the end of a session, a similar wish came up in her about me. She was horrified at it, spent a sleepless night, and at the next session, though she did not refuse to be treated was quite useless for work. (Breuer and Freud 1895:301–303)

Freud then discovered that when the patient recalled the memory, the block in the working relationship was removed. He postulated that the wish to be kissed by him appeared first, disassociated from the memories of the past events. He assumed that only because the wish to be kissed was disassociated from its historical moorings was it displaced upon him. Freud thought that when the historical connection was restored, the transference manifestation would disappear. If the patient recognized that she at one time had wanted to be boldly kissed by a particular man, she would no longer wish to be kissed by Freud. But matters did not turn out to be as simple as Freud had anticipated. An analysand is more apt to think, "Even though I recognize that my wish to be kissed is based on a childhood memory of the wish to be kissed by my father, I still want to be kissed by you now."

Freud found three typical occasions when the treatment process became complicated through the appearance of the transference: (1) when the patient felt slighted or neglected; (2) when the patient was seized with the dread of becoming too dependent on the therapist; and 3) when the patient was frightened at finding that she was transferring to the figure of the physician the distressing ideas that were arising from the content of the analysis. The reader should note that in that early phase of psychoanalysis, transference is the prerogative of woman patients. However, beyond this historical anachronism, the three occasions cited by Freud contain a wealth of material that shows how complex the phenomenon of transference already was at the moment when it was recognized by Freud in 1895.

Freud's first example deals with narcissistic injuries that are experienced for the first time because the therapist has forgotten about an appointment with the patient or has failed to respond to a communication by the patient, in short, neglected her. These may or may not connect to earlier disappointments. There may also be events, harmless in themselves, that assume a special significance because they conceal painful memories of the past. The second example, the fear of dependency, although universal, contains for every analysand residues of numerous recollections of anxiety feelings that are the result of the dependency of the child on an adult who proved to be unreliable. Here the transference is the vehicle for the reappearance of anxiety feelings that belong to childhood. The third example embodies what Freud in 1926 called transference resistance, a resistance to the recall of painful childhood memories. Already at the moment of its first appearance, transference was a complex phenomenon, an amalgam of childhood memories, fears, wishes, and real events that occur in the relationship to the analyst, all set in motion by the psychoanalytic experience.

It is likely that the phenomenon of transference, so puzzling to Freud at the turn of the century, supplied the dynamic force for his inquiries into the nature of love. The Dora case (Freud 1905) contains the first statement on the transference beyond the conceptualization in 1895. Dora's premature termination of her treatment was retrospectively attributed by Freud to his failure to master the transference. We might add that at that time his understanding of love was also rudimentary. Freud thought that if a normal girl of 14 years were suddenly and unexpectedly kissed by a close associate of her father, whose wife was her father's paramour, this kiss should have evoked sexual excitement rather than displeasure (1905:28). Today, because of our better understanding of adolescence, we can see both Mr. and Mrs. K. as Dora's adolescent displacement figures, standing for her parents. They offered Dora what Blos called a "second chance" to work out her positive and negative oedipal feelings with her substitute parents. Freud interpreted to Dora that she summoned her love for her father as a defense against her love for Mr. K. At that time, he failed to understand that Mr. K.'s advances evoked in Dora an intrapsychic conflict precisely because he was too close to the father-image not to evoke the incest taboo, forcing her to reject Mr. K. despite her attraction for him.

In the Dora case, Freud distinguished two types of transference. In the first type, feelings are displaced from a parent to analyst, and so the analyst remains a mere reprint of the parent. In the second type, the need for transference takes advantage of some real characteristic of the therapist which is similar to that of the parent. This characteristic resembles revised editions of the original (1905:116).

The two categories of transference can easily be translated into two types of love. In the first, in which the real character of the beloved plays only an insignificant role, we call such relationships *infatuations*. In the second type of love a real similarity to one or both parents forms a bridge to a new love.

In an important paper on technique (1914), Freud became aware of a further complicating factor destined to play a role in the history of psychoanalytic technique. He realized that analysands cannot remember all that is repressed in them, and at times they may not be capable of remembering even the most essential material that would lead the psychoanalyst to understand their illness. Fortunately for the treatment process, what the patients cannot remember, they reenact and relive in the transference as well as in real life. They repeat instead of remember. Thus, infantile neurosis is replaced by the transference neurosis (Freud 1914b and 1920:18). It becomes the analyst's task to decipher the manifestations of the transference neurosis and thus to translate it back into past behavior and past feeling states. The way Freud conceptualized transference in 1914 gives us a chance to understand a new aspect of love. Love can be seen as a form of reliving past feeling states that may not be accessible to direct memory. It is one form in which what was repressed has found a new, altered way of returning into consciousness.

Freud recognized that under such conditions, transference was only a special example; a much earlier force operated in psychic life: the compulsion to repeat.

In 1915, in a paper entitled "Observations on Transference Love," Freud brought together his insights into the nature of transference and his understanding of love in real life. In reading it one can sense the difficulties that confronted Freud in writing it. By 1915, Freud's isolation was over, the Psychoanalytic International Organization was five years old. A new generation of young psychoanalysts was eager for guidance. Few problems in the realm of psychoanalytic technique appeared as urgent as the question of transference love. Nearly all psychoanalysts at the time were young men, and most of the patients were young women. Under these conditions the problem of transference love took on a particular urgency. What was the analyst to do when, as a result of successfully applying the psychoanalytic technique, his female patient declared that she was in love with him? Not only were the practitioners in need of guidance, but the good name of psychoanalysis itself had to be protected; nothing aroused as much derision as did the popular assumption that every woman had to fall in love with her psychoanalyst.

Freud advised steering a careful course between the Scylla of not wounding the woman patient who has declared her love and the Charybdis of yielding to the all-too-tempting situation. He advised the therapist to renounce his pride in having made a conquest and to recognize that the patient's falling in love had been brought about by the analytic situation. Having mastered the countertransference, the therapist must be careful not to steer away from transference love or to repel it, but just as resolutely to withhold any personal response to it. He must demonstrate to the patient that she fell in love at a time when particularly distressing events in her life were about to emerge without her being aware of it. Freud thus discovered something new about love: that it can be summoned as a defense. Freud wrote:

The treatment must be carried out in abstinence. By this I do not mean physical abstinence alone, nor yet the deprivation of everything that the patient desires, for perhaps no sick person could tolerate this. Instead, I shall state it as a fundamental principle that the patient's need and longing should be allowed to persist in her, in order that they may serve as forces impelling her to do work and to make changes, and that we must beware of appeasing those forces by means of surrogates. (1915a:164–165)

Freud believed that ungratified wishes can be turned into motivation for psychic change, whereas gratified wishes are conducive to inertia. Without saying so directly, this view amounted to a theory of sublimation.

The more plainly the analyst lets it be seen that he is proof against every temptation, the more readily will he be able to extract from the situation its analytic content. The patient, whose sexual repression is of course not yet removed but merely pushed into the background, will then feel safe enough to allow all her preconditions for loving, all the phantasies springing from her sexual desires, all the detailed characteristics of her state of being in love, to come to light; and from these she will herself open the way to the infantile roots of her love. (1915a:166)

Up to this point, one would conclude that transference love is a form of resistance, by its very nature different from love in real life. However, toward the end of that paper, Freud made a striking observation:

I think we have told the patient the truth, but not the whole truth regardless of the consequences. The part played by resistance in transference-love is unquestionable and very considerable. Nevertheless the resistance did not, after all, create this love; it finds it ready at hand, makes use of it and aggravates its manifestations. Nor is the genuineness of the phenomenon disproved by the resistance. It is true that the love consists of new editions of old traits and that it repeats infantile reactions. But this is the essential character of every state of being in love. There is no such state which does not reproduce infantile prototypes. It is precisely from this infantile determination that it receives its compulsive character, verging as it does on the pathological. Transference-love has perhaps a degree less of freedom than the love which appears in ordinary life and is called normal; it displays its dependence on the infantile pattern more clearly and is less adaptable and capable of modification; but that is all, and not what is essential. (1915a:168).

This statement represents a break with Freud's previously held conviction that transference is a form of resistance. Freud now gave to transference love the status of a species of love. In real life, the repressed infantile images that give rise to falling in love remain unconscious and, though unconscious, they provide the energy for a new love. In the analytic situation, the early images are made conscious and are thereby deprived of their energizing potential. In analysis, the uncovering of the incestuous fixation behind transference love loosens the incestuous ties and prepares the way for a future love free from the need to repeat oedipal triangulation. Under conditions of health the infantile prototypes merely energize the new falling in love while in neurosis they also evoke the incest taboo and needs for new triangulations that repeat the triangle of the oedipal state.

Freud conceded that even if the (male) psychoanalyst is as tactful as he can be, not every woman will consent to have her love be the subject for psychological inquiry. Ruefully and philosophically, he observed:

There is, it is true, one class of women with whom this attempt to preserve the erotic transference for the purposes of analytic work without satisfying it will not succeed. These are women of elemental passionateness who tolerate no surrogates. They are children of nature who refuse to accept the psychical in place of the material, who in the poet's words, are accessible only to "the logic of soup, with dumplings for arguments." With such people one has the choice between returning their love or else bringing down upon oneself the full enmity of a woman scorned. In neither case can one safeguard the interests of the treatment. One has to withdraw, unsuccessful; and all one can do is to turn the problem over in one's mind of how it is that a capacity for neurosis is joined with such an intractable need for love. (1915a:166–167)

It is noteworthy that in this passage Freud does not speak of transference love, but uses the term erotic transference. Later on he lapses again and speaks of returning this love rather than responding to their erotic wishes. The difference between transference love and erotized transference is not yet sharply drawn.

If under the pressure of the erotized transference or an erotized counter-transference, the psychoanalytic relationship becomes a sexual love relationship, the beneficiary, in Freud's view would be only the repetition compulsion.

She would have succeeded in acting out, in repeating in real life, what she ought only to have remembered. In the further course of the love-relationship she would bring out all the inhibitions and pathological reactions of her erotic life, without there being any possibility of correcting them; and the distressing episode would end in remorse and a great strengthening of her propensity to repression. The love-relationship in fact destroys the patient's susceptibility to influence from analytic treatment. A combination of the two would be an impossibility. (1915a:166.)

## Erotized Transference

The women whom Freud described in the last quoted passage as having elemental passions have often been discussed in the later psychoanalytic literature under the heading of erotized transference. Greenson (1967) described women who come to analysis not to seek insight but to enjoy the physical proximity of the analyst (pp. 338–341). Such patients relate appropriately during the initial interview. They have a good history of achievement and an adequate social life, but an unsatisfactory love life. They develop a strong sexual transference in the first hour on the couch. Their sexual demands show wishes for incorporation, possession, and fusion. Verbalization and interpretation are frustrating to them. Their sexuality, Greenson believes, turns out to be a last-ditch defense against "the abyss of homosexual love for the mother" (p. 340). It is not difficult to discern between Greenson's lines that these women failed to evoke his empathy. I have found that if the analyst can accept these women's early wishes and can regard them as a very early form of love, and if they are explained as such to these women, the treatment situation need not become hopeless.

In states of erotized transferences, I have found it useful to encourage such analysands to imagine what it would be like if their wishes were granted. One finds that they believe that the analytic relationship would continue for twenty-four hours a day, but all the attention will be focused on their needs, that under this exquisite care their problems will vanish as if by magic; life will begin anew, free of toil, care, or neurosis. One then can show these analysands the early nature of their love and help them understand that infancy cannot be relived. If analyzed, erotized transference turns out to be what Balint (1937) called primary love. If the question is asked in a matter-of-fact way, there is ordinarily no danger that it will be taken as seduction.

Blum (1971) described a woman who, early in analysis, developed an erotized transference. She rejected all interpretations related to the revival of the past and felt that she had fallen completely in love with the analyst. She declared that she was ready to "leave her husband and drown her children if only the analyst would marry her." Despite the erotized transference, the patient continued to be a good wife and mother.*

Socarides (1978) believes that female homosexuals are more likely than male homosexuals to develop an erotic transference in their relationship with male analysts. He warns the male analyst that he must interpret the meaning of female homosexual patients' erotic and dependency demands before they can attain an overwhelming peak of intensity. Once the transference feelings reach a high pitch, they will be mixed with bitter and retaliatory feelings directed against the father-psychoanalyst. The lesbian patient is then in danger of experiencing once more the same humiliation at the hands of the analyst that she experienced from her father and that led her to transfer her love back to the mother. Socarides believes that lesbian women once reached the oedipal phase and felt passion toward their father, but because of his rebuff, retreated to preoedipal love relationships and to a maternal representative.

I have had opportunities to observe the consequences of a love relationship between an analysand and her former therapist. Already during treatment, she felt that she was special to her therapist. Toward the end of the treatment, the work of mourning, the necessary working through of the loss of the infantile love object, did not take place. Typically in such cases, feelings of jealousy, envy, and wishes to be victorious over rivals, other analysands, wife or daughters, were not analyzed. The fate of these patients represents a variant on the theme of the "exception" (Freud 1916; Jacobson 1959) which may be paraphrased as "unlike the rest of humanity I am entitled to disobey the incest taboo, circumvent the work of mourning, and possess my parent sexually. I am entitled to do so because I suffered so much or simply because I am an exception." From the analyst's point of view, I assume that the relationship with a former analysand represents a variant on the Pygmalion theme. Like Pygmalion, these analysts wish to create love objects rather than to find them in the outside

---

*Oral communication from Blum. The fact that an analysand can continue the routines of everyday life, despite the transference storm, is an important criterion of analyzability.

world. Such analysts themselves fear and mistrust the outside world. When the transference relationship becomes a sexual one, it represents symbolically and unconsciously the fulfillment of the wish that the infantile love object will not be given up and that incestuous love can be refound in reality. A reanalysis of such cases shows that a new sense of guilt was created, which in turn stimulated superego aggression and resulted in depression. They seek analysis only if the relationship leads to a new disappointment. The fact that they once succeeded in circumventing the oedipal prohibitions makes reanalysis difficult.

## Economics of Love

Blanton (1971) reported that when he was Freud's analysand, Freud used the term *economics of love* (p. 39). The metaphor follows Freud's libido theory. Every person that enters treatment can be seen as bringing with him or her libidinal and aggressive "capital." Aggression as well as love is "invested" in the important persons in everyone's life, such as spouse, children, parents, friends, teachers, pupils, fellow workers, and physicians. It also consists of "investments" in the self, that is, narcissism. In addition to these investments in current objects, psychoanalysis regularly shows that past objects have also remained invested. Not only infantile love objects but also former lovers constitute part of this investment.

During a psychoanalysis, transference changes the libidinal investment in current objects. The possibility of an erotized transference warns us that transference love can create a new deficit in the existing object relationships. It is usually easier to love the analyst and express dissatisfaction with persons in real life. It takes therapeutic skill to reverse the process and safeguard existing relationships. Furthermore, in cases of greater disturbance, the therapist must also protect the representations of past objects from too-rapid disillusionment. If we choose to emphasize the economics of love, analysands will fall into a number of reasonably distinct groups.

First, there are those whose libido is still attached to parental figures. The spinster who devotes her life to the care of her mother or father and the bachelor who lives at home are familiar examples. Here the work of the therapist is to pry loose the libido from its entrapment in the original object, temporarily hold the libido in the transference, and then let the libido seek a more satisfactory person in real life.

Narcissistic personalities comprise the second group that is so self-preoccupied that there is not enough libido available to others. The literature on narcissism is vast; it mostly pertains to the ways in which narcissists can establish a meaningful transference to the therapist. The question of whether once transference love has been established, the narcissist can also transfer out into persons in the real world has received less attention.

In the third group are those who have detached their libido from parental figures, who are not narcissistic, but whose ego cannot master the integrative function of centering the libido on one other person.

The fourth group comprises men and women who have established a lasting relationship, who have become parents, but who are nevertheless unhappy in their marriage. Strife, discontent, and disappointment in the partner predominate. We know that relationships create their own pathology, which is to some extent independent of the neurosis of each partner. There was a time in the history of psychoanalysis when it was fashionable to believe that the repetition compulsion was so powerful that divorce was futile, because the partners would rediscover the same neurotic partner under a new name (Bergler 1949). But under the impact of object relations theory, this extreme view no longer predominates.

Blanton (1971) reported that when he was in analysis with Freud, Freud told him, "It has been my experience that when women have a love affair they are absolutely lost to analysis. Men on the other hand can have affairs without total immersion" (p. 53). What Freud says about women subsequent experience has shown to be true in adolescents and borderline personalities. In two other situations, at the height of falling in love and after the birth of a baby, I have found that love may absorb all of the libido that is available. In such cases analytic work usually yields to daydreams about the beloved, expressions of love toward him or her, and wishes to end the hour so as to be reunited with the beloved. In extreme cases it may be necessary to give the analysand a furlough from treatment. This is particularly true in borderline patients who cannot sustain more than one relationship at a time. Analytic work can resume after the love affair has lost some of its intensity and when the symbiotic phase has come to an end, and, in the case of a baby, the separation process has started.

To what extent the transference love is transferable to objects in the real world during and after treatment is a question that has not received the attention it deserves. If the image of the analyst has been internalized and the separation and mourning work was done, psychoanalytic theory postulates that the analysand will be internally ready to love a person in the real world. For some analysands, the analyst becomes a new ego ideal, replacing that of the parent. When this takes place, the analyst can become the basis of a new falling in love and a bridge to a new object relationship in the outside world. A new love object selected after an analysis often bears the features and personality traits of the analyst.

We also encounter cases in which this replacement takes place while the analysis is still in progress. I am familiar with a case in which a man started therapy, became frightened by transference love, left treatment, established a love relationship with another therapist, and then returned to treatment. Striking are those cases in which homosexual analysands in treatment with women therapists establish their first heterosexual relationship based on the model of their therapist. When such falling in love takes place while the analysis is still in progress, the role of resistance is greater. Without saying so explicitly, the analysand's behavior can be deciphered as "I do not need your love, I have found a substitute therapist who is the right sex and the right age and who, unlike you, does not withhold sexual gratification." Such patients do not sexualize the transference but build a barrier to the deepening of transference feelings. There is a tendency to call such fallings in love "acting out" because the therapist feels that they interfere with the full unfolding of the transference relationship. When thus in love, the analysands accept the interpretation, but it has little effect on his or her love; they resent the analyst's interference and questioning about this relationship. Analysands rightly resent the interpretation that their love is a resistance. The resistance plays a role but it is not the sole force determining the falling in love. In these cases there is a danger that the mourning and working through of the terminal phase of the analysis has been circumvented. It may also happen that a relationship that was satisfactory while the analysis was in progress is insufficient to carry the relationship after terminating, and a new love object must be sought.

I have found that transference love is a very early and dependent form of love. Such loves are not unknown in real life, but they are ill-suited to the slings and arrows of every day experience. Many analysands who cannot find love in real life nevertheless can experience transference love; it is a mistake to assume that those who are capable of transference love have achieved the capacity to find love under ordinary conditions. Transference love can be the beginning of a capacity to love, but by itself, it is not life's equivalent. In psychoanalysis, one frequently observes that analysands who can relate only ambivalently and who continuously fight with their partners nevertheless in transference relate positively to the analyst. Toward the analyst, they display an attitude reminiscent of what Abraham (1924) called preambivalence. They may be critical of everybody in the outside world but find the psychoanalyst above reproach. Because they idealize the psychoanalyst, they repress or deny their negative feelings.

In the analytic situation, the channels for expressing concern and reciprocity from the analysand to the analyst are radically curtailed. It is especially designed for the purposes of cure but is unsuitable for meeting the analysand's mature needs. In states of narcissistic depletion, however, when other fixations on early developmental stages dominate, transference love has the great advantage of demanding less reciprocity from the analysand than does love in real life. It is the inability of transference love to meet the adult needs of the analytic patient that propels the analysand to redirect the libido freed through the analytic process to love objects in the real world. Ultimately the analysand's yearning for adult love and his or her willingness to substitute adult love for the gratification and frustration of his or her infantile love mobilized in the transference makes termination an inner necessity.

Bak (1973) stressed that one is most apt to fall in love after a love object has been lost. The termination of treatment is conducive to falling in love, whereas its unnecessary prolongation has the opposite effect. The termination thus can be difficult in all cases where prospects for a new love are not favorable. These issues should be discussed so that the patient can be prevented from suddenly feeling empty after the termination.

Loewald (1962) suggested that, ideally, termination of treatment should lead to the relinquishing of the analyst as an incestuous object and the transformation of this relationship into a new relationship between superego and ego. It can then undergo further development as an internal relationship within the superego-ego system. Relationships with internalized objects are real, psychologically speaking, because they lead to internalized structures, whereas relationships with fantasy objects remain fantasies. Termination is incomplete as long as the psychoanalyst remains an object of fantasies.

There is still another danger that should be worked through before termination. The analytic situation focuses entirely on the analysand. The psychoanalytic relationship demands that everything be said; by implication, the analysand should not censor his or her thoughts because the analyst's feelings may be hurt. Many ex-analysands demand in their behavior the same rights from their spouses. In some cases a couple can successfully function as dream interpreters for each other. But even in these cases, I suspect that the process of emotional growth from transference love to love in real life has not been completed.

## Transference Love and Sublimation

When we look back at Plato's ideas on sublimation, it becomes evident that the analysand who cannot gratify his or her direct libidinal or erotic wishes within the treatment situation sublimates them in the service of insight.

Freud did not use the term *sublimation* to describe the work of either the psychoanalyst or the analysand. However, during psychoanalysis, sexual and aggressive wishes continually emerge during transference, and interpretations are converted into a recollection of the past and greater self-knowledge. Therefore I find no justification for denying the term sublimation to the work of the analysand. The burden of sublimation is not as great on the analyst; nevertheless in many analyses, countertransference feelings are continually evoked. If the analyst remains creative, these feelings will become conscious in an ongoing process of self-analysis. If they are used in the service of analysis, this process too deserves the name sublimation. The sublimation of the analyst and analysand differs from the artist or scientist. Although in order to become converted into useful therapeutic work such sublimation has to become conscious, artists and scientists can pursue their sublimations best if their wishes remain preconscious or even unconscious.

I find it useful to differentiate between two types of sublimation. The first usually takes place sometime between adolescence and early adulthood, and it resolves competing needs and culminates in the choice of an occupation. (Every occupational choice contains some sublimation of sexual and aggressive wishes, some gratification of the demands of the superego, and includes answers to traumatic events and an acceptance of reality limitations.) As therapists we are familiar with cases in which such a compromise solution cannot be brought about by the ego. The commitment to an occupational choice thus remains tenuous and ambivalent. In other cases, the occupational choice has to be balanced by a hobby or a second occupation.

The second type of sublimation is a continuously ongoing process within the occupational choice. If the artist is creative, every new work of art will represent a new victory for sublimation. For less creative artists, such works are mere variations on a theme, because the problems which were resolved long ago have become routinized. In psychoanalysis, too, we encounter patients who can be treated with knowledge acquired long ago that has become routinized, whereas other analysands make new demands on the analyst's psychic equilibrium, calling for a new capacity for sublimation.

My experience in treating professional therapists has taught me that almost every therapist, depending on his or her psychic structure, has the same attitude toward all patients. Thus therapists who have a strong superego tend to see all patients as judging them. Those who are narcissistic tend to feel that all patients are demanding and lack gratitude. In addition to characterological attitudes, different patients evoke different responses.

In supervisory work, one encounters time and again a conflict which causes younger psychoanalysts a great difficulty. At a stage in the analysis the analysand (usually female) insists that her feelings for the analyst are not transference but real love. The analyst remains adamant that this is transference, evoking the analysand's hostility. I believe that it would be more useful at this point to introduce the concept of sublimation and instead of denying the reality of the love feelings to respond with, "It does not matter whether you experience your feelings toward me as love or as transference love because we are going to use this love as a way of exploring your past, including your neurotic patterns of loving." This reply is closer to the clinical truth and it spares the analysand unnecessary feelings of humiliation.

# 19

## Psychoanalytic Contributions to Love After Freud

In the previous chapters, I have pointed to some developments within psychoanalysis after Freud. In this chapter, I will attempt a systematic treatment of these developments. During Freud's lifetime, he was so towering a figure in psychoanalysis that the contributions by other analysts usually were extensions of projects he had initiated. The climate of opinion during the early decades of psychoanalysis was less orthodox than is generally assumed. There were controversies in many areas, notably around the approach to female sexuality, where Jones and Horney held opinions very different from those of Freud. There were also disagreements on technique, with Ferenczi questioning the value of the rule of abstinence. In the realm of metapsychology there were also disagreements. When Fenichel and others questioned Freud's death instinct theory, nevertheless, what Freud said was where psychoanalysis stood. After Freud's death, there was no longer an indisputable center. Love was not a topic of psychoanalytic interest in the first decades after Freud's death but the picture changed in the seventies when new formulations about the development of the infant, and new concepts about the nature of narcissism, radically changed the picture.

When one deals with thoughts of psychoanalysts who came of age after 1939, the year Freud died, I find it useful to differentiate between extenders and modifiers. The extender bases his work on concepts already well established by Freud and extends them into areas Freud has left unexplored. By contrast, the modifier begins his own line of thought with an addition to, or modification of, one of Freud's basic assertions. Needless to say that the division is not absolute; the extenders differ with Freud on some points and the modifiers do not completely reject Freud. But, in general, the distinction is useful. Thus, I regard Nunberg and Fenichel as extenders, Hartmann and Klein as modifiers. On the subject of love, the significant modifier is Balint. Typical extenders are Eissler and Bak.

Since modifiers disagree on basic issues, my task as a reviewer is more complex. I have given each modifier a subheading of his own, but I have not hesitated to criticize the modifiers. I believe that readers who are not committed to one school or another will find that every modifier has thrown new light on one aspect of love. They all deserve a hearing. The reader will further find that I have discussed in this chapter two types of contributors to love, those who have written directly on the subject, and those who have made essential contributions elsewhere in the field that in turn could be used to deepen our understanding of love. I will begin with two psychoanalysts, Eissler and Bak, who added to our understanding of love but whose views require no other assumptions beyond those made by Freud.

Eissler's (1963) observations on love appeared as an appendix to his two-volume biography of Goethe. The chapter dealing with love is entitled "The Emotion of Amorousness and the Principle of Repetition." Eissler begins with an observation usually taken for granted; that lovers repeat in countless variations the simple statement: "I want to assure you that I love you." Eissler asks: "It is really not self-evident why an adult should feel the urge to repeat the same statement despite the fact that the person to whom it is addressed is already fully aware of its content" (p. 659). He answers: "There are strong forces in the psychic apparatus that work against an exclusive attachment. With each repetitive step in the state of amorousness, the image of the love object becomes more firmly attached to and integrated by the ego" (p. 661).

It was Freud's emphasis on the mobility of the libido that made it possible for Eissler to decipher why lovers continuously repeat their vows of love. From the libido theory Eissler also drew the conclusion that those who mourn and those who love have much in common. Mourner and lover feel the need to concentrate all their thoughts, words, and actions upon the partner. If the mourner forgets for a moment that the object no longer exists, he feels like a passionate lover who forgets the beloved. In other ways, the two emotions are opposite. For the mourner the thought of the lost beloved evokes the greatest pain; for the lover, the thought of the beloved evokes the greatest joy. The mourning process, as Freud observed in 1917, leads to severing of the tie. In love, the same repetitive process leads to the anchoring of the tie. This may seem paradoxical: the explanation is that it takes the same "work" to detach as it takes to attach the libido.

Anthologists of love poetry (Stallworthy 1974) inform us that more poems have been written about love than about any other subject. Traditionally it has been assumed that most people who are in love turn to love poetry because words fail them. What they themselves cannot express, they hope to find in poetry. Poetry, by using the right words in the right order, crystallizes the emotions that love has provoked. All this is traditional wisdom and beyond dispute. Eissler has added a hitherto unsuspected reason why lovers read love poetry: they do so in order to overcome ambivalence and to withdraw libido from their usual interests and concentrate it on the beloved. Reading love poetry and going on a honeymoon have much in common.

Eissler's book deals with ten years in Goethe's life between 1775 and 1786. During these years Goethe was deeply in love with Charlotte von Stein, a married woman, mother of many children. In Eissler's opinion this relationship remained sexually unconsummated. For this reason and because the love relationship brought about a profound personality change in Goethe, Eissler called it "proto-psychoanalysis." Eissler showed that Goethe transferred his libido step by step from his beloved sister to Frau von Stein. When the transfer of the libido was completed Goethe could leave her, and soon afterwards established his first genital sexual relationship at the age of forty. In this way Frau von Stein fulfilled the intermediary role of helping the libido to pass on from incestuous to nonincestuous objects analogous to the role of a psychoanalyst in the analytic situation.

Among Goethe's poems there is a posthumously published poem of great beauty. The beauty is achieved by an extraordinary condensation. In Eissler's view, Goethe intended it as a personal poem to Frau von Stein, too personal to be published.

> Only to our poor selves, full of love as we are,
> The eternal bliss was denied,
> To love each other without knowing each other
> And to see in the other what he never was.
> Oh tell! What faith has in store for us!
> For you must have been in times lived out long ago
> My sister or my wife.
>
> (my translation)

In the first four lines, Goethe complains that he cannot idealize the beloved enough. What Freud discovered to have been the incestuous tie of infancy, Goethe poetically transferred to a life lived out long ago. This device enabled Goethe to simultaneously admit and deny the incestuous basis of his love for Frau von Stein. A few months earlier, Eissler informs us, Goethe expressed in a letter to his beloved his hope that his sister should find a brother just as he had found a sister in her. The letter as well as the poem is a fascinating example of what Freud described as the process in which the libido is being transferred from incestuous to new love objects. During this period Goethe developed an inhibition against writing to his sister even though she was mortally ill. He could not relate to the two women at the same time. We should not, however, make the mistake of assuming that Goethe was as conscious of this transfer as psychoanalytic patients become when the incestuous nature of their transference love has been interpreted. An important question remained open. Frau von Stein enabled Goethe to transfer the incestuous wishes from the sister and, after that love, genital sexuality became possible. But did Goethe ever love another woman as he loved her? Or must we conclude that for some men and women the first recipient of the transference love is also the person who remains most deeply loved? Many analysands report that they loved someone early in life and never loved anyone else as deeply. In such cases, Freud's two streams, the tender and the sexual, never coalesce.

One gains the impression that for some people the first nonincestuous love object recapitulates the fate usually reserved to the incestuous one. One can never love as deeply as one loved for the first time. Such men and women usually feel guilty toward all subsequent loves because they know that they do not love them as deeply as they loved for the first time. It seems that in such cases the guilt properly reserved for incestuous love objects has been transferred and lingers with the memory of the first nonincestuous love.

For Eissler such a striking transfer of the libido was part of the psychology of genius. Goethe's capacity to use the emotional state in which the libido is being transferred for artistic purposes is of course unique, but I see no reason to assume that the process itself is unique. In 1980 I postulated that what Freud called transfer of libido from incestuous to nonincestuous objects probably takes place in every falling in love, whether consummated or not. A process that Freud saw as taking place once and for all during adolescence, I see as taking place in stages throughout the life cycle, whenever one falls in love. Intrapsychically every new love represents such a transfer.*

---

*What Freud called transfer of the libido can sometimes be observed in dreams. When a dreamer dreams of a sexual or a love relationship with a person who combines features of the love object recently abandoned with features that belong to the new object, a transfer of libido is taking place.

Eissler's contribution can be seen as an extension of Freud's second stage of theorizing on love: it extends ideas Freud found in the papers on narcissism (1914) and the paper on mourning and melancholia (1917).

Bak (1973) stressed the connection between love and melancholia. His point of departure was Freud's statement: "In the two most opposed situations of being most intensely in love and of suicide the ego is overwhelmed by the object, though in totally different ways" (1917:252). In being in love, Bak observed, the self is overwhelmed by the "good object" and in suicide the self is overwhelmed by the "bad object"; in both instances the object has been taken into the self.

Bak saw love as a midway station between mourning and melancholia. In mourning the person who was loved has died, a real object was lost. In melancholia the loss is unconscious, intrapsychic, and symbolic. In being in love, there is a real person in the real world, but the emotion of being in love is only in small part a response to that person. The urgency of love comes from the need to avoid experiencing object loss. Bak sees love as a precarious state, for if the attempt to find a substitute for the lost person fails, love may turn into melancholia or suicide. Goethe's Werther, an alienated and depressed young man, commits suicide when love fails. He is the outstanding example of such a love-suicide in literature.

Erotomania, the pathological equivalent to love, illuminates for Bak others forms of love. Erotomania is the last and most desperate attempt to regain the lost object; when this attempt fails, a further regression toward de-differentiation of self and object takes place. Failure to regain the last outpost of libidinal cathexis may then lead to suicide or schizophrenia. Bak believed that all too often a breakdown was already on its way before the falling in love took place: love was a desperate attempt to forestall the breakdown.

The separation between self and object representations, Bak also observed, "is never complete and traces of primary identifications will remain in the most highly developed object relationships." Bak reiterates Freud's observations that men and women need intense object cathexes in order to feel a strong sense of aliveness. Due to the intensification of the object cathexes, nature, music and art, as well as sexuality, are experienced with greater intensity in a state of love.

In the early states of symbiosis the infant, Bak noted, is, as far as our observations go, intensely preoccupied with mother's face. Throughout our lives the face remains the most individualized part of the body, and in love, the preoccupation with the face of the beloved returns. In sexual relationships the so-called part-objects, penis, breast, or vagina, may become the greatest source of sexual attraction, but in love it is always the face. In love it is the face of the beloved we yearn for most intensely.

Bak's approach to love is topographic. He assigns no role to the ego in falling in love. As a result, the personality of the beloved plays only a minor role.

In psychopathology, there is a midway station between the bliss of love and suicide: masochistic love. The subject of masochistic love is vast. During the age of the Troubadours it found a significant literary and musical expression. Bak cites the case of Oscar Wilde, who was in love with Lord Alfred Douglas, whom Bak sees as a homosexual variant on the "femme fatale." Wilde was ten years old when his father, Sir William Wilde, was brought to court in a scandalous libel suit for having had sexual relations with a young patient. These proceedings greatly excited the child Oscar. When he heard about it he fantasized that he would one day have to appear in court: "Regina versus Wilde." His wish was fulfilled in circumstances almost identical with those of his father except that they were homosexual rather than heterosexual. *De Profundis* is one of the most heart-rending documents of love, portraying the masochistic submission alternating with desperate rebellion toward a lover to the point of moral if not physical suicide.

Bak has added a universal precondition to Freud's preconditions for loving, namely, object loss. In Bak's view, the personality of the beloved plays only a subordinate role. What matters is that he or she shall be present at the time when the loss of a loved one has taken place.

I have found that some women know this intuitively. Contrary to custom, they do not hesitate to approach a widower in the first stages of his bereavement. If the widower is capable of mourning, he will rebuff such attempts until his work of mourning is complete; but if he avoids mourning, the early intruder may well succeed in replacing the lost love object. The old bachelors who marry after the death of a parent tend to support Bak's thesis.

## The Role of the Ego and Superego in Love

The topographic point of view as formulated by Freud divided the psyche into conscious, preconscious, and unconscious. The structural point of view divides the psychic apparatus into ego, id, and superego (Freud 1923). The topographic is the older of the two. For a long time psychoanalysts were, so to speak, bilingual, employing either the topographic or the structural frame of reference. The topographic dominated dream psychology while the structural was used to understand symptoms. In 1952, Lewin suggested that symptoms like dreams could be conceptualized in topograhic terms. In 1964, Arlow and Brenner argued that it would be more economical to treat all psychic phenomena, including dreams and psychoses, within the structural frame of reference. In an earlier chapter I pointed out that Freud's ideas on love were expressed within the topographic frame of reference. In this section I will discuss what changes were brought about in the understanding of love by the structural point of view. Even though Freud himself originated the structural point of view, to discuss love in this frame is already a modification, although not a basic one.

The first psychoanalyst to discuss love from a structural point of view was Waelder in his classical paper of 1930. This paper was written directly under the influence of Freud's *The Ego and the Id* (1923). It stands apart from Hartmann's ego psychology. The paper was very influential in shaping later views on love. To Waelder, love was an act of integration of a high order, a tribute to the ego's capacity to bring together harmoniously wishes of the id, demands of the repetition compulsion, the demands of the superego, and the claims of reality. The love object chosen must be sexually gratifying, connected unconsciously to love objects in the person's past, sufficiently admired to meet the approval of the superego, and appropriate in meeting the demands of reality. When one of the partners to this "coalition" remains in opposition, love may still be experienced as blissful, but it will not be free of conflict.

Following Waelder, we can see felicitous falling in love as simultaneously satisfying potentially conflicting needs. These can be enumerated as: in happy love the best that the original love objects have bequeathed to the child has been refound. The beloved is not so much idealized as she or he represents realistic aspects of the lover's ego ideal. When this happens, the lover can experience a sense of pride in the person he or she has chosen. Finally the choice must meet the requirements of the ego in the sense that it is a realistic choice that assures the prospect of a continuous happy relationship in the future.

A paper of Altman (1977) highlights the role assigned to the ego in contemporary psychoanalytic thinking. He states that the ego imparts to love a sense of duration. "Without the interference of ego functions, love would be merely an exercise in erotic as well as sadistic techniques, or a repertoire of perversions" (p. 38). It is worth noting that the task that Freud and Abraham assigned to the libido in its autonomous process of maturation Model (1968) and Altman assign to the ego. The ego is here conceptualized as the guardian of our uniqueness as human beings. Altman also suggested that women can with greater ease commit themselves to a stable relationship because they already once before renounced the first object, the mother, for the father, while men, for whom the mother remains the love object until adolescence, are more prone to continue to search for the ideal mother.

It is the ego and not the libido in Altman's view which is charged with the function of bringing together the sexual and the tender currents during adolescence. It is the ego that synthesizes the pregenital stages under the primacy of the genital phase; it is the ego that gives to love the capacity to tolerate differences between partners and endure frustration. Altman assigns a significant role to the superego as well. It is the superego that gives to love the capacity for compassion and remorse and enables a person to continue loving even when gratification is not forthcoming.

In a 1980 paper, I stressed five additional functions the ego has to perform: first, reality testing is one of the most important functions of the ego. Although the ego has lost much of its power in falling in love, its first task is to observe the real qualities of the love object and to evaluate the future of the relationship. This task is particularly difficult, since falling in love is dominated by displacement and projection. The proverbial blindness of love is due to these mechanisms. I have observed cases in which the refinding process was experienced so powerfully that the analysand, psychologically speaking, lost sight of the fact that the woman he loved was not really his mother. He had to be helped to realize that certain "calamities of childhood" (Brenner 1982) which he or she experienced with mother or father will not necessarily repeat themselves in an adult love relationship. The participation of the ego is experienced as a change from falling in love as a dream state to experiencing the relationship as real. This transition is difficult to make for many lovers. On the other hand, when object choice is dominated by realistic ego considerations—talent, social position, health, or wealth—love is seldom experienced. The same difference was stated in a different vocabulary by Singer (1984) when he differentiated between appraisal and bestowal. In psychoanalytic terms, love can be experienced only when the refinding process works unconsciously and is sanctioned by ego and superego.

The second task I assigned to the ego was that of integration. Typically, the growing child has a number of love objects: mother, her substitutes, father, siblings, etc. Under favorable conditions, the object representations of these love objects become integrated and do not compete for supremacy later on in life. However, if there has been disharmony between these objects, their representations will tend to be at war with each other within the former child. The choice of the adult love object may be modeled on one of these early love objects, but love is richer if it can draw upon a significant number of them. In the topographic model, drawing on a number of significant objects of infancy takes place by chance through condensation. Using the structural model, it can be seen as being achieved by the integrative functions of the ego, working unconsciously.

Particularly when the early maternal functions were performed by more than one person and there was conflict between the original objects, the task of integration can be beyond the capacity of the ego. To resolve the intrapsychic strife, more than one love object will be sought at the same time or in rapid succession. Under such conditions, each object of infancy has remained cathected separately and demands its own refinding. There are other tasks of integration which the ego must perform. Sometimes even the image of the mother- or the father-figure is not a unified one and fragments of that image press for a separate refinding. Bisexuality is a universal human endowment, but individuals differ in the strength of their respective masculine and feminine components, and they seek in the partner a corresponding mixture of the two components. Contradictory wishes may also be present. For example, the wish for the mirroring of the self in the love object is opposed to the wish to find the characteristics one lacks. Philosophers (Hazo 1967: 31–33) have argued for centuries over whether love seeks complementarity or similarity, when in fact both forces are active to varying degrees in most people.

A third task of the ego is to counteract the force of the superego so that the love object does not succumb to the incest taboo, even though the similarities to the original incestuous love object are present. I recall an analysand who at 17 fell in love but at the same time heard an inner voice commanding him to give up the girl he had fallen in love with and to accept another with whom he was not in love. This pattern remained a lifelong characteristic of his love relationships. Whenever he tried to establish a relationship with the woman he loved, he encountered the same mysterious inner voice demanding he give her up. Psychoanalysis revealed that the "voice" was that of the superego, which vetoed each choice as being too close to the image of the mother.

A fourth task of the ego consists of counteracting the extreme demands of the id that insist on refinding the impossible, the replica of the longed-for symbiosis. In the course of her analysis an analysand reflected, "I can't go on comparing X with my ideal man. We will never make it." Thus began an intrapsychic process in which the ego negotiated with the ego ideal as to what shortcomings in the man could be tolerated and what were the demands that were, so to speak, nonnegotiable.

Finally, when one is under the pressure of the repetition compulsion and a new object is sought that will have the same pain-evoking qualities that characterized the old, every effort will have to be made to transform the new object to conform to the original object. The fifth task of the ego then becomes to oppose the "candidate" chosen by the destructive repetition compulsion.

If the original objects were good enough, the refinding process can run more or less smoothly. For those who had unempathic or neglectful parents, the refinding process will lead to pathological object selection unless the ego intervenes. Thus, an already burdened person is under pressure to direct the choosing of an object in opposition to infantile prototypes. The ego must exercise a protective as well as anticipatory function. Beleaguered, it may fail to observe the total personality of the love object and take cognizance only of its opposition to the old. Even when the object is in fact different, under the pressure of the repetition compulsion, the individual may succeed in eliciting responses characteristic of the defective parent (Lipin: 1963). In 1971, I called this reactive type of object choice "counterselection."

Attempts at counterselection represent a vulnerable solution. Frequently the repetition compulsion opposes the efforts of the ego, and a state of conflict arises between the two opposing groups of wishes. Under such pressure, two love objects may be selected simultaneously, one representing counterselection, the other the dangerous refinding. In such a situation the person clings to the counterselected object for safety, but will seek sexual gratification from another, based on refinding. For example, when a mother was seductive, exciting, but unreliable, the man may marry a woman that offers safety and loyalty, having thus found a "safe harbor" to which he can always return; he may feel safe enough to have love affairs with women who are modeled after the mother. The greater emphasis on the ego as a psychic structure that weighs conflicting claims, reaches compromises, and takes reality into account when it selects a partner has modified Freud's topographic view of love.

## The Effect of New Formulations Outside the Field of Love

After World War II, under the leadership of H. Hartmann, a group of psychoanalysts modified many of Freud's formulations and succeeded in throwing new light on the transformation of libido into love. This is known in psychoanalytic history as psychoanalytic ego psychology.

In 1945 and 1946 Spitz observed infants in a foundling home where the infants received above-average physical care in terms of food, hygiene, and medical care, but little love because one nurse was responsible for the care of twelve babies. These babies first developed an anaclitic depression which was followed by a marked motor retardation, marasmus, and eventually a high death rate (Spitz 1965: 280 ff.). These observations were unexpected in the light of Freud's assumption that the infant is at birth narcissistic. Spitz drew no radical conclusions from his observations but they confirmed what Balint (1937) has surmised, that the libido is object-directed from birth. In time the observations of Spitz gave rise to a psychoanalytic object relations theory (Blanck and Blanck 1979; Kernberg 1980). Contemporary psychoanalysts recognize what Freud did not know: that the type of daily interaction between mother and child as well as the way the other significant persons interact with the baby creates a matrix upon which the later interactions with adult love objects will take place. They will influence significantly the extent of the adult's capacity to love.

In 1952, Hartmann suggested another line of development which has important implications for loving. During the first half year of life the infant has a smiling relationship with any adult that meets his needs. At this stage, the object exists psychologically only as long as the need exists. This happy state culminates between the sixth and eighth month in what Spitz called "stranger anxiety." The infant becomes frightened when he realizes that he was picked up by a stranger with an unfamiliar face. Under normal circumstances this stranger anxiety lasts a few months. This anxiety is the signal that the infant is beginning to differentiate between the mother whose face evokes pleasure and a stranger whose face evokes anxiety. This stage of development can be seen as the first precursor to what will become the capacity to love. From now on, emotions will develop and become stabilized as they involve in the relationship between the baby and those who take of him. The mother who ministers to the needs of an infant is both gratifying and frustrating; the infant at first splits her image into a good and a bad mother (this split survives in fairy tales where the witch and the wicked stepmother represent the bad mother and the fairy the good one). Eventually, this splitting is overcome and the next stage, the stage of object constancy, is reached (Fraiberg 1969). Although adults are not children, some adults in their love lives function on a need-gratification level; others are prone to split the image of the loved one into idealized and debased. This splitting is in turn responsible for idealized desexualized love and debased sexuality. It is also the base for an earlier split between the good and bad object.

Psychoanalytic developmental psychology assumes that when a firm object constancy has been achieved in childhood, the adult lover will not resort to splitting. The hypothesis is difficult to test. Psychoanalytic theory further assumes that the need to idealize the beloved—so common a feature in falling in love—is designed to protect the beloved from ambivalence and is conducive to splitting.

Jacobson (1964) stressed that, as a result of inner development, the child gradually learns to separate intrapsychically self representations (feelings, ideas toward and about the self, and a growing realistic appraisal of the self) from object representations (an increasingly realistic appraisal of the parents and their internalized images comprising love as well as hostile feelings). Only after the separation between self and object representations has been achieved can one speak of a cohesive self. If adulthood is reached before there is an intrapsychic separation between self and object representations or while the separation is still going on, there will be fear of reengulfment by the intrapsychic representation of the parent and this fear is then displaced on the adult love object. Such men and women have to curtail their contact with those they love. They have to live in different towns, meet at infrequent intervals, have other relationships, take separate vacations, or develop other unique ways of dealing with the fear of engulfment.

Mahler and her coworkers (1963, 1968, 1975) and Pine (1979) have shown that separation between object and self representations is achieved in the first years of childhood as a result of a gradual process of separation and individuation from the mother or her substitutes. Initially, the infant is described as passing through a state of autism, followed by the state of symbiosis. In this state there is as yet no psychic separation between mother and infant. Out of this symbiotic dual unity of mother and infant, and through complex development of separation-individuation phases, the self as a psychological entity gradually emerges. Normal separation-individuation is the first crucial prerequisite for the development of a healthy sense of identity. The rhythm associated with the availability of the mother lays the foundations for the development of object constancy (Mahler 1963). To varying degrees the process of separation from the mother also leaves a residue of sadness that under unfavorable conditions becomes a source of depression (Pine 1979).

In my 1971 paper, I suggest that the symbiotic phase leaves a psychic residue in the form of a longing for merger and this state of longing is reevoked when one falls in love. It was this longing that Plato described so well over 2500 years ago. Bak's (1973) views on this subject are similar to mine. He writes: "Being in love is a uniquely human, exceptional emotional state, which is based on undoing of the separation between mother and child" (p. 6).

Mahler's subphases of separation-individuation have thrown new light on many difficulties in loving. One of the subphases, which she calls the "rapprochement" subphase, is of importance in understanding a particular difficulty in loving. During this phase the toddler continuously goes away from the mother but needs her to be there when he or she returns for what Mahler so aptly called refueling. When the mother for her own reasons is not there to receive the toddler joyfully when he or she returns, the toddler's development may remain arrested on this period. Many college students repeat the rapprochement crisis when they leave home for the first time and are seized with an anxiety to come home. Homer's *Odyssey* can be seen as the epic poem of this phase of development with Penelope as the ideal mother of the rapprochement subphase. When the rapprochement subphase has not been navigated successfully, lovers will repeat the need to leave and return only to leave again, subjecting their partner to an infinite number of waiting tests.

A recently published love poem by E.B. White has captured this phase.

### Love Poem to Katherine

The spider, dropping down from twig,
Unwinds a thread of her devising:
A thin, premeditated rig
To use in rising.

And all the journey down through space,
In cool descent, and loyal-hearted,
She builds a ladder to the place
From which she started.

Thus I, gone forth, as spiders do,
In spider's web a truth discerning,
Attach one silken thread to you
For my returning.
(*New York Times*, October 27, 1985)

In keeping with these ideas developed by the psychologists of the Hartmann school, Model (1968: 88) finds that the greatest obstacles to happy love are the heavy demands we make on our love objects. Love is possible to the extent that we are capable of tolerating separateness from our love object. If one has been fortunate enough to receive "good enough mothering" in the first and second years of life, a positive sense of identity has been formed. If these conditions prevail, we accept a sense of separateness and have a better capacity to find a realistically suitable partner.

When the mother out of anxiety or loneliness opposes the specific needs of the infant for separation and individuation, a fear of future closeness and a hypersensitivity about intrusion are likely to result. I have the impression that American society today with its emphasis on the mother's early return to work does not provide the optimal needs of a child for the necessary closeness upon which future love relationships will be based. It remains to be seen what the effects of the two parents sharing the traditionally maternal functions will have on the development of gender identity.

## Love Among Those Who Are Psychically Ill

Because we idealize love, we tend to recognize love only when it takes place under favorable conditions, when the intrapsychic conflict has been resolved. If we wish to study love objectively, we must also include in our observations love associated with psychopathology. Already in antiquity, it was known that insanity and suicide may follow spurned love. The insight, however, that love can be summoned as a desperate defense against impending psychic disintegration is a recent discovery of psychoanalysis.

In 1936 Schmideberg noted that falling in love is a "normal cure" for paranoid anxieties and depression. She speaks of normal cure because the cure is given by life itself and not with the help of a therapist. In love she finds that both the "good objects" and the good parts of the self are projected on the loved person. Ambivalences are countercathected by idealization. She even postulates that the lover can be a counterphobic object* (Fenichel 1939). In such cases one loves a person one unconsciously fears.

Since paranoid anxiety underlies the state of being in love, love can turn into hate. Arlow (1980) described the role of pathological identification in those who cannot love. He cites the case of a successful Don Juan who pursues women ardently but drops them abruptly after they yield to him. The genetic basis for this need to drop the woman after sexual gratification was an identification with a promiscuous mother and a nursemaid that abandoned him. The opening phase in the relationship of this young man was typical romantic love with intoxication and heart sickness. Sexual intercourse was inevitably followed by disappointment. Arlow's case

---

*Fenichel (1939) wrote a classic paper on counterphobia. An example of counterphobia is a person who suffers from fear of heights becoming a mountain climber or a stammerer being an orator.

recalls the biblical Amnon and Tamar. That consummation of sexual intercourse can be a prelude to disappointment in a hitherto idealized woman is well known. The idealized woman is unconsciously believed to be a phallic woman. After intercourse she loses this status and may become no different from other women; seen as castrated, she has to be discarded. Mozart's *Don Giovanni* claims to be permanently in love with the species woman but not with one of its individual representatives. The syndrome of the perpetual seducer is complex and is based on individual biographical history. All these cases, however, present phallic-narcissistic fixation, a counterphobic attitude toward women. It is as if they were saying, "I am not afraid of you, I can conquer you. By seducing you, I show how faithless you are to your own loves." The disappointed child "masters" his disapointment by becoming a disappointing lover.

Marcel Proust's *Remembrance of Things Past* described such a figure. The hero is in love with Albertine as long as he believes she is inaccessible.

Jacobson (1954a; 1954b) wrote no specific paper on love. Her description of cyclothemic disorders (extreme fluctuations between depression and mania), however, and her interest in psychotic identification led her to discover much that is relevant to the subject of love. Cyclothemics, before their break with reality or during their free intervals, have many interests. They make delightful companions and are capable of full genital response. They retain, however, an infantile narcissistic dependency on their love objects. They live, so to speak, through the idealized partner. They are proud of their capacity to idealize and believe that this capacity is part of their uniqueness. As long as they can, they hypercathect the image of their partner with love and deprive their own self representations of necessary narcissistic love. They then hope to gain back, through the love they receive from their partner, their inner libidinal deficiency. (The reader will note that Jacobson here describes a pathological process, the very process Freud thought to be normal in falling in love.) When these cyclothemic personalities can no longer idealize their love objects, they break off the relationship and blame the previously loved person. They attempt to reverse the process and recapture as much as possible of the libido for themselves. As a rule, however, this process is not successful. What happens is that both the person and the previously loved person become devalued, worthless, and empty. Furthermore, they develop guilt feelings for the psychological destruction of the love object, which increases their feelings of worthlessness.

In psychotic identifications the pathology goes even deeper. Jacobson quotes one of her patients: "I am so confused, I don't know whether I am complaining about my husband or myself. In my mind, his picture is all mixed up with that of myself, as if we were the same person. . . . we cling to one another like two babies, each expecting the other to be a good mother. I don't know anymore what sort of a person he really is or what I am like" (1971:248).

For such people the possibility of losing self-boundaries and becoming merged with another person represents a psychic danger. These patients help us realize that one of the prerequisites for an enduring love is the sense of certainty in one's self-boundaries. The tendency to shift both aggression and libido back and forth between what Hartmann called self representation and object representation makes love relationships difficult.

A very large number of poems could be cited to demonstrate that love has its origin in depressive feelings. I cite a passage from Matthew Arnold's (1822–1888) "Dover Beach."

> The Sea of Faith
> Was once, too, at the full, and round earth's shore
> Lay like the folds of a bright girdle furled.
> But now I only hear
> Its melancholy, long, withdrawing roar,
> Retreating, to the breath
> Of the night-wind, down the vast edges drear
> And naked shingles of the world.
>
> Ah, love, let us be true
> To one another! for the world, which seems
> To lie before us like a land of dreams,
> So various, so beautiful, so new,
> Hath really neither joy, nor love, nor light.
> Nor certitude, nor peace, nor help for pain;
> And we are here as on a darkling plain
> Swept with confused alarms of struggle and flight,
> Where ignorant armies clash by night.

## Love and Narcissism

In 1937, ten years before Balint wrote the paper "On Genital Love," which I discussed at some length in a previous chapter, he challenged Freud in another crucial area: that of primary narcissism. Unlike Freud, Balint did not see the child as born in a state of primary narcissism but rather in a state of intense relatedness to the maternal caretaker. He called that state primary object love. (At the time Balint did not have the experimental data that Spitz found at his disposal.) Balint assumed theoretically that this state prevails in infancy; clinically he described adults who function on the level of primary object love.

Balint defined primary object love as: "I shall be loved and satisfied without being under any obligation to give anything in return." This regressive wish was for Balint the final goal of all erotic strivings. How primary love manifests itself in adult life was described by Balint in a clinical vignette.

She has always been terribly in need of love and affection; several times it has happened that she has thrown herself away at the first signs of some slight attention. The person in question was then equipped with "angel wings" and for a while she lived in blissful expectation. Then because the other person not being identical with her expectations, certain privations were unavoidably imposed upon her, which she interpreted as heartlessness and cruel neglect. The result has always been painful disappointment. This soon turned into hatred. The partner was discarded as bad, heartless, rotten and cruel. (1951:142)

Such a primitive form of love has, according to Balint, certain characteristics: (1) weakness of the ego which manifests itself in the inability to bear frustration; (2) faulty reality testing which does not permit realistic evaluation of the beloved; (3) a quick shift in attitude in the evaluation of the loved one from marvelous to very bad; (4) preponderance of earlier scars from previous disappointment and proneness to withdrawal; (5) absolute dependence on the love object and absolute demands that one's needs be met totally and immediately.

Balint conceptualized narcissism as a defensive detour for one who is disappointed in his or her search for primary object love: "If I am not loved sufficiently by the world or given enough gratification, I must love and gratify myself" (1937:98–99).

This reformulation by Balint had significant implications for psychoanalytic technique. Narcissism was seen by him as due to injury in the primary relationship between infant and caretaker. This was a significant break with the traditional Western attitude toward narcissism, where narcissism was seen both as a vice and as a form of love.

Balint's concept of primary object love was in turn derived from Ferenczi's (1933) "passive object love." Ferenczi observed that in the state of passive object love the infant is highly vulnerable and can respond to the mother's love only if she intuitively meets his need. Should the mother's love be excessively passionate or should she be too withdrawn, the baby's response will become pathological (1933:164).

Ferenczi and, following him, Balint were the first psychoanalysts to suggest that the interaction between infant and mother is crucial to a person's further development. They should be looked upon as the forerunners to the psychoanalytic school of object relations.

Balint's differentiation between primary object love, with all its childish features and genital love, introduced into psychoanalysis a new way of looking at the phenomenon of love. It was self-evident, yet no one before him formulated so clearly the idea that different people love differently: that love cannot be isolated from the rest of the personality. Childish people love childishly and mature people show maturity in the way they love.* That the state of primary love may antedate narcissism was also new and had a significant effect on subsequent thinking. Balint influenced both Kohut and Kernberg in their reformulation of narcissism.

It will be recalled that Freud saw love and narcissism as antagonistic forces. This view was challenged by Van der Waals (1965). He noted that well-matched couples intuitively satisfy each other's narcissistic needs. When couples stay together, they find ways of modifying their respective narcissistic needs so that it becomes compatible with the relationship. The couple itself in time becomes a narcissistic unit. I have observed that the disappearance of such a narcissistic bond within a couple is often the prelude to a break-up.

The French psychoanalyst, Grunberger (1971), went a step beyond Van der Waals in his view. No object is sexually gratifying unless it also contributes to narcissistic enhancement. Every love relationship consists of an instinctual aspect mingled with an "elative gratification" of a narcissistic nature (p. 223–224). Grunberger sees human beings as suffering permanently from a narcissistic wound. This wound manifests itself with particular strength in states of depression. Love heals this wound to some extent when the partner supplies the missing narcissistic enhancement.

Joffe and Sandler (1965) introduced the concept of "an ideal state of well-being" in which biological and mental structures are functioning harmoniously. They considered this feeling state to be associated with Freud's primary narcissism. In this state, the object is seen primarily as a vehicle for the attainment of the ideal state of well-being. They believe that even after object constancy has been reached, the object is not loved as an end in itself but only as a vehicle for the attainment of the ideal state. Thus, to them object love is a roundabout way to the attainment of the state of feeling which accompanies the primary narcissistic state. When a love object is lost, one experiences not only the loss of the object but also the

*I am indebted to Dr. William Grossman for this clarification.

loss of the object-complementary aspect of the self. Like Grunberger, Joffe and Sandler reemphasize the narcissistic aspect inherent in the loss of the love object.

Along similar lines, Mahler (1963) found that children who suffer from "a basic depressive mood" have experienced insufficient "secondary narcissism." (In current psychoanalytic terminology, primary narcissism refers to a state where there is as yet no separation between self and caretaker. Secondary narcissism implies that the separation has taken place but the child is still very dependent on love and appreciation from the parent.) When secondary narcissism is missing, there is a danger that the hostility to the parent will rise and the child will be forced to resort to splitting, separating the idealized parents from the "bad" parents. When this remains as a point of fixation, one can only love one person when another is hated.

In a sensitive study, Bach (1980) highlighted difficulties some encounter in integrating love with self-feelings. He contrasts self-awareness with object awareness. Some people in the sexual act can feel either "all themselves" or "somebody's lover" but cannot integrate the two. Some are continuously plagued by self-observation even at the moment of orgasm, while others have the opposite difficulty, they cannot observe themselves objectively. Normal sexuality, Bach points out, requires the capacity to enjoy oneself as a subject and as an object at the same time. The experience of being an object is achieved through identification with the partner. In perversions this state is accomplished by denial of gender differences, through fantasies of bisexuality. In some neuroses and perversions, to solve this problem the partners alternate between masturbation in each other's presence and object-directed sexuality. Simultaneous orgasm is so cherished because it celebrates the overcoming of the painful dichotomy of perpetual separateness.

The Argentinian psychoanalyst, Bleichmar (1981), noted that sometimes another person, not the partner, supplies the narcissistic enhancement. He cites as example Fellini's movie *Casanova,* where in the presence of guests Casanova is urged to compete with a servant as to who can have intercourse more often during a fixed period of time. When Casanova emerges triumphant in this competition, the woman realizes that she has been only the instrument to prove Casanova's superiority. It is the bystanders who watched the competition who supplied the narcissistic enhancement that Casanova needed. In Shaw's *Pygmalion,* the same relationship prevails in a desexualized form: Eliza is merely the object through which Professor Higgins gratifies his narcissistic needs. The significant object of his narcissism is an admiring male.

To this discussion, I would like to add the concept of "narcissistic space" as a significant element in the functioning of a couple. To take an everyday experience: a man wishes to describe a trip he and his wife have taken to visiting guests. His wife interrupts and describes the same trip with greater vivacity. The man feels left out. Or, the man is praised for a culinary feat which was in fact done by the wife. She feels deprived. As a rule, such minor infringements do not affect the couple, but in some cases one of the partners usurps a disproportionate share or even the total "narcissistic space" available to the couple, inflicting injury on the other partner. Deprivation of narcissistic space can lead to marital conflict and alienation between partners.

## Love and Gratitude

Melanie Klein and her followers have developed a view of love that stands apart from the views of other psychoanalysts. In Klein's view (1957) love emerges from the infant's feeling of gratitude toward the good mother and particularly toward the gratifying breast. This feeling forms the basis for the appreciation of all goodness in the self and in others. In her view the feeling of gratitude arises very early in the infant. Pleasurable feelings are transformed into feelings of gratitude and undisturbed enjoyment of the breast leads to the introjection of the good breast. When fully gratified, the infant feels he has received a unique gift which he wants to keep. This gratitude slowly evolves into love. Under unfavorable conditions, this feeling of gratitude can be destroyed either by greed or strong envy (p. 17). Excessive idealization in love denotes to Melanie Klein a reaction formation against feelings of persecution. The idealized breast is the counterpart of the feared, devouring breast.

I will limit myself to two comments on these views. Some creative writers have expressed similar views. Balzac in *Pere Goriot* remarks that love represents the warmth and gratitude that all generous souls feel for the source of their pleasures. On the other hand, while the emotions attributed to infants are of necessity speculative, psychoanalytic data have in my experience shown that gratitude and love do not always go together. Many men and women feel a sense of gratitude to their mates for the love and the care that they have received but they feel just as strongly that this gratitude is not love. This is not to say that love does not contain feelings of gratitude but the fact that gratitude can so often be experienced without love and is then associated with guilt feelings argues that the two emotions are in a more complex relationship to each than the Kleinian view would postulate. Nevertheless, gratitude for the love and the pleasure received is normally a major component that sustains the continuation of the love relationship.

## Love and Self Psychology

Among those whom I have classified as modifiers of Freud, Kohut is currently, at least in the United States, the most influential. To Freud, the main goal of the therapeutic effort was the widening of consciousness in topographic terms, or the expansion of the ego at the expense of the id and superego in terms of the structural theory. To Kohut, the main aim of treatment is the strengthening of the structure of the self.

In 1971 Kohut introduced the concept of "selfobject" into psychoanalysis. The selfobject is another person who shores up our sense of self (Kohut 1984:49). The selfobject is therefore incompletely differentiated from the self. The selfobject is another person who is psychologically experienced as part of the self. The self-selfobject relationship is the original state of relatedness that in Kohut's formulation characterizes the mother-child relationship. Out of that matrix the self as well as object relations develop. It is significant that in his later writings Kohut dropped the hyphen between self and object.

Kohut emphasized that there is a philosophical bias in psychoanalysis in favor of growth, independence, and maturity as desirable life goals. Freud was undoubtedly influenced by Goethe's famous dictum: the greatest happiness available to mankind is the personality itself ("Das grosste Gluck der Menscheit is doch die Personlichkeit"). From this basic Western bias, which has come down to use from Enlightenment, Kohut dissents.

> In the view of self psychology, man lives in a matrix of selfobjects from birth to death. He needs selfobjects for his psychological survival, just as he needs oxygen in his environment throughout his life for physiological survival. Certainly, the individual is exposed to the anxiety and guilt of unsolvable conflict and to the miseries of lowered self-esteem following the realization that he has failed to reach his aims or live up to his ideals. But so long as he feels that he is surrounded by self-objects and feels reassured by their presence—either by their direct responses to him or, on the basis of past experiences, via his confidence in their lasting concern—even conflict, failure, and defeat will not destroy his self, however great his suffering may be. Self psychology does not see the essence of man's development as a move from dependence to independence, from merger to autonomy, or even as a move from no-self to self. (Kohut 1980:478–479)

In his last book, published posthumously (1984), Kohut took up once more his disagreement with the formulations of psychoanalytic ego psychology. The development from symbiosis to autonomy he regards as impossible (p. 52). There is, however, a development from "archaic mergers" with "archaic selfobjects" and the establishment of a bond of emphathic resonance between self and selfobject (p. 76). Love strengthens the self and conversely a strong self makes possible an intense experience of love. Kohut assigns greater significance to hope than do other analysts. (Hope may well be the most neglected emotion in the psychoanalytic literature.) The daydreaming about the ideal love object Kohut sees as the yearning for a selfobject who will help consolidate the structures that were formed but not completed during childhood (p. 132).

The controversy between Kohut and psychoanalytic ego psychology is one of the most interesting ones in contemporary psychoanalysis. Mahler has emphasized that we long for the lost mother of symbiosis from cradle to grave. Kohut thinks that we refind her in the selfobject.

Kohut cites as an ideal selfobject relationship that of Eugene O'Neill toward his third wife, and that of Proust to his housekeeper, Celestine. The biographies of both writers, however, suggest that they showed little regard for the independent needs of these women.

Kohut cites no source for his view of O'Neill's marriage. Gelb and Gelb (1960), Eugene O'Neill's biographers, report that he married his third wife Carlotta Monterey in 1929 and stayed married to her until his death in 1953. Their biography as well as the psychoanalytic study of O'Neill by the Lichtenbergs (1972) give a very different picture. O'Neill's demands on Carlotta were heavy. She had to be wife, mistress, mother, secretary, all in one, and devote her life entirely to him. There is little evidence that he actually found with her the bliss attributed to him by Kohut. For in spite of her great devotion he seems to have treated his third wife no better than his two previous wives. After each mistreatment, however, he experienced bouts of guilt. As to his creativity, O'Neill did indeed write some of his best plays during this marriage, but also some of his worst, for example, *Days Without End* (Lichtenberg and Lichtenberg 1972).

O'Neill has described love profoundly in many of his plays, but was he capable of loving? The question is relevant for our topic, for O'Neill suffered many traumatic experiences; he also had creative capacity that opened to him channels of sublimation not ordinarily available. The question remains whether he did, as Kohut believes, find the curative selfobject that helped cure his traumatic past. Upon reading of the evidence I suspect that a selfobject, even when it can be refound in real life, is less curative than Kohut had hoped.

O'Neill in *The Iceman Cometh* described Hickey, the central character, as a man who killed his wife even though she forgave him all his misdeeds. He killed her supposedly out of love to give her the peace she longed for and to free her from the painful pipe dream that life would ever be better. Hickey's wife is as good a representative of a selfobject as we are likely to find in literature. And yet she was so hated that she had to be killed. This raises an interesting dilemma: Did the psychoanalyst Kohut in his optimistic appraisal of relationships between two selfobjects to one another come closer to the truth than did the artist O'Neill?

Because Kohut sees love relationships as self-selfobject relationships, he has a different view on love. Kohut's view is in sharp contrast to Binstock (1973), who stresses that the capacity to survive without the love object is the sign of healthy love.

Terman (1980) delivered a paper on love at the meeting of self psychologists in Chicago. Terman begins with a criticism of Freud. The term libido refers to an intrapsychic process and cannot therefore adequately describe an interpersonal relationship like love. He sees Ferenczi, Balint, and Saul (1950) as forerunners of self psychology. Saul emphasizes that being loved is a basic need of childhood. Terman holds that Balint's primary love and Kohut's self-selfobject relationship have much in common. (He ignores the differences, for to Balint, primary love in an adult is a prescription for disaster.) "Loving," Terman finds, "bears a special proximity to the conditions of our psychological birth" (p. 357). For the love relationship to be productive both partners have to refind the self-selfobject relationship they had in childhood. As adults they now can experience actively what they lived through passively during childhood. When a correct balance is established by the couple for their complementary needs, a deep hitherto unknown feeling of happiness is experienced. Out of this refound self-selfobject relationship an "independent center of initiative" develops, giving each partner a new and creative sense of self. Kohut as well as Terman is optimistic about the chances of adults to supply for each other what they respectively missed in the selfobjects of childhood.

## Love in the Service of Healing a Damaged Self

Dicks and associates (1967) were not interested in the phenomenon of love but in the disturbed marriage. They approached marital tensions from the concept of "internal object relations" and "projective identification" as these concepts were developed by Bion. Precisely because they focused on the failure of love, they have enlarged our understanding of it. As they see it, a successful adaptation to modern marriage requires a blend of dependency and a capacity for autonomy (p. 29). In a good marital relationship the partner can be experienced as different from the self without threatening the union of the couple (p. 31). In a successful marriage both partners experience the affirmation of the other as lovable. When marital tensions occur there is a mistrust of the partner's good will, coupled with a possessive jealousy. There is also a need to deny ambivalence and hostile feelings. Idealization of the partner becomes a reaction formation against the hostile feelings. The need to idealize does not allow the partner to become real and in order to maintain the idealization, aggressive and sexual feelings must be denied.

Up to this point, Dicks and his coworkers confirm observations and beliefs held by other psychoanalysts. They go on to describe a psychic phenomenon that I have not found described elsewhere. The men and women they portray search unconsciously for a missing part of themselves. Love is for them a reparative mechanism based on a deficiency in the self that was brought about by repression or denial. The partner attracts, because he or she promises to rediscover a lost aspect of the person's own self. Such people fall in love with what they once were, specifically, what they were before repression or reaction formation set in. They unconsciously believe that in the partner they will refind an aspect of themselves that had been given up in the course of development. Thus the strongly independent seeks out a dependent partner with the hope that this union will allow the reexperience of the dependency wishes he or she had to repress. Such relationships rarely fulfill these hopes, for the need to repress arises once more. The person that was loved has to be expelled just as the original wishes had to be repressed. An earlier intrapsychic battle is refought as a marital one. The person reexperiences the same need to rid himself of the partner who stands for the part of the self that had to be expelled.

Dicks describes a case where love began with the displacement on the husband of the image of a stern father. However, as time went on, the husband began to personify the persecuting mother. The change of the transference from father to mother was responsible for the deterioration of the marriage. This was a significant new insight. Freud, when he postulated that "all finding is refinding," based love on the infantile prototypes. He did not, however, realize that in the course of an adult love relationship, one infantile prototype can replace another. Now that we know that this is indeed possible we can explain either the improvement or the deterioration of a love relationship by the replacement of one infantile prototype by another.

One of Wallerstein's (1967) patients had a similar experience in her transference relationship. She told him: "I came to psychoanalysis looking for a loving father and what do I run into, but a denying mother" (1967:559). Ritvo (1966) described a young man who was phobic as a child and compulsive as an adult. During his analysis he married a phobic woman who like him had suffered from intense separation anxiety as a child. The marriage to a phobic woman enabled this patient to refind the phobia from which the analysis had ostensibly freed him. It would seem that an identification with the therapist played a role in selecting this woman for now he was himself no longer phobic and was actively taking care of a phobic wife just as a therapist had taken care of him.

Like all loves, this type offers a second chance; the extent to which an adult can internalize that kind of love and undo the trauma of childhood will differ from person to person. Love does not conquer all. Its power is limited by the depth and damage that was inflicted by the original objects in the life of the child.

A Sanskrit poem expresses this state of feeling:

> Praise to Vishnu, his hands fondle in
> secret the large breasts of Lakshmi as
> though looking there for his lost
> heart.
> (Merwin and Masson, 1977)

## Love and Psychoanalytic Diagnosis

Otto Kernberg, like Balint a generation earlier, stresses psychoanalytic object relations theory. In his 1980 book he has traced his own intellectual journey. His object relations theory combines earlier influences of Melanie Klein with a later interest in the work of Jacobson and Mahler.

Kernberg brought concepts derived from systems theory to the psychoanalytic literature on love. More than other psychoanalysts he emphasizes the role of integration. In Kernberg's view, mature love is reached through a complex series of such intrapsychic integrations. The emphasis on integration in turn makes it possible for Kernberg to construct a psychoanalytic diagnostic hierarchy for love. On the lowest end of the ladder he classified narcissistic personalities incapable of establishing either hetero- or homosexual object relations (Kernberg 1975: chapters 7 and 8). These narcissistic people fail in their attempts to love because they are consumed by envy and greed. They wish to devalue and spoil what they have conquered. (In earlier classifications, these personalities were described as having pregenital fixations.)

On the next step on this developmental ladder Kernberg envisions narcissistic personalities whose narcissism is essentially a defense against a disappointment on the oedipal level. After analysis such narcissistic personalities can become capable of loving. Kernberg presents a clinical example: A young woman considered herself to be ugly, but felt unconsciously that she was an extremely beautiful woman toward whom men would feel impelled to pay homage. On this unconscious level she saw herself as a "mother-queen-goddess" who would achieve a perfect relationship with a "father-husband-son." In the transference she experienced the analyst as such an ideal mate (1975:241). Unmodified, this fantasy could not serve as a basis for a realistic relationship. It was only after the analysis had led her to recognize that this fantasy was a defense against her oedipal disappointment that the fantasy could be given up and the patient become capable of loving.

In Kernberg's view, borderline personalities "whose sexuality is chaotic, polymorphus perverse, nevertheless have a better capacity to invest their libido in others" because they are capable of idealization (1975:215).

The fourth group comprises neurotics who have reached a better integrated stage of development, their object representations are coherent and separated from their self representations. These people are capable of loving but they cannot combine love with sexuality without feeling guilty because they have remained fixated on the oedipal level. Freud dealt with this group in his papers on love (Freud 1910; 1912).

Those capable of mature love, the final group in Kernberg's classification, have fully integrated their genital sexuality into a total capacity for object relations. Here tenderness expands into full sexual enjoyment. The partners have established a sense of identification with each other. The need to idealize has been transmuted into a mature commitment. (Here Kernberg follows Balint's lead.) Kernberg shares the view of those analysts who, like Van der Waals (1965) and Chasseguet-Smirgel (1983), believe that normal love increases both object and narcissistic libido (1980:281). The depletion of narcissistic libido which Freud thought was typical of all forms of love is, in Kernberg's view, typical only in pathological loves. Kernberg also believes that only in romantic adolescent love is the ego ideal projected. In mature love the projection gives way to the sharing of ideals. Kernberg does not believe that mature love blurs the boundary between self and non-self. He states categorically: "There can be no meaningful love relationship without the persistence of the self, without firm boundaries of self which generate a sense of identity" (1980:290).

In spite of the fact that the self remains strongly cathected, love brings about "the crossing of the boundaries" in sexual passion. Lovers in Kernberg's description also experience a sense of transcendence. In this state a number of psychic events take place simultaneously: identification with a sexual partner, "fantasized union" with the oedipal parents, a temporary experience of dying, by which Kernberg means the famous French designation of orgasm as the "little death." Such a crossing of the boundaries Kernberg differentiates from regressive merger phenomena which take place in the loves of borderline patients. All these complex intrapsychic processes take place during sexual intercourse when one is in love and are experienced as profound sexual passion. Sexual passion keeps the couple together but it is as unstable as it is complex. Relationships based on quiet harmony endure longer than the passionate ones. (Kernberg here follows Freud.)

I admire the clarity that Kernberg brings into the world of bewildering phenomena. Kernberg's five basic groups—narcissistic, moderately narcissistic, borderline, oedipally fixated, and mature lovers—represent a significant advance over the classification by Abraham (1924) which was based exclusively on psychosexual phases and the dominant points of fixation. In the historical perspective that I have developed in this book, Kernberg's definition of narcissism represents a break with the Western tradition, for, in Kernberg's view, the narcissist no longer loves even himself. Rather than gazing with pleasure upon his own image he is consumed with envy, jealousy, and aggression toward the significant people in his life.

Kernberg's last category, mature love, was criticized by Arlow (1980) as being ideal rather than clinical. Psychoanalysts are in no position to assume that it exists in real life: Kernberg, it seems, has not allowed enough space for the childlike part in men and women and for the unresolved conflicts we all carry within us. Mature love does not leave room for the essential human tragedy that bliss, once experienced in infancy, is resought but seldom found in adulthood. In the world of real relationships, every love contains recognizable infantile remnants in abundance. Within the historical perspective I have developed in this book, it is interesting to note that Kernberg's mature lovers are no less utopian than were Abraham's and Wilhelm Reich's "genital characters." Utopians have a tenacity of their own. It is not easy to reconcile his statement that there can be no love without firm boundaries of the self with his concept of crossing of boundaries. I will return to consider the problem in the next chapter.

These criticisms do not obscure the achievement that is implicit in Kernberg's classification. He outlined three distinct clinical categories that have different difficulties in loving. The narcissist cannot love because his envy and his wish to destroy are overwhelming. The borderline cannot love because the intrapsychic structure is too fragile to resist the regressive pull of love. Neurotic personalities cannot combine love with sexuality because their unconscious attachment to parental figures has remained too strong.

# 20

## Varieties of Love and Loving

The fruit of love, it is a book too mad to read,
Before one merely reads to pass the time.

Like a dull scholar, I behold in love
an ancient aspect touching a new mind.
It comes, it blooms, it bears its fruits and dies.
—Wallace Stevens, *Le Monocle de Mon Oncle.*

### Recapitulation

In this book we have followed man's quest to understand the nature of love. I traced love's prehistory back to the magic of fertility figurines believed to be potent to bring a good harvest. Out of these emerged goddesses of fertility and sexual desire, and out of these in turn the Greeks created gods concerned only with love. Hymns to the goddesses of fertility preceded the first songs of love.

The first to find words for love were the Egyptians who 3,500 years ago wrote poems of love. They discovered the metaphor as the vehicle to express love. Some of their metaphors, such as comparing love to sickness, and a sickness that only the presence of the beloved can cure, have remained with us. The Egyptians also created the metaphor of love as a sweet entrapment.

In a leap of imagination, the Greeks brought about a separation of the typical goddess of fertility found throughout the Near East. They created two gods of love to personify the intensification of the sexual passion we call love. I stressed that the Greeks did not attempt to combine what we call falling in love with the capacity for a prolonged and sustained love relationship. The fact that Eros became a child was a mythological antecedent to Freud's concept of infantile love. The arrow of Amor condensed the metaphor of the sudden appearance of love with the feeling that the reason why one person rather than another is selected remains unconscious. The arrow, therefore, tended for centuries to downgrade the role of the beloved. It is striking how the ability of the Greeks to project love on gods in turn enabled their poets to describe love and its conflicts in a language never discovered before. The Greek tragedians enlarged the horizon of love by bringing it in contact with incestuous desires and the battle against yielding to incest.

The most influential explorer of love was Plato. I have shown how he influenced Christian thinkers as well as Freud. He dethroned the god of love by showing that love is based on a feeling of insufficiency, on wanting, and on longing. He also introduced into the sphere of love the recognition that it is based on a wish for union, on the wish to undo our separateness, our individuality, and our lonely existence. Plato also discovered that the energy of love can be deflected to other channels than the sexual union. Freud will call this plasticity sublimation. It is the force that all religions, social movements, and philosophers have used when they deflected love to other purposes.

The Roman poet, Catullus, articulated the emotions of ambivalence when love and hate for the same person are active at the same time. Ambivalence greatly interferes with the ability to love and psychoanalysts devoted a great deal of thought to the nature of ambivalence. The next great contribution came from the Roman poet Ovid who showed in a mythological form the dangers of self-love. He opened the way to the understanding of the conflict between narcissism and love.

The Hebrews and, following them, the Christians showed that man could create the image of a god whom he endows with the capacity of love, and then feel loved by the god he has created. They thus showed that a concrete object is not always necessary for the emotion of love to take place. The nineteenth century, through Schopenhauer and Stendhal, enlarged our understanding by stressing that idealization of the beloved is a characteristic of love. In love, one person and that person alone has the capacity to make us blissful; or by not reciprocating our love, they can inflict upon us a great deal of pain. Psychoanalysis further developed this insight to show that love can be a defense against depression, envy, or aggression.

The Middle Ages developed the concept of romantic, that is, sexually unconsummated love. For the bliss of orgasm they substituted a consummation at the point of a joint death. Romantic love stands midway between profane and sacred love.

Somewhere between the seventeenth and the nineteenth centuries, it became clear that man alone is capable of loving. Planets no longer rotate around the sun out of love, nor is the iron drawn to the magnet because of love. Poets still use this former language, but they know they are speaking metaphorically. Nevertheless, at the turn of the century, Sir Julian Huxley still maintained that gregarious animals show social love for other individuals of the same species. They also show signs of distress when they become separated from other animals. But even he concedes that whatever love can be found in the animal kingdom is directly governed by instincts. Freud derived love from the sexual drive. But drive is not instinct, and in Freud's view, the sexual drive was already a highly complex structure built out of many components.

I have argued in the previous chapters that Freud deciphered much that was enigmatic about love that had eluded previous observers. His basic discovery that connected adult love to infancy will endure. That love is a necessity and that it absorbs for both men and women a useless surplus of narcissism is, in my opinion, an enduring contribution even though we no longer find that the flow back and forth between narcissistic libido and object libido is as simple as Freud had assumed. Current psychoanalysis sees the child as far more related to his caretaker and creating his world in continuous interaction with this caretaker than Freud had envisioned. Primary narcissism, in the sense and vision of Freud, does not correspond to the reality of an infant's life. The connection between love and genitality also had to be given up, for, as I will recapitulate in this chapter, not all forms of love are genital in nature. This is not to deny what many genital lovers know: that ambivalences disappear and a new love is born each time after a genitally satisfying orgastic experience has taken place.

## Definition of Love

In the introduction, I mentioned Cherubino's aria in Mozart's *Figaro*, "Tell you who know if this be love." There are many who wonder if the emotion they feel is love. Psychoanalysis does not have a phenomenological definition of its own. Freud never attempted to define love. For definitions of love we have to consult philosophers and poets. Any selection will, of necessity, reflect my personal bias. I choose the following from the platonic fable: the yearning to be forever united with another person. I paraphrase Schopenhauer's definition of love to read, "endless bliss associated with the possession of one particular person and unutterable pain associated at the thought that the possession is unattainable." From Roland Barthes' (1978) *A Lover's Discourse* I select "He praises the other for being perfect, he glorifies himself for having chosen this perfect other." And: "I encounter millions of bodies in my life; of these millions I desire some hundreds: but of these hundreds I love only one." From Octavio Paz,

I take "Love is a point of intersection between desire and reality. Love reveals reality to desire and creates the transition from the erotic object to the beloved person" (quoted by Kernberg 1980). Plato emphasized the merger aspect of love, Schopenhauer, the uniqueness of the beloved, and Barthes, the narcissistic enhancement in love. Paz emphasized the transformation of fantasies into a real relationship, and the evolution from sexual desire to a love relationship.

So far, psychoanalysis has not developed a definition of love of its own. I take this to mean that psychoanalysts have not succeeded in explaining the nature of love. However, in spite of this difficulty I believe that psychoanalysis can explain what goes on intrapsychically when one loves. First, there is a refinding of some hitherto repressed aspect of the parent. Then there is a recalling, however dim, of the very early symbiotic phase. This is followed by the inclusion of the other within the boundaries of the expanding self, the undoing of some degree of separateness. There is a transfer of the idealization of the self or the idealization of the parent that makes one feel that this person is perfect or at least perfect for me. Hope is awakened that this person so selected will heal all or many of the wounds earlier disappointments have inflicted.

## Toward a Psychoanalytic Theory of Love

Following the lead of Thomas Kuhn (1962) in his book, *The Structure of Scientific Revolution*, I will propose that psychoanalysis is in a position to outline a theory of love. Kuhn has taught us that a theory need not answer all the questions put to it, but it must answer more questions than any other rival theory. It will continue to be accepted unless the contradictions within the theory itself become too glaring and until another theory that answers the questions better and more parsimoniously is proposed. Psychoanalysis today has reached the point where a theory of love becomes possible.

Man's need to love is due to his prolonged helplessness as an infant and equally due to the great intellectual development that takes place during this early period. It seems beyond dispute that after a few months when the baby responds to any caretaker, the baby is happy in the presence of the person or persons that take care of him and sad and miserable when they are away. Under normal conditions, the capacity to enjoy and be happy in the presence of the main caretakers is an inherent capacity in the human being equivalent to the capacity to walk and speak. Out of the alternation between the presence and absence of the caretaking person the emotion of longing emerges. Psychoanalysis demonstrates how difficult it is for many adults to experience longing. Many people get angry rather than lonely when they are separated. Longing for the absent person one loves has to be differentiated from a longing for a state that once existed and exists no more. The wish to merge, to be one with the beloved, can be understood as a yearning for the very early symbiotic phase even though this phase was so early that it left no clear-cut memories. It is a longing that can never be entirely satisfied in a state of love. The opposite feeling is also experienced. Lovers who feel that they are as one person can also experience themselves, contrary to the image of Plato, as lonely.

One of the main characteristics of the state of being in love consists in the beloved being psychically present and emotionally available at all times even when the beloved is not physically present. The paradox consists of the ability to reproduce intrapsychically the image of the beloved and at the same time long for the physical presence. The Hebrew poetess, Rachel, has captured this state in a poem I here render in a free translation.

To you and about you I have sung my songs.
To you and about you I have sung my songs.
There were brief moments when I failed to hear your replying voice.
There were brief moments when the chain binding us nearly broke.
But within the moment my songs returned to you,
Returned to you singing of love and disdain.

The next important capacity that makes love possible is the ability of man to use symbols. This was not a concept familiar to Freud, who used the term symbol in a more restricted sense. We owe the recognition of the significance of symbols to the philosopher Cassirer and his American disciple Suzanne Langer. Because we can use symbols, we can also transfer our love from one object to another, from the animate to the inanimate, and finally also direct this love toward abstract ideas.

There is a built-in developmental timetable that leads the infant first to recognize, and then to love and name those who take care of him. At the same time, certain erogenous zones, the mouth, anus, and genitals, become sources of pleasure. When these pleasure zones are aroused within a loving relationship, sex and love will go hand in hand. The erogenous zones reach their peak in a preordained succession: mouth, anus, and genitals—that is, penis and testicles in the boy, clitoris and vagina in the girl. Under unfavorable conditions, fixation can take place on any of these zones, making this zone the main carrier of the sexual and love gratification.

The human being is also capable of taking himself as his own love object. Some self-love is necessary and desirable as the basis from which a healthy self-esteem will develop. But when there is deprivation or excessive sexualization on the part of the caretaker, the attachment to one's own body and one's self as a love object will inhibit the ability to love another.

Gender awareness begins early in life but reaches a high point in the phallic phase when the genital organs become the main source of sexual gratification. At this point, a polarization between love and hate takes place, one parent receiving the love, the other the aggression. The child now enters the oedipal stage. Anxiety over castration and guilt feelings over aggression force the oedipus complex into repression. With the repression of the oedipus complex, the child enters latency. The tender component of love develops during latency. Those who have a disturbed latency, psychoanalytic experience has demonstrated, have difficulty in loving tenderly.

In adolesence there is an increase in the sexual urges. Now the battle between the hold of the infantile incestuous love objects and the need to find new love objects outside of the incest taboo takes place. How this battle is resolved will determine to a significant extent freedom from neurosis and the capacity to love. Falling in love, I suggest, is the way we know that in the unconscious this battle to transfer from incestuous objects to nonincestuous ones is raging. Some can do it once and for all and find happiness with the new partner; others can transfer only some component of the parental attachment. They need a number of loves to finish the process. Seen in this light, love has a significant intrapsychic function to fulfill—to detach love from the original incestuous love objects and transfer it to the new nonincestuous adult object. Such a transfer cannot take place quietly; turmoil is inevitable, as in any revolution. It can take place only in a state of heightened intensity that we call falling in love. Every new love draws once more upon the storehouse of what has remained attached to the incestuous objects of infancy or to the self. Every falling in love can be conceptualized as a new raid upon the incestuous and narcissistic treasure house.

Plato was right when he assumed that the bisexual predisposition of men and women contributes to falling in love. It seems that gender identity never reaches into the deepest layers of the id. To a greater or lesser extent, we fall in love with what we perceive to be the gender half we were forced to relinquish in the course of development. Some mirroring seems to be a component of every love.

Freud's understanding of love makes it possible for us to see the difference between love and lust in a new light. In lust, little if any transfer of the attachment takes place; love, however, signals a major change from incestuous to nonincestuous love objects. Since Plato and, following him, St. Paul, the absolute dichotomy between love and lust has held Western thinking in its grip like a vise, out of which Freud's thinking offers a liberation. While it is customary to contrast the two states as love and lust, it will be more accurate to state that there are a number of intermediary states where different quantities of libido are being transferred. Thus "the economic approach" used by Freud enables us to see lust and love on a continuum, rather than as opposites.

It follows that love and mourning have much in common. We mourn the old as we find the new. Here my view is somewhat different from that of Freud, who believed that mourning must precede the refinding of a new love object. My own clinical experience has convinced me that often the finding of a new love is associated with a renewal of mourning for the previously lost love.

The relationship between love and the oedipus complex was never fully resolved by Freud. In the essay entitled "The Dissolution of the Oedipus Complex" written in 1924, Freud differentiated repression from the more radical term "going under." (The German title uses the word *Untergang*, the same term that Spengler used as a title in his famous book. The word *Untergang* means literally going under and refers first of all to the sun's disappearance behind the horizon.) Repression is not sufficient, for repression can always return while dissolution or going under makes the complex disappear. Freud advanced two main reasons for the going under of the complex. First, the young lover does not receive the gratification he hoped for. The other force is the superego, who, as the heir to the oedipus complex, demands the annihilation of the complex. Freud's argument runs into contradictions. Clinically we know that neurotics have a very severe superego and yet it fails to annihilate the oedipus complex. Furthermore, and this is crucial for the theory of love, if indeed the oedipus were truly demolished, how could love be explained since it is based on refinding? The term repression plays a central role in psychoanalysis but the term dissolution or going under runs contrary to Freud's belief in the unconscious in which nothing can be destroyed.*

I have expanded Freud's finding in another direction. Love has another function besides refinding: to make up for what was missed in childhood, to make up for the many shortcomings and cruelties which the parents sadistically or inadvertently inflicted upon the child. Consciously or un-

---

*For a different view on the dissolution of the Oedipus complex see Loewald (1978).

consciously we all ask that the love partner be also the healer of our earlier wounds. This is an additional reason why the psychological healer is so often experienced as a lover. At times the wish to have one's own child-hood wounds healed by love appears in a reverse form, that is, to be the healer of one's partner. That this can be realized only on a limited scale is a source of disillusionment to many lovers. What I am saying about love applies also to transference love. Even a psychoanalyst, who more than a lover in real life represents the past, is loved because he is experienced as the healer of past wounds.

The dialectics of love can be understood as a tension between these groups of wishes, the first operating in the direction of refinding, so that the new love object will be as similar as possible to the early parental images, the other opposing this process and wishing to find a person who will heal the wounds the major objects in childhood have inflicted. If a good balance between these contradictory wishes can be found, happy love becomes possible. However, at other times the conflict remains unresolved and various compromise formations take place.

## Why Love Is So Often Painful

Freud (1912) offered two main reasons for the prevalence of unhappiness in loving. Both were rooted in the tension between the infantile and the adult love. When the oedipus complex remains strong, the adult partner is experienced only as a surrogate for the early love, never quite equaling it. A lifelong search for the originally loved parent remains active in the unconscious. The second reason is due to the inability to transfer love without also transferring the guilt of the oedipus complex. The guilt often prevents the transformation of a premarital relationship into a marriage. In other situations oedipal guilt results in sexual inhibition. A third reason can be added. When the original relationship to the parent was painful, the refinding results in a refinding of the early pain of the child. A fourth reason is based on the work of Margaret Mahler. The lost symbiotic love of childhood can never be reexperienced fully in adulthood.

When childhood was reasonably happy, the intrapsychic conflict be-tween the refinding process and the wish to heal the wounds need not be severe. But if there were traumata, the need to refind and reexperience the pain which now operates under the domination of the repetition compul-sion clashes with its opposite, the wish to heal the wounds. To give a clinical example, a woman who has had an alcoholic father has refound her infantile love object when she found an alcoholic man. However, this refinding is not a signal for bliss but the beginning of conflict. She then proceeds to empty out his liquor bottles, or to hide them. The aim may have been to repair but the results are repetition. For example, the woman says, "If you love me you will marry me and give me a child." The man replies, "On the contrary, if you love me you will give up your wish to be a married woman and a mother and devote yourself totally to my needs." To this man, love that does not sacrifice all is not the kind of love he is seeking. In innumerable variations, a clash of needs is reenacted in the lives of many couples.

*clash of both partner Oedipal remnants.*

Much unhappiness with the love partner is due to the conflict between the wish to refind and the wish to have a love object very different from the old. Love's inability to heal all that it is charged with healing is one of the unhappy features with which every adult must come to terms. Love is especially charged with eliminating feelings of envy, jealousy, and rivalry. Indeed the feeling that now when one has found one's love one need no longer envy or be jealous of anyone else is one of the most exhilarating feelings connected with love.

In many analyses, we can find the moment in which the disappointment in the parental love object took place. These analysands recall that after a certain act on the part of the parent, their love was withdrawn. After prolonged crying, they reached the stage of caring no more. In this development, two nodal points can be discerned. At the first, nonambivalent love becomes ambivalent. At the second stage, the child or even an infant resolves to break the love tie to the disappointing mother or father, never share secrets with them, and never trust them. In transference, psychoanalytic patients relive this stage with a great deal of pain.

Most psychoanalysts today see the antagonism between love and narcissism only in pathological cases. As a rule a healthy self-love accompanies and grows with love for the other. In a love relationship the partners enhance each other's narcissistic well-being.

## Love as a Process

I will now describe the process of falling in love. A stage prerequisite to falling in love consists of a vague feeling of dissatisfaction with one's self, a feeling that something is missing in one's life. A mild depressive feeling emerges. The feeling of depression should not be so severe that any potential suitor is rebuffed. Mourning over the loss of some person or a disappointment in the self if they are not too severe are conducive to falling in love. Another prerequisite seems to be not to be excessively involved with one's parents, or a former lover, either positively or negatively. Divorced mothers of a young child may be so taken up with the child and invest so much love in the child that no other love is possible until the child has individuated himself. A psychic space must be available for a new person.

At a certain stage in falling in love, the beloved is experienced as the masculine or feminine part of the self, now ready to be projected on the partner. Discoveries of similarities play a crucial role. One loves the same music, the same books and films, the same countries, and the same nature. Every discovery of similarity enhances falling in love. Idealization of the partner's perfection takes place. There is a feeling of two bodies with one soul. One understands the other, often without explanation, and feels supported and understood.

Like Stendhal, I too believe that love has two crystallizations or, to put it more simply, two phases. In the second phase, differences begin to emerge, unexpected fragilities in the partner are observed. Doubt, as Stendhal has pointed out, enters and other people become attractive again. Old fears are revived: fear of commitment, fear of being taken over by the partner, fear of having to give up one's freedom. At this stage, lovers become two again and the need to take into account another person's needs becomes evident. There are many casualties in this phase of love but when love survives, a quieter stage of longer duration becomes possible, a stage that may lead to a permanent tie.

Once the second phase has been navigated, love will endure if derivatives of the oedipus complex are not carried over into the new love; if the beloved can heal at least some of the earlier traumata that were incurred; if the balance between love and aggression is intrapsychically favorable; and if the partners have a similar capacity for growth.

## Love's Aftermath

I no longer love her, that's certain,
But now I love her
Love is so short, forgetting is so long
(Pablo Neruda in Stallworthy 1974)

Psychoanalysts are familiar with a type of analysand who needs help after the breakup of a love relationship. These cases usually show a deeper disturbance going beyond the loss of someone once loved. These lovers have built their whole world, their interests, and above all, their inner self-esteem on the love they had received. The loved person has become the representative of the loving part of the inner psychic structure. Because this happened, they cannot mourn the loss of the beloved. The end of the love brought with it an increase in anger and aggression which is directed at times toward the deserting lover and at other times toward the self. One has the impression that hate was held back by love but now the floodgates of hate and depression threaten to overwhelm the bereaved person.

Finally, when psychopathology goes deep, falling in love is followed not only by a disappointment, but by a feeling of being misled, taken advantage of, and misused. The formerly loved person is now hated with equal passion. Jacobson and Bak have suggested that when this happens love is not as much to blame as popular wisdom would have it, because the process of an inner breakdown was already on its way before the person fell in love: love was a desperate attempt to stem or at least delay the impending breakdown.

When couples are in a process of separation, one often sees the struggle to maintain the good image of the former beloved. When this is possible, the future capacity to love is safeguarded. Unfortunately, the offer of friendship in exchange for the loss of love is usually easier for the partner who initiates the separation as he or she may already have a new love object or is separating with the belief that such a new partner can be found.

At other times, falling in love does not lead to a permanent tie but it is an important transitional phase in which the feelings of attachment of childhood become permanently loosened. Such a love prepares the person for the love objects to come. Many relationships of young men to older women and younger women to older men have this transitional character. In the opera *Der Rosenkavalier,* Richard Strauss has translated this emotional state into music. The Marschallin represents psychologically a mother figure who renounces her son-lover to her young rival. In the opera, the Marschallin may be a bit more generous than older women in real life are likely to be when a younger lover abandons them in favor of an age-appropriate partner.

Eissler's description of Goethe's love for Frau von Stein discussed in the preceding chapter is another example of a type of love that has the character of a transitional love. To the extent that love is in the service of healing past injury, the partners replay for each other the role of parent and child for each other. Such loves leave no space for a child. When a child is born to such needy parents, they must exclude or reject the child or alternatively transfer their love from the partner to the child. Thus, the capacity to combine love with parenthood is a major achievement not reached by everybody. Psychologically speaking, parenthood implies a yearning for continuity from one generation to another. Homosexuals undergoing an analysis, unless they become heterosexual, go through a period of mourning over the fact that their homosexuality excludes parenthood.

We have noted how in the sonnets Shakespeare tried to separate love from generativity. The same can be said about extra-marital relationships. They often derive their intensity from the mother-child model, undisturbed by reality considerations, be they financial or problems of parenthood.

## Refound Love

Freud emphasized that every love is a refinding. As if to confirm this theory, many lovers must lose their love object first, only to rediscover him or her at a later period in their lives. Cases are known where lovers met in their teens or early adulthood, broke up, and refound each other decades later. Less dramatic but more frequent is the breakup that precedes a resolution to stay together. Unconsciously, such breakups have the same function to lose and refind, and thus repeat in adulthood our fate as children.

## The Renewal of Love

I have quoted from a Latin poem "Perviglium Veneris": "Tomorrow let him love who never loved / He who loved let him love tomorrow." The poem was sung at a festival to Venus celebrating her power to renew love and fertility. Psychoanalytic experience teaches us that the capacity to love again depends to a significant extent on what happens intrapsychically to previous love objects.

In Sonnet 31, Shakespeare expressed the triumph of such a refinding.

> Thou art the grave where buried love doth live,
> Hung with the trophies of my lovers gone,
> Who all their parts of me to thee did give;
> That due of many now is thine alone.
> > Their images I loved I view in thee,
> > And thou, all they, hast all the all of me.

Not everyone experiences such a happy resolution of his love history. Many carry throughout life the image of a love and yearn back to what they lost. On the other end of the spectrum, we find men and women who keep old love letters they have received or even copies of those they have written as a kind of talisman against a lonely period to come. These letters represent an external symbol of the inner fear that one will end bereft of internalized love objects and will need such letters as witnesses that once one was capable of feeling love.

## The Incapacity to Love

The incapacity to love is as complex and multifaceted as love itself. It would deserve a book of its own. Only a few remarks on this subject will be made here. Much that psychoanalysts have learned about love comes from those who undergo psychoanalysis because they realize that they cannot love. Usually they do not know this but experience the feeling that something repetitively goes wrong in their love relationships. Women at the end of their fertility cycle are often seized with anxiety that they will not find marriage or maternity (M.V. Bergmann 1985). So far there has been no systematic psychoanalytic study of the inability to love. The best we have is Kernberg's classification discussed in the previous chapter. Most analysands who seek analysis because they cannot love belong to an intermediate category where they very much wish to be able to love but cannot. They turn to analysis for help.

Seen from the vantage point of childhood, those who cannot love are likely to have been children who were deprived of a deep tie to one person in the early years of their life. They were frequently raised by changing nurses or grew up in institutions. Then there are those who were raised by one person but that person was markedly detached or depressed so that the caretaker was physically present but emotionally absent. From a dynamic point of view narcissism is the greatest obstacle to loving. Those who cannot experience the tension between what they are and what they wish to be, who insist on being treated as if they already were what they imagine they are, have difficulties in loving. Finally, more hopeful are those who cannot love because they did not succeed in combining into one person the love they received as children from many often contradictory adults. In these cases the inherent capacity is there, but what is missing is the ability to integrate.

## Varieties of Love

It will be recalled that Freud made two attempts to classify types of love. The first was in 1914 when he differentiated anaclitic from narcissistic love. The second was in 1931 when he described three libidinal types, the erotic, the narcissistic, and the obsessional. I have argued in this book that love is a compound of many emotions, diverse memories, and many needs that remain ungratified in childhood that seek resolution in adulthood. People love on various levels of intrapsychic maturity. The level of development that a person has reached will to a significant degree determine the fate of adult love, what he or she will find or will elude him.

The realization that there are different kinds of love does not come easily to us. The jealous husband finds it difficult to accept the fact that his wife's love for the newborn is a different kind of love than for him. Or that a love for a sibling is not the same kind as the love for a partner. In psychoanalytic language, we can say that the id knows only one kind of love and the beloved should relinquish all previous ties.

*Infatuation.* The *Oxford English Dictionary* defines infatuation as "an extravagantly foolish and unreasoning passion—to make somebody fatuous." Infatuation, like a disease, runs a certain course. It usually has a sudden and violent beginning and an equally sudden end. It is characterized by a sudden dropping of previous ties. Early in Western history, Homer described the violence of infatuation when Helen left her husband, child, and country to join Paris. An infatuation resembles a waking dream. The flight from transference love often gives rise to an infatuation. There one can observe how infatuation rests on complex fantasies. These are no less complex than fantasies that lead to love, but what is unique to infatuations is that these fantasies are in no way connected to the person selected. The infatuated person usually repeats actively what happened to him as a child. He drops one love object and exchanges it for another the way he was dropped as a child.

Some men and women can experience love only as long as the love object is reluctant. They lose interest in the partner when love is reciprocated. I am familiar with a case of a middle-aged man who went shopping with his sister. The saleslady assumed that the sister was his wife. At the moment in which she addressed the sister as a wife, he was struck by the idea, "No, you are my wife." He proceeded then to court and propose marriage to the saleslady. In this case one can see that the infatuation was a necessary defense against the incestuous wishes toward the sister mobilized by the mistake of the saleslady. The loves of the poet Shelley, discussed earlier, probably were such infatuations. The erotized transference case reported by Blum probably also belongs to this category.

The dramatic quality of the infatuation suggests a desperate attempt to transfer the libido from incestuous moorings to a new object. The term infatuation connotes that the transfer failed to take place.

*Love and the Proximity of Death.* We are accustomed to associate falling in love with youth. Romeo and Juliet and Tristan and Isolde are on the threshold of adulthood. I have suggested an explanation for the association between love and youth, for this is the time when the earlier incestuous attachment must find a new outlet. This is also the time when bisexual wishes must be renounced, love accomplishes the projection of countergender wishes on the beloved. But love in old age is not unknown and it has a poignancy all its own.

> Now, old & near my end,
>    I have known you,
> And, knowing you,
> I have found both ecstasy & peace
>    I know rest
> After so many lonely years,
>    I know what life & love may be
> Now, if I sleep
>    I shall sleep fulfilled.
> (From Bertrand Russell's *Autobiography*)

Russell's poem testifies that the capacity to fall in love is not extinguished in old age. It may even be that this is one of the prerogatives of creative individuals. The poem captures the association that Freud made between love and the sleep of the gratified infant. It also shows that love may be enhanced by the proximity of death. Creative writers have known how to intensify their portrayal of love by the proximity of death. It was well known to poets and novelists before Freud. Andrew Marvel's poem to his "coy mistress" and Hemingway's novels come to mind. Freud also knew of this task of love—to reconcile us with our mortality. He alluded to it in the essay "The Theme of the Three Caskets."

*Triangular Love.* Love, unlike friendship, is by its very nature dyadic, confined to a couple, but there are many who can love only when in a triangle. This precondition for loving, to use Freud's term, demands the presence of a third person. Rebecca, the heroine of Ibsen's *Rosmersholm*, is a mistress who cannot replace the wife out of oedipal guilt. To psychoanalysts, the ability to love only within a triangle suggests a continued fixation within the oedipal triangle. Some people know that they are in love only because they experience jealousy.

*Conflictual Love.* In this group, we find men and women who feel that they can love one person uniquely but not exclusively. Other supplemen-

tary love objects are needed. When people with such conflicts are analyzed, it usually becomes clear that they failed in the task of integration,
and different childhood love objects, even different aspects of the mother
or the father, each seek their own object of refinding. For example, men
who were raised predominantly by maids "refind" less educated women
and yearn to refind the ideal woman who represents the yearned-for
mother. An intrapsychic conflict can also take place between homo- and
heterosexual impulses or between different phases of development: one
sexual partner can be genital, while another gratifies earlier pregenital
sexual wishes. Whether different love objects can coexist in reasonable
harmony depends on the virulence of the intrapsychic conflict, on the ratio
of love and hate within the person, and also on the capacity of a person to
accept as necessary a less than ideal solution.

Many people who fear that loving one person will make them too
dependent on the love object or cause them to lose their sense of self find
safety in dividing their love between different people. Some know love
only as a state of indecision between two or more people. They need not
be promiscuous; every one of their loves has its own history and stretches
over many years, but what characterizes every one of these relationships is
that they can love only when they love more than one person at a time.

*Loveless Sexuality.* One of Freud's significant contributions to the understanding of human sexuality that differentiates it from animal sexuality
was the realization that "the sexual instinct itself may be no simple thing,
but put together from components which have come apart in perversions"
(Freud 1905a:162). The insight that our sexuality is a complex amalgam
of components led to a new understanding of what human beings are
seeking in sexual union. For, if the sexual act is to gratify the various
components making up human sexuality, it must receive gratification in
the order of their strength. The sexual act therefore is a highly individualis-
tic one. It explains why sex with one partner can be so much more gratifying than with another. The fact that two people discover a unique compatibility in their sexual needs is by itself a source of happiness and gratitude.
It often but not always can lead to falling in love.

Loveless sexuality is the experience of intense sexuality without the
concomitant feeling of love. I have analyzed a number of men and women
who experienced passionate sex with one person only, over a long period
of time, but remained convinced that they never loved each other. The
analysis of such cases has taught me that unconsciously these men and
women feel entitled to have sexual experiences but not entitled to feel love

and be loved and certainly not entitled to have both love and sex with the same person. Loveless sexuality differs from love in that superego prohibitions are directed not against sex but against love. In passionate sex as in love, the partner too stands for and has replaced the parent; it differs from love because the inner permission or the superego's approval for the replacement has not been won. Therefore, there is a feeling of sexual bliss but not a feeling of love. One of the ways in which a love relationship can be differentiated from a merely sexually passionate relationship is that lovers develop a language all their own, including names for the sexual organs, while sexual couples employ the slang names. By developing a language of their own, lovers recapitulate the pleasure of the child who learns to speak. In a purely sexual relationship the two partners remain adults. There is no partial regression to childhood.

When such relationships are examined in the course of a psychoanalysis they either become transformed into love or they lose their unique sexual meaning. After analyzing a number of such cases, I concluded that human beings are incapable of having a sexual experience without endowing it with a narcissistic and symbolic meaning. In contrast to what seems to prevail in the animal kingdom, humans need to experience either consciously or preconsciously something beyond the relief from sexual tension. Every happy sexual experience is also a form of self-enhancement and represents at least a temporary resolution of a state of intrapsychic conflict. To many men and women their capacity to experience sexual orgasm comes as a surprise. In such cases one often finds that they believe that they are not entitled to this happiness: sexual orgasm then takes place over the objections of an antisexual superego.

*Masochistic and Sadistic Love.*

> Hippolyta I wooed thee with my sword,
> and won thy love doing thee injuries
> But I will wed thee in another key
> (Shakespeare, *A Midsummer Nights Dream.*)
>
> Love is a smoke made with the fume of sighs.
> (Shakespeare, *Romeo and Juliet*)

Masochistic love is an exaggeration of normal falling in love where everything is sacrificed for the partner; the person lives only through the partner; the partner is magnificent; the person himself or herself is insignificant. For the masochist, falling in love and loving are in the service of suffering. Such people love in order to suffer and to have pain inflicted upon them. While sadism is often experienced as antagonistic to loving, to love masochistically is not only possible but for many enhances the feeling that one is greatly in love. Much of the proverbial pain of love does not come from love itself, but from the need to suffer. Troubadour love, institutionalized and glorified during the Middle Ages, is a special form of masochistic love. Those who "kill the thing they love" are people whose love contains too much sadism.

*Hermaphroditic Love.* Discussed by Plato in the *Symposium* and by Ovid in the *Metamorphoses,* hermaphroditic love represents the earliest conceptualization of love. Psychoanalysis has found that it rests on the powerful wish to be both sexes. The wish exists in all people but not in the same strength. We accept our own sense of gender identity, slowly and incompletely. The wish to remain both sexes survives in many perversions. Hermaphroditic love is a "solution" to this limitation. It is based on the fantasy that the other represents a missing half and, together, one reaches a sense of completion and heals the wound of separateness and confinement to one gender. This love becomes problematic when the beloved shows unexpected signs of independence and one is forced to recognize that the other is more than a mirror image. Plato speaks of the wish of lovers to be melted into one another. An analysand expressed her fear of loving as a fear of a "meltdown." Her term didn't come from Plato but was associated with the danger posed by the Three Mile Island accident. In such cases men and women have a highly specific picture of the person they are looking for when they are searching for the love object. They fall in love when they feel the other represents their feminine or masculine part. A search for the missing hermaphroditic part of one's self can lead to falling in love, but the capacity to stay in love depends on the ability to tolerate and enjoy in the other what is not part of the self. A woman daydreams that she has found a man amazingly like herself. They have the same tastes, interests, and hobbies. Then the horrifying thought occurs to her: if he will be like me, he will be too effeminate.

*Pygmalion Love.* In this form of love, first recorded by Ovid, one loves what one has created. Men's envy of women's procreative capacities is often the basis behind Pygmalion love. Pygmalion-type lovers need to teach and mold the beloved, showing him or her places the other had never visited, books the other had never read, and pleasures the other had never experienced, improving their speech, manners, and the way they dress. I am familiar with a case of a woman who as a precondition for loving asked the man to change his whole wardrobe to conform to her taste; his willingness to oblige her made her love possible. Loves based on the Pygmalion model are more viable than hermaphroditic types of love. They often lead to lasting happy relationships. Pygmalion love becomes endangered when the disciple wishes for equality, and individuality asserts itself. The concept of having saved the beloved from monsters, unsympathetic parents, or from mental illness and to have made a new life possible for the beloved can be a variant on the theme of Pygmalion love. In psychoanalysis a special type of Pygmalion love is encountered when one of the partners is willing to stay in the relationship if the other promises to undergo treatment or when a heterosexual relationship is undertaken with a homosexual partner with the belief that love can change the sexual orientation.

*Narcissistic Love.* The concept as well as the term comes from Freud. In this form of love, one loves what one is or what one was, what one wished to have been, and finally someone who was once part of oneself. The love for what one would like to be, Freud discovered, has the advantage of lowering the tension at least temporarily between ego and ego ideal. Here the lover says, "I love you because you are what I could never be." Narcissistic love is a vulnerable form of love. It is threatened when, for reasons of illness or otherwise, the partner is unable to perform the tasks he or she once did. It is also vulnerable to narcissistic rage when the performance falls below expectation. But it reaches its greatest vulnerability when one of the partners develops interests or aspirations the other cannot share. For, in narcissistic love the other exists only insofar as he or she meets the demands of the person. When this happens, the narcissistic lover feels betrayed—as if an oath never to be different had been taken and broken. Narcissistic love need not be sexual love. A child can also be loved narcissistically as an extension of the parent. Here too a crisis ensues when the child develops wishes of his own.

*Primary and Anaclitic Love.* The term primary comes from Balint. This form of love recapitulates, although in a distorted form, early love. One person is selected to gratify all the love and sexual wishes without requiring reciprocity. This form of love closely resembles the infantile stage of need-gratification; but object constancy has been attained since only one person is selected to be the supplier of love. In this form of love, the demand is made that the partner should have no other interests in life and be devoted entirely to the gratification of one's own needs. If such lovers are men, they do not desire and often cannot tolerate having a child. When they are women they view with dread the possibility that a future child will make inordinate demands upon them. They see the future baby as permanently demanding and insatiable for love, as a competitor and destroyer of the couple's love. Anaclitic love was delineated by Freud as opposed to narcissistic love; it is the continuation of the love of the child for an adult, the love of the weak for the strong; it is the love of the person with feelings of inadequacy for the person who is powerful, rich, and who has achieved a great deal in life. It is characterized by deep dependency needs. It enables the person to love without having to become an adult. The fixation point of this love is the wish to be permanently taken care of and remain dependent on the other.

*Addicts of Love.* The term was discussed by Fenichel (1945:382). These people need love as others need food or drugs. Being loved is essential but the capacity to love is limited. Addicts of love are usually attached to a person they consider ungratifying. They are angry and unhappy without being able to free themselves from the frustrating partner. Fenichel saw addicts of love as orally fixated character neurotics.* They continually nag to obtain more love and usually achieve the opposite results.

*Transference Love.* Since I have devoted a chapter to this type of love, I will here say only that transference love is the normal byproduct of an unfolding relationship to an analyst. It presents difficulties when the analysand wants to love and be loved instead of doing analytic work. If this love is not to turn into masochistic love, it has to be sublimated into a striving for understanding and for future health.

*Aim-Inhibited Love.* In this form of love the sexual component is either absent or repressed, or, at the very least, censored. Dante's love for Beatrice is the celebrated example of such love. I have discussed such a love between Goethe and Carlotta von Stein. Another famous example of aim-inhibited love was that between the aging Michelangelo and the austere and devout widow, Vittoria Colonna, Marchioness of Pescara. In Michelangelo's life, this love was associated with his renunciation of neoplatonism and its permissive attitude toward homosexuality and with a growing preoccupation with Christ as judge and saviour. Aim-inhibited love is often associated, as it was for Michelangelo, with a profound intrapsychic

---

*Freud discovered that psychosexual fixations can be transformed into typical character structures of which the addicts of love are one.

change in the artist (Liebert 1983: chapter 17). Such love has been the inspiration to many artists. If this form of love is entirely desexualized and without jealousy, we may speak of friendship.

*Sublimated Love.* Sublimated love differs from aim-inhibited love in that it contains the full quantum of passion. However, the passion is directed away from a real person to a more abstract aim. Saint Catherine's love for Jesus was an outstanding example of such a love. The vocabulary of mystical love is often astonishingly clsoe to the vocabulary of sexual love.

*Ideal Love.* Idealization is a major component of love. We have seen how the beloved is idealized, how in a reciprocal love, the lover himself becomes idealized. Furthermore, one can also be in love with love itself. The wish for ideal love seems inherent in the human condition. I have shown in previous chapters how the early psychoanalysts also fell under the spell of idealization when they idealized genital sexuality and orgasm.

With the advent of ego psychology, love appeared in a new light. It became evident that love was of necessity a compromise formation between diverse and sometimes even incompatible needs. Happy or ideal love meets many of these diverse needs to a significant degree. It resembles a coalition government with no party in opposition. Such a love is a major achievement of the integrative capacities of the ego and, justifiably, a source of happiness. Neurotic or unhappy lovers' kind of love is also a compromise formation, but major components and basic needs have not been included in this love.*

In ideal love, sexual gratification is passionate and culminates for both partners in orgasm. Pregenital wishes are experienced harmoniously and free from aggression during foreplay. Sexual intercourse is associated with feelings of tenderness and regard for the other. The relationship is based on compatible interests and a persistent feeling that the partners understand, esteem, and love each other. This love is free from hate, wishes to humiliate, and envy. The beloved is experienced as unique in his or her capacity to gratify, and supplementary love objects are not needed. Insofar as a refinding took place, the partner represents symbolically many and perhaps all the important love objects of childhood. There is a balance so that the partner can meet one's adult needs at the same time that he or she also gratifies wishes left unfulfilled during childhood. The two coexist in reasonable harmony.

The partner is regarded as unique to the lover but not so unrealistically

---

*For a detailed discussion of compromise formation, see Brenner (1982).

idealized that a disappointment is inevitable. Mutual identification plays a significant role but one partner does not give up his or her sense of self for the other as is the case in masochistic love. The partners are sufficiently similar in their personality and in the way they see the world so that the outside world does not continuously create conflicts. At the same time, they do not experience themselves as mirror images of each other. I have observed that feelings of loneliness ensue either when the partners fail to understand each other or when they do no more than mirror each other.

Symbiotic feelings of merger, oneness, and bliss are experienced but the lovers nevertheless retain their independent self-boundaries, except during sexual intercourse. They do not regress to the point where self-boundaries have become blurred. Self-love is held in check by love for the other. Feelings toward earlier love objects have been successfully transferred to the new one, but this transfer does not include the need to repeat early disappointments and to recapitulate past trauma. Such lovers delight in teaching each other, but the need to teach is not carried so far as to wish to transform the beloved as in Pygmalion love. Idealization, identification, and regression to infancy all partake in the love experience without being allowed to go beyond a certain limit. Seen in this perspective love constitutes an ideal compromise formation of a great variety of wishes and needs. What is surprising, therefore, is not that it often falls short of the ideal, but that in spite of these numerous checks and balances, many lovers succeed in transforming falling in love into an approximation of ideal love.

Insofar as we had a happy infancy we were all once our own ego ideal. We then idealized our parents. We idealize the symbiotic phase and we yearn to refind it when we love. We idealize our partner. We idealize love itself. We cannot forgo idealization entirely, but the transformation of falling in love into a permanent tie depends significantly on the ability to establish an inner peace between the idealization we bring with us from infancy and our capacity to accept the limitations of reality.

Few lines in the history of love are as famous as Shakespeare's Sonnet 116:

> Let me not to the marriage of true minds
> Admit impediments. Love is not love
> Which alters when it alteration finds,
> Or bends with the remover to remove;
> . . . It is an ever-fixed mark,
> That looks on tempests and is never shaken

When Shakespeare wrote these lines, he was not a psychologist but a poet, especially licensed to idealize love.

# Bibliography

Abraham, K. 1909. Dreams and myths. In *Clinical Papers and Essays in Psychoanalysis*. New York: Basic Books, 1955.
—— 1913. On neurotic exogamy: similarities in the psychic life of neurotics and primitive man. In *Clinical Papers and Essays in Psychoanalysis*. New York: Basic Books, 1955.
—— 1916. The first pregenital stage of the libido. In *Selected Papers*. London: Hogarth Press, 1948.
—— 1924. A short study of the development of the libido in the light of mental disorders. In *Selected Papers*. London: Hogarth, 1948.
—— 1924a. The influence of oral erotism on character formation. In *Selected Papers*. London: Hogarth, 1948.
—— 1925. Character formation on the genital level. In *Selected Papers*. London: Hogarth, 1948.
Alberoni, F. 1983. *Falling in Love*. New York: Random House.
Alberti, L. B. 1972. *On Painting and Sculpture*. London: Phaidon.
Altman, L. 1977. Some vicissitudes of love. *J. Amer. Psychoanal. Ass.*, 25: 35–52.
Arlow, J. A. 1964. The Madonna's conception through the eyes. *The Psychoanalytic Study of Society*, 3: 13–25.
—— 1980. Object concept and object choice. *Psychoanal. Quarterly*, 49: 109–133.
Arlow, J. A., and Brenner, C. 1964. *Psychoanalytic Concepts and the Structural Theory*. New York: International Universities Press.
Auerbach, E. 1946. *Mimesis*. Princeton: Princeton University Press Paperbacks, 1974.
Bach, S. 1980. Self-love and object-love: some problems of self and object constancy, differentiation and integration. In *Rapprochement*, Lax, Bach, and Burland, eds. New York: Jason Aronson.
Bak, R. 1973. *Being in Love and Object Loss*. *Inter. J. Psychoanal.*, 54:1–7.
Baily, J. 1960. The characters of love. Quoted in Hagstrum 1980.
Balint, M. 1936. Eros and Aphrodite. In *Primary Love and Psycho-Analytic Technique*. New York: Liveright, 1953.
—— 1937. Early developmental stages of the ego primary object loss. In *Primary Love*.
—— 1947. On genital love. In *Primary Love*.
—— 1951. Love and hate. In *Primary Love*.
—— 1956. Perversions and genitality. In *Perversions, Psychodynamics, and Theory*, S. Lorand ed. New York: Gramercy Books.
Barnstone, W. 1965. *Sappho*. New York: Doubleday.
Barthes, R. 1978. *A Lover's Discourse*. New York: Hill & Wang.
Benedek, T. 1977. Ambivalence, passion and love. *J. Amer. Psychoanal. Ass.*, 25:53–79.

Berezin, M. A. 1969. The theory of genital primacy in the light of ego psychology. *J. Amer. Psychoanal. Ass.*, 17:968–987.

Bergler, E. 1949. *Conflicts in Marriage; The Unhappy Divorced.* New York: Harper and Row.

Bergmann, M.S. 1953. Recall and distortion of legendary material in the course of psychoanalysis. In *Explorations in Psychoanalysis*, R. Lindner, ed. New York: Julian Press, 1953.

—— 1966. The intrapsychic and communicative function of the dream. *Int. J. Psychoanal.* 47:356–363.

—— 1971. Psychoanalytic observations on the capacity to love. In *Separation-Individuation: Essays in Honor of Margaret Mahler*, J.B. McDevitt, C.G. Settlage, eds. New York: International Universities Press.

—— 1973. Limitations of Method in Psychoanalytic Biography: A Historical Inquiry. *J. Amer. Psychoanal. Ass.*, 21:833–850.

—— 1980. On the intrapsychic function of falling in love. *Psychoanal. Quarterly*, 49:56–76.

—— 1982. Platonic love, transference love and love in real life. *J. Amer. Psychoanal. Ass.*, 30:87–111.

—— 1984. The legend of Narcissus. *American Imago*, 41:389–411.

—— 1986. Transference love and love in real life. *Int. J. Psychoanal. Psychotherapy*, 11:27–45.

Bergmann, M.V. 1985. The effect of role reversal on delayed marriage and maternity. *Psychoanalytic Study of the Child*, 40:197–219.

Bernfeld, S. 1922. Bemerkungen uber "Sublimierung." *Imago*, 8:333.

—— 1949. Freud's scientific beginnings. *American Imago*, vol. 6.

Binstock, W.A. 1973. Two forms of intimacy, *J. Amer. Psychoanal. Ass.*, vol. 21.

Bird, B. 1958. *A study of the bisexual meaning of the foreskin*, *J. Amer. Psychoanal. Ass.*, 6:287–304.

Blanck, G., and Blanck, R. 1979. Drive theory reconsidered. In *Ego Psychology II*. New York: Columbia University Press.

Blanton, S. 1971. *Diary of My Analysis with Sigmund Freud.* New York: Hawthorn Books.

Bleichmar, H. 1981. *Narcismo.* Buenos Aires.

Bleuler, E. 1910. Vortrag uber die Ambivalenz. *Zertralblatt fur Psychoanalyse*, 1:266.

Bloom, H. 1982. *The Breaking of the Vessels.* Chicago: Chicago University Press.

Blum, H.P. 1971. Transference and structure. In *The Unconscious Today*. M. Kanzer, ed. New York: International Universities Press.

—— 1974. The borderline childhood of the Wolf Man. *J. Amer. Psychoanal. Ass.*, 22:721–742.

Bornstein, B. 1949. The analysis of a phobic child. *Psychoanal. Study Child*, 3–4:181–226.

Bornstein, M. and Meissner, W.W. eds. 1985. Freud's legacy: science and humanism. *Psychoanalytic Inquiry*, 5(3).

Bowra, C.M. 1944. *Sophoclean Tragedy.* London: Oxford University Press.

—— 1962. *Primitive Song.*

—— 1964. *In General and Particular.* Cleveland: The World Publishing Company.

Brenner, C. 1982. *The Mind in Conflict.* New York: International Universities Press.

Breuer, J., and Freud, S. 1895. *Studies in hysteria.* S.E., vol. 2. London: Hogarth Press, 1955.

Brownlee, A. 1960. *William Shakespeare and Robert Burton.* Reading: Bradly and Sons.

Bunker, H.S. 1947. Narcissus: a psychoanalytic note. *Psychoanal. and the Social Sciences* 1:159–162.

Burkert, W. 1985. *Greek Religion.* Cambridge, Massachusetts: Harvard University Press.

Burton, R. 1627. *The Anatomy of Melancholy.* F. Dell, ed. P.J. Smith. New York: Tudor, 1927.

Butcher, S.H. 1904. Greece and Israel. In *Harvard Lectures on Greek Subjects*. London: Macmillan.

Butler, E.M. 1935. *The Tyranny of Greece Over Germany.* Cambridge, England: Cambridge University Press.

Cassirer E. 1946. *Language and Myth,* S. F. Langer, tr. New York: Dover.

—— 1964. *Philosophie Der Symbolischen Formen.* Wissenschaftliche Buchgesellschaft Darmstadt.

Chasseguet-Smirgel, J. 1970. *Female Sexuality.* Ann Arbor: University of Michigan Press.

—— 1983. Perversions and the universal law. *Int. Rev. Psychoanal.,* 10:293–301.

Clark, K. 1956. *The Nude: A Study in Social Form.* Bollingen Series, No. 35. New York: Pantheon.

Cornford, F.M. 1950. *Greek Religious Thought.* Boston: Beacon Press.

Deutsch, H. 1930. Hysterical fate neurosis. Reprinted in *Neurosis and Character Types.* New York: International Universities Press, 1965.

—— 1942. Some forms of emotional disturbance and their relationship to schizophrenia (as if). Ibid.

—— 1973. *Confrontations with Myself.* New York: W.W. Norton.

Dicks, H.V., et al. 1967. *Marital Tensions.* New York: Basic Books.

Dodds, E.R. 1951. *The Greeks and the Irrational.* Boston: Beacon Press.

Dover, K.J. 1978. *Greek Homosexuality.* London: Duckworth.

Edwards, C.R. 1977. The Narcissus myth in Spenser's poetry. *Studies in Philology,* 74:63–88.

Eisenstein, V. 1956. *Neurotic Interaction in Marriage.* New York: Basic Books.

Eissler, K.R. 1951. An unknown autobiographical letter of Freud and a short comment. *Int. J. Psychoanal.,* 32:319–324.

—— 1961. *Leonardo Da Vinci.* New York: International Universities Press.

—— 1963. *Goethe: A Psychoanalytic Study 1775–1786.* Detroit: Wayne University Press.

—— 1971. *Discourse on Hamlet.* New York: International Universities Press.

Eliot, T.S., 1951. Virgil and the Christian World. In *Poetry and Poets.* New York: Farrar Strauss and Cudhay.

Ellenberger, H.F. 1970. *The Discovery of the Unconscious.* New York: Basic Books.

Ewen, F. 1948. *Heinrich Heine: Self Portrait and other Prose Writings.* Secaucus: Citadel Press.

Ewen, F., ed. 1969. *The Poetry of Heinrich Heine.* New York: Citadel Press.

Fenichel, O. 1939. *The Counterphobic Attitude.* Int. J. Psychoanal., 20:263–274.

—— 1945. *The Psychoanalytic Theory of Neurosis.* New York: W.W. Norton.

Ferenczi, S. 1933. Confusion of tongues between adults and the child. In *Final Contributions to the Problems and Methods of Psycho-Analysis.* Hogarth Press, 1955.

Flaceliere, H.F. 1970. *Love in Ancient Greece.* New York: Crown.

Fraiberg, S. 1969. Libidinal Object Constancy and Mental Representations. *Psychoanal. Study Child,* 24:9–47.

Frazer, J.G. 1918. *Folklore in the Old Testament.* London: Macmillan.

Freud, A. 1952. *Studies in passivity.* In *The Writings of Anna Freud,* vol. 4. New York: International Universities Press, 1968.

—— 1954. Problems of infantile neurosis. In *The Writings,* vol. 4.

Freud, E. 1960. *Letters of Sigmund Freud.* New York: Basic Books.

Freud, S. 1899. Screen memories. *S.E.* 3.

—— 1900. The Interpretation of dreams. *S.E.* 4 and 5.

—— 1901. The psychopathology of everyday life. *S.E.* 6.

—— 1905. Fragment of an analysis of a case of hysteria. *S.E.* 7.

—— 1905a. Three essays on the theory of sexuality. *S.E.* 7.

—— 1907. Delusions and dreams in Jensen's *Gradiva. S.E.* 9.

—— 1908. Civilized sexuality and modern nervous illness. *S.E.* 9.

—— 1908a. Hysterical phantasies and their relation to bisexuality. *S.E.* 9.

—— 1908b. Character and anal eroticism. *S.E.* 9.
—— 1909. Notes upon a case of obsessional neurosis. *S.E.* 10.
—— 1910. Leonardo da Vinci and a memory of his childhood. *S.E.* 11.
—— 1910a. A special type of choice of object made by men (Contribution to the psychology of love 1). *S.E.* 11.
—— 1910b. Five lectures on psychoanalysis. *S.E.* 11.
—— 1911. Psychoanalytic notes on an autobiographical case of paranoia. *S.E.* 12.
—— 1911a. Great is Diana of the Ephesians. *S.E.* 12.
—— 1912. On the universal tendency to debasement in the sphere of love. *S.E.* 11.
—— 1912a. The dynamics of tranference. *S.E.* 12.
—— 1913. Totem and taboo. *S.E.* 13.
—— 1913a. The theme of the three caskets. *S.E.* 12.
—— 1914. On narcissism: an introduction. *S.E.* 21.
—— 1914a. On the history of the psychoanalytic movement. *S.E.* 14.
—— 1914b. Remembering, repeating and working-through. *S.E.* 13.
—— 1915. Instincts and their vicissitudes. *S.E.* 14.
—— 1915a. Observations on transference love. *S.E.* 12.
—— 1916. Some character types met with in psychoanalytic work. *S.E.* 14.
—— 1916/1917. Introductory lectures on psychoanalysis. *S.E.* 16 and 17.
—— 1917. Mourning and melancholia. *S.E.* 14.
—— 1918. The taboo of virginity. *S.E.* 11.
—— 1918a. From the history of an infantile neurosis. *S.E.* 17.
—— 1919. The uncanny. *S.E.* 17.
—— 1920. Beyond the pleasure principle. *S.E.* 18.
—— 1921. Group psychology and the analysis of the ego. *S.E.* 18.
—— 1922. Some neurotic mechanisms in jealousy, paranoia and homosexuality. *S.E.* 18.
—— 1923. The ego and the id. *S.E.* 19.
—— 1923a. The infantile genital organization. *S.E.* 19.
—— 1923b. The libido theory. *S.E.* 18.
—— 1924. The dissolution of the oedipus complex. *S.E.* 19.
—— 1926. Inhibition, symptom and anxiety. *S.E.* 20.
—— 1927. Fetishism. *S.E.* 21.
—— 1927a. The future of an illusion. *S.E.* 21.
—— 1927b. Humour. *S.E.* 21.
—— 1930. Civilization and its discontents. *S.E.* 21.
—— 1931. Libidinal types. *S.E.* 21.
—— 1931a. Female sexuality. *S.E.* 21.
—— 1933. New introductory lectures. *S.E.* 22.
—— 1938. Moses and monotheism. *S.E.* 23.
—— 1950. From the origins of psychoanalysis. London: Hogarth Press.
Friedman, L. 1966. From Gradiva to the death instinct. *The Psychoanalytic Forum,* 1(1).
Friedrich, P. 1978. *The Meaning of Aphrodite.* Chicago: University of Chicago Press.
Fromm, E. 1956. *The Art of Loving.* New York: Harper & Row.
—— 1959. *Freud's Mission.* New York: Harper & Row.
Furness, H.H. 1961. *Shakespeare: The New Variorum Edition.* New York: American Scholar.
Gay, P. 1983. *The Bourgeois Experience: Victoria to Freud.* New York: Oxford University Press.
Gardiner, M., ed. 1971. *The Wolf-Man by the Wolf-Man.* New York: Basic Books.
Gedo, J., and Pollock, R. 1976. Freud: the fusion of science and humanism. *Psychological Issues.* 9 (2/3). New York: International Universities Press.

Gelb, A., and Gelb, B. 1960. *O'Neill*. New York: Harper & Row.

Gibbons, R. ed. 1979. *The Poet's Work*. Boston: Houghton Mifflin.

Giedion, S. 1964. *The Beginnings of Architecture*. Bollingen Series. Princeton: Princeton University Press.

Gitelson, M. 1958. On ego distortions. *Int. J. Psychoanal.*, 39:245–257.

Glover, E. 1931. The therapeutic effect of inexact interpretation. *Int. J. Psychoanal.*, 12:347–411.

Goldberg, A., ed. 1980. *Advances in Self Psychology*. New York: International Universities Press.

Goldin, F. 1964. *The Mirror of Narcissus in Courtly Love*. Ithaca: Cornell University Press.

Gombrich, E. 1960. *Pygmalion's Power*. Bollingen Series. New York: Pantheon.

Gomperz, T. 1896. *Greek Thinkers*. 4 Vols. London: John Murray, 1901.

Gould, T. 1963. *Platonic Love*. London: Routledge and Kegan Paul.

Graves, R., and Patai, R. 1963. *Hebrew Myths*. New York: McGraw Hill.

Greenacre, P. 1957. The Childhood of the Artists: Libidinal Phase Development and Giftedness. In *Emotional Growth*, vol. 2. New York: International Universities Press.

Greenson, R. 1967. *The Technique and Practice of Psychoanalysis*. New York: International Universities Press.

Gross, G.E., and Rubin, I.A. 1973. Sublimation. *Psychoanal. Study Child*, 27:334–357.

Grunberger, B. 1971. Narcissism. In *Psychoanalytic Essays*. New York: International Universities Press, 1979.

Hadas, M. 1959. *Hellenistic Culture*. New York: Columbia University Press.

Hagstrum, J.H. 1980. *Sex and Sensibility: Ideal and Erotic Love from Milton to Mozart*. University of Chicago Press.

Handelsman, I. 1965. The effect of early object relationships on sexual development. *Psychoanal. Study Child*, 20:367–383.

Harrison, J. 1903. *Prolegomena to the Study of Greek Religion*, third edition. New York: Meridian Books, 1922.

Hartmann, H. 1952. The mutual influences in the development of ego and id. In *Essays on Ego Psychology*. New York: International Universities Press, 1964.

—— 1955. Notes on the theory of sublimation. In *Essays on Ego Psychology*.

Hazo, R.G. 1967. *The Idea of Love*. New York: Praeger.

Higham, T.F., and Bowra, C.M. 1938. *The Oxford Book of Greek Verse*. London: Clarendon Press.

Hitschmann, E. 1952. Freud's conception of love. *Int. J. Psychoanal.*, 33:421–428.

Holland, N.N. 1966. *Psychoanalysis and Shakespeare*. New York: McGraw-Hill.

Horney, K. 1937. Chapter 6: The neurotic need for affection; and chapter 9: The role of sexuality in the neurotic need for affection. In *The Neurotic Personality of Our Time*. New York: W.W. Norton.

Humphries, R., tr. 1955. *Ovid, Metamorphoses*. Bloomington: Indiana University Press.

Huxley, J. 1964. What do we know about love? In *The World of Love*, I. Schneider, ed. New York: George Braziller.

Isay, R.A. 1985. On analytic therapy of homosexual men. *Psychoanal. Study Child*, 40:235–254.

Jacobson, E. 1937. Wege der Weiblichen Über-Ich-Bildung. *Internationale Zeitschrift*, 23:402–412.

—— 1950. The development of a wish for a child in boys. *Psychoanal. Study Child*, 5:139–152.

—— 1954a. Contributions to the metapsychology of psychotic identifications. *J. Amer. Psychoanal. Assn.*, 2: 239–262.

—— 1954b. Transference problems in the psychoanalytic treatment of severely depressive patients. *J. Amer. Psychoanal. Assn.*, 2:595–606.

—— 1959. The exceptions. *Psychoanal. Study Child,* 14:135–154.

—— 1964. *The Self and the Object World.* New York: International Universities Press.

—— 1971. Chapter 9: On the psychoanalytic theory of cyclothemic depression (1953); and chapter 10: Psychotic identification (1954). In *Depression.* New York: International Universities Press.

Jaeger, W. 1945. *Paidea: the Ideals of Greek Culture.* 3 Vols. New York: Oxford University Press.

Janson, H.W. 1963. *The Sculpture of Donatello.* Princeton: Princeton University Press.

Jekels, L., and Bergler, E. 1934. Transference and love. *Psychoanal. Quarterly,* 18:325–350.

Joffe, W. R., and Sandler, J. 1965. Notes on pain, depression and individuation. *Psychoanal. Study Child,* 20:394–424.

Jones, E. 1914. The Madonna's conception through the ear. In *Essays in Applied Psychoanalysis,* vol. 2. London: Hogarth Press.

—— 1953–1957. *The Life and Work of Sigmund Freud.* 3 vols. New York: Basic Books.

Kaufman, W.A. 1950. *Nietzsche: Philosopher, Psychologist Antichrist.* Princeton: Princeton University Press.

Kelly, H.A. 1975. *Love and Marriage in the Age of Chaucer.* Ithaca, N.Y.: Cornell University Press.

Kernberg, O. 1975. *Borderline Conditions and Pathological Narcissism.* New York: Jason Aronson.

—— 1980. *Internal World and External Reality.* New York: Jason Aronson.

Kestenberg, J. 1968. Outside and inside, male and female. *J. Amer. Psychoanal. Ass.,* 16:457–520.

Kirk, G.S. 1970. *Myth.* Cambridge: Cambridge University Press.

Khan, M. M. R. 1979. *Alienation in Perversions.* New York: International Universities Press.

Klein, M. 1957. *Envy and Gratitude.* New York: Basic Books.

Kohut, H. 1971. *The Analysis of the Self.* New York: International Universities Press.

—— 1972. Thoughts on narcissism and narcissistic rage. *Psychoanal. Study Child,* vol. 27.

—— 1977. *The Restoration of the Self.* New York: International Universities Press.

—— 1980. Two letters. In *Advances in Self Psychology.* A. Goldberg, ed. New York: International Universities Press.

—— 1984. *How Does Analysis Cure?* Chicago: University of Chicago Press.

Kramer, S. N. 1969. *History Begins in Sumer.* New York: Doubleday.

Kramrish, S. 1981. *The Presence of Siva.* Princeton: Princeton University Press.

Kris, E. 1955. Neutralization and sublimation. *Psychoanal. Study Child,* vol. 10.

Kubie, L. S. 1974. The drive to become both sexes. *Psychoanal. Quarterly,* 43:349–426.

Kuhn, T. S. 1962. *The Structure of Scientific Revolutions.* Chicago: University of Chicago Press.

Lacan, J. 1978. *The Four Fundamental Concepts of Psychoanalysis.* American edition. Chapter 15: From love to the libido. New York: W.W. Norton, 1981.

Laplanche, J., and Pontalis, J. B. 1967. *The Language of Psychoanalysis.* New York: W.W. Norton, 1973.

Lawick-Goodall, Jane, Baroness van. 1971. *In the Shadow of Man.* Boston: Houghton Mifflin.

Leeuwen, K. 1966. Pregnancy envy in the male. *Int. J. Psychoanal.,* 47:319–324.

Lehmann, H. 1970. Sigmund Freud and Thomas Mann. *Psychoanal. Quarterly,* 39:198–214.

Lewin, B. D. 1952. Phobic symptoms and dream interpretation. In *Selected Papers.* J. A. Arlow, ed. New York: Psychoanalytic Quarterly, 1973.

Lewis, C. S. 1936. *The Allegory of Love.* Oxford University Press, paperback edition, 1971.

Licht, F. 1979. *Goya.* New York: Universe Books.

Lichtenberg J. D., and Lichtenberg, C. 1972. Eugene O'Neill and falling in love. *Psychoanal. Quarterly,* Vol. 41.

Lichtheim, M. 1976. Ancient Egyptian literature, a book of reading. In *The New Kingdom,* vol. 2. Berkeley: University of Calif. Press.

Liebert, R. 1983. *Michelangelo: A Psychoanalytic Study.* New Haven: Yale University Press.

Lipin, T. 1963. The repetition compulsion and maturational drive representation. *Int. J. Psychoanal,* vol. 44.

Loewald, H. 1962. Internalization and the superego. *Psychoanal. Quarterly,* vol. 31.

—— 1978. The waning of the Oedipus complex. In *Papers on Psychoanalysis.* New Haven: Yale University Press, 1980.

Lucretius. 1968. *De Rerum Natura (The Way Things Are).* Humphries tr. Bloomington: Indiana University Press.

MacAlpine, I. 1950. The development of the transference. *Psychoanal. Quarterly,* vol. 14.

MacCary, W.T., 1985. *Friends and Lovers,* New York: Columbia University Press.

Mahler, M.S. 1963. Thoughts about development and individuation. In *Selected Papers of Margaret S. Mahler.* New York: Aronson, 1979.

Mahler, M.S., and Furer, M. 1968. *On Human Symbiosis and the Vicissitudes of Individuation.* New York: International Universities Press.

Mahler, M.S., Pine, F., and Bergman, A. 1975. *The Psychological Birth of the Infant.* New York: Basic Books.

Mandelstam, O. 1970. *Hope Against Hope: A Memoir.* New York: Atheneum.

Marcuse, H. 1955. *Eros and Civilization.* Boston: Beacon Press.

McDougall, J. 1980. *A Plea for a Measure of Abnormality.* New York: International Universities Press.

McGuire, W., ed. 1974. The Freud/Jung letters. *Bollingen Series* 94. Princeton: Princeton University Press.

Merwin, W.S., and Masson, J.M. 1977. *Sanscrit Love Poetry.* New York: Columbia University Press.

Milano, P., ed. 1947. *The Portable Dante.* Penguin Books, 1979.

Model, A. 1968. *Object Love and Reality.* New York: International Universities Press.

Momigliano, A. 1981. Greek culture and the Jews. In *The Legacy of Greece: A New Appraisal.* M.I. Finly, ed. London: Clarendon.

Murray, G. 1935. *Five Stages of Greek Religion.* London: Watt.

Murray, J.M. 1921. Shakespeare and love. In *Countries of the Mind.* London: Collins.

Nachmanson, M. 1915. Freud's libido theorie verglicken mit der Erloslehre Platos. *Int. Z. for Psychoanalyze,* 3:65–83.

Newbolt, H. 1909. The book of Cupid. *Being an anthology from the English Poets.* London: Constable.

Novey, S. 1955. Some philosophical speculations on the concept on the genital character. *Int. J. Psychoanal.,* vol. 36.

Nunberg, H. 1926. The will to recovery. In *Practice and Theory of Psychoanalysis.* New York: Nervous and Mental Disease Monograph, 1948.

Nunberg, H., and Federn, E. 1962–1975. *Minutes of the Vienna Psychoanalytic Society.* 4 vols., 1906–1918. New York: International Universities Press.

Oates, W.J., and O'Neill, E.G., eds. 1938. *The Complete Greek Drama.* New York: Random House.

O'Flaherty, W.D. 1975. *Hindu Myths.* Baltimore: Penguin Books.

Onians, R.B. 1954. *The Origin of European Thought.* Cambridge: Cambridge University Press.

Ortega y Gasset, J. 1957. *On Love.* T. Talbot, tr. New York: Meridian Books.

Otto, W.F. 1979. *The Homeric Gods.* M. Hadas, tr. London: Thames and Hudson.

Ovid (Pioblus Ovidius Naso). 1955. *Metamorphoses.* R. Humphries, tr. Bloomington: Indiana University Press.

—— 1958. *Amores.* R. Humphries, tr. Bloomington: Indiana University Press.

Painter, G. D. 1965. *Proust: The Later Years*. Boston: Little Brown.

Panofsky, D., 1969. *Problems in Titian*. New York: New York University Press.

Panofsky, E. 1939. Blind Cupid. In *Studies in Iconology*. New York: Harper, 1962.

—— 1955. Albrecht Durer and classical antiquity. In *Meaning in the Visual Arts*. New York: Doubleday.

Persson, A. W. 1942. *The Religion of Greece in Prehistoric Times*. Berkeley: University of California Press.

Pfister, O. 1921. *Plato als vonnlaufer der Psychoanalyze*. Inter. Z. Psychoanal., 7:264–269.

Pine, F. 1979. On the pathology of the separation-individuation process as manifested in later clinical work. *Int. J. Psychoanal.*, 60:225–242.

Pritchard, J.B., ed. 1969. *Ancient Near Eastern Texts*. Third edition. Princeton: Princeton University Press.

Radin, P. 1957. *Primitive Man as a Philosopher*. New York: Dover.

Ranelagh, E.L. 1979. *The Past We Share*. London: Quartet Books.

Rank, O. 1907. *Der Kunstler*. Vienna: Heller.

Reich, A. 1940. A contribution to the psychoanalysis of extreme submissiveness in women. In *Psychoanalytic Contributions*. New York: International Universities Press, 1973.

Reich, W. 1927. *The Function of the Orgasm*. New York: Oregon Institute Press, 1942.

—— 1929. The genital character and the neurotic character. In *The Psychoanal. Reader*. R. Fliess, ed. New York: International Universities Press, 1948.

Reik, T. 1944. *A Psychologist Looks at Love*. New York: Farrar & Rinehart.

Ritvo, S. 1966. Correlation of a childhood and adult neurosis. *Int. J. Psychoanal.*, 47:130–131.

Rollins, H.E. 1944. The sonnets. In *Variorum Shakespeare*. New York: American Scholar.

Ross, N. 1970. The primacy of sexuality in the light of ego psychology. *J. Amer. Psychoanal. Ass.*, 18:267–284.

Rozelaar, M. 1954. *Shir ha Shirim al Neka ha Shira ha ero tit Hayevanit* (The Song of Songs on the Basis of the Greek Erotic Lyric). Jerusalem: Eshkolot.

Rougemont, D. De. 1956. *Love in the Western World*. New York: Doubleday.

Saul, L. 1950. The distinction between loving and being loved. *Psychoanal. Quarterly*, 19:412–413.

Schafer, R. 1974. Problems in Freud's psychology of women. *J. Amer. Psychoanal. Ass.*, 22:459–485.

—— 1977. The interpretation of transference and the conditions for loving. *J. Amer. Psychoanal. Ass.*, 25:335–362.

Schmideberg, M. 1936. A note on suicide. *Inter. J. Psychoanal.*, vol. 17.

Schneider, L. 1985. Mirrors in art. *Psychoanalytic Inquiry*, vol. 5.

Schopenhauer, A. 1858. The metaphysics of sexual love. In *The World as Will and Representation*. E.F.J. Payne, tr. New York: Dover, 1966.

Schur, M. 1972. *Freud Living and Dying*. New York: International Universities Press.

Seibel, S. 1924. *The Religion of Shakespeare*. London: Watts.

Sharpe, E. 1943. Cautionary tales. In *Collected Papers on Psychoanalysis*. London: Hogarth, 1950.

Shelley, P. B. 1952. *The Complete Poetical Works of Percy Bysshe Shelley*. T. Hutchinson, ed. Oxford: Oxford University Press.

Silver, D. 1983. The Dark Lady, sibling loss and mourning in the Shakespearean sonnets. *Psychoanalytic Inquiry*, 3:5B–527.

Silverman, L.H.: Lachmann, F.; and Milich, R.H. 1982. *The Search for Oneness*. New York: International Universities Press.

Simon, B. 1973. Plato and Freud: the mind in conflict and the mind in dialogue. *Psychoanal. Quarterly*, 43:91–122.

—— 1978. *Mind and Madness in Ancient Greece*. Ithaca, N.Y.: Cornell University Press.

Simpson, W. K., ed. 1973. *The Literature of Ancient Egypt*. New Haven: Yale University Press.

Singer, I. 1984. *The Nature of Love I: Plato to Luther*. 2d ed. Chicago: University of Chicago Press.

Slochower, H. 1970. *Mythopoesis*. Detroit: Wayne University Press.

Snell, B. 1953. *The Discovery of the Mind*. Cambridge: Harvard University Press.

Socarides, C. W. 1978. *Homosexuality*. New York: Jason Aronson.

Solomon, R. C., 1981. *Love, Emotion, Myth, and Metaphor*. New York: Doubleday Anchor.

Speiser, E. A. 1969. Akkadian myths and epics. In *Ancient Near Eastern Texts Related to the Old Testament*. J. B. Pritchard, ed. Third edition. Princeton: Princeton University Press.

Spitz, R. 1945. Hospitalism, an inquiry into the genesis of psychiatric conditions in early childhood. *Psychoanal. Study Child*, vol. 1.

—— 1946. Hospitalism, a follow-up report. *Psychoanal. Study Child*, vol. 2.

—— 1965. *The First Year Of Life*. New York: International Universities Press.

Stallworthy, J., ed. 1974. *A Book of Love Poetry*. New York: Oxford University Press.

Stanesau, T. 1971. Young Freud's letters to his Rumanian friend Silberstein Israel. *Ann. Psychiatry*, Vol. 9.

Steinberg, L. 1983. *The Sexuality of Christ in Renaissance Art and in Modern Oblivion*. New York: Pantheon.

Stendhal. 1842. *On Love*. 3d ed. New York: Liveright, 1947.

Sterba, R.F., 1984. Discussion of Martin Bergmann's "The legend of Narcissus." *American Imago*, vol. 41.

Stone, L. 1985. The strange history of sexuality; sex in the West. *New Republic*, July 8, 1985.

Sulloway, F. J. 1979. *Freud, Biologist of the Mind*. New York: Basic Books.

Taylor, A.E. 1926. *Plato*. London: Methuen.

Terman, D. M. 1980. Object love and psychology of the self. In *Advances in Self Psychology*, A. Goldberg, ed. New York: International Universities Press.

Van Der Waals, H. G. 1965. Problems of narcissism. *Bull. Meninger Clinic*, 29:243–275.

Virgil. 1983. *The Aeneid*. R. Fitzgerald, tr. New York: Random House.

Waddell, H. 1955. *The Wandering Scholars*. New York: Doubleday.

Waelder, R. 1930. The principle of multiple function: observations on overdetermination. *Psychoanal. Quarterly* (1936):45–62.

Wallerstein, R.S. 1967. Reconstruction and mastery in the transference psychosis. *J. Amer. Psychoanal. Ass.*, vol. 15.

Wangh, M. 1950. Othello: The tragedy of Iago. *Psychoanal. Quarterly*, vol. 19.

Weissman, P. 1969. Creative fantasies and beyond the reality principle. *Psychoanal. Quarterly*, vol. 38.

Werman, D.S., and Jacobs, T.J. 1983. Thomas Hardy, The Well-Beloved and the Nature of Infatuation. *Int. Rev. Psychoanal.*, 10:447–457.

Wieseler, F. 1856. *Narkissos Eine Kunst Mythologische Alhandlung*. Gottine.

Wilson, J. D. 1966. The sonnets. In *The Works of Shakespeare*. Cambridge: Cambridge University Press.

Wolkstein, D., and Kramer, S. 1983. *Inanna: Queen of Heaven and Earth: Her Stories and Hymns from Sumer*. New York: Harper & Row.

Woolf, V. 1928. *Orlando: A Biography*. New York: Harcourt Brace

# Index